Enforcing Normalcy

Enforcing Normalcy

Disability, Deafness, and the Body

LENNARD J. DAVIS

VERSO

London • New York

First published by Verso 1995
© Lennard J. Davis 1995
All rights reserved

Verso
UK: 6 Meard Street, London W1V 3HR
USA: 180 Varick Street, New York NY 10014–4606

Verso is the imprint of New Left Books

ISBN 1–85984–912–1
ISBN 1–85984–007–8 (pbk.)

British Library Cataloguing in Publication Data
A catalogue record for this book is available from the British Library

Library of Congress Cataloging-in-Publication Data
Davis, Lennard J., 1949–
Enforcing normalcy : disability, deafness, and the body / Lennard
J. Davis
    p.   cm.
Includes bibliographical references.
ISBN 1–85984–912–1 (hbk.). — ISBN 1–85984–007–8 (pbk.)
1. Sociology of disability. 2. Handicapped—Social conditions.
3. Deaf—Social conditions. 4. Deafness—Social aspects.
5. Discrimination against the handicapped. 6. Body, Human—Social
aspects. I. Title.
HV1568.D39 1995
362.4′2—dc20   95–31509 CIP

Typeset by Keystroke, Jacaranda Lodge, Wolverhampton
Printed in Great Britain by Biddles Ltd, Guildford and King's Lynn

As for the exposure and rearing of children, let there be a law that no deformed child shall live.

Aristotle, *The Politics*

Contents

Dedicated to my daughter, Francesca Eva Mirabella-Davis, who fights for justice every day, and to my CODA (Children of Deaf Adults) brothers and sisters, who provided an oasis for me where I could dwell with my Deafness.

Preface

This book tries to think through some of the complex issues raised by concepts such as the body, the normal, the abnormal, disability, the disabled, people with disabilities. I wrote this book because I believe deeply that people with disabilities, Deaf[1] people, and others who might not even consider themselves as having a disability have been relegated to the margins by the very people who have celebrated and championed the emergence of multiculturalism, class consciousness, feminism, and queer studies from the margins.

In the few years that I have been associated with disability studies, I have noticed that books about disability are usually little read; academic sessions at professional conferences, and other types of meetings about disability are usually poorly attended. When I talk about culturally engaged topics like the novel or the body I can count on a full house of spectators, but if I include the term 'disability' in the title of my talk or of a session the numbers drop radically. This is not only my experience: I received a cautionary warning from a colleague who uses a wheelchair as we planned a session at the Marxist Scholars Conference in New York in 1994. 'People don't come to sessions on disability. They think it is a specialized area and only the disabled come.' It has been true that when I speak about disability inevitably people drift up from the audience to tell me about themselves and their family members who are deaf, blind, and so on. There is always an eagerness in their approach, because disability is the bodily state that dare not speak its name in professional circles.

My response to my colleague was that our goal should be to help 'normal' people to see the quotation marks around their assumed state. The fact is that disability as a topic is under-theorized – a remarkable fact for this day when smoking, eating a peach, or using a bodily orifice are hyper-theorized. Because of this under-theorization, which is largely a consequence of the heavy control of the subject by medical and psycho-social experts, the general population does not understand the connection between disability and the status quo in the way many people now understand the connection between race and/or gender and contemporary structures of power. I hope that as a result of the efflorescence of studies on disability from within the community of people with disabilities the day is not far off when the majority will dismiss the current dominant view as 'antiquated' and find it hard to believe that such a regressive understanding of the body could ever have been held by intelligent, progressive people.

In writing this book, I focus among other impairments on deafness particularly. In some sense, I consider deafness as the best-case scenario to describe general attitudes toward people with disabilities. Some may argue, and indeed many in the Deaf community will argue, that deafness is not a disability. It has become increasingly common for deaf people to deny the term 'disabled,' and to dissociate themselves from other people with disabilities. So before I discuss anything else, I must deal with this set of issues.

It should be said that the term 'disabled' is not a very good one. It was used to replace the worse term 'handicapped.' That word itself derives from the phrase 'hand i' cap,' according to the *Oxford English Dictionary*, and originally appeared in the seventeenth century to describe a kind of lottery in which 'one person challenged some article belonging to another, for which he offered something of his own in exchange.' The drawing of items from a hat was involved, and an umpire was chosen to note the difference of value between the two objects exchanged. Then in the eighteenth century, the term came to refer to horse races in which an umpire would assign extra weight to be carried by a superior horse, and lots would be drawn from a hat to see if the race was 'on' or 'off.' The idea of the lottery drawn from the hat dropped out, but the sense of unequal contestants, the superior one being 'handicapped' to equalize the race, survived in the late nineteenth century. It was only a very late sense that switched from the idea of a superior competitor being weighed down to a newer sense of an inferior unduly burdened with a disability. 'Disability' is by far the older term, dating from the period of the first printed works. As a term it is more broadly used to indicate any lack of ability – fiscal, physical, mental, legal, and so on. We can with this knowledge tag 'handicap' as a term that arises in the context of an ableist[2] establishment specifically to link impairment to the notion of competition and unfair inability to compete, a model that will fit well with capitalist notions of the functionality of the human body, as we will see. 'Disability,' on the other hand, survives from a usage that links any impairments – not pigeonholed as physical limitation – together without creating a discourse of disability.

The term 'differently abled' has been recently used, but strictly needs to be applied to everyone, since all people, not just those who are paraplegic or autistic, are differently abled. (One person is a better artist; another better at sports.) The principle of difference is in fact the principle of meaning in linguistics: things mean by differing from each other. In this usage, therefore, the term 'abled' describes everyone – not just those with physical limitations – and the term 'ability' includes but does not stigmatize 'disability.'

The term 'person with disabilities' is preferred by many to 'disabled person' since the former term implies a quality added to someone's personhood rather than the second term's reduction of the person to the disability. In this text, I will use the former term as much as possible, but it is not a felicitous term for a writer, and I ask readers for some forbearance here. I will use the term 'disabled person' only when I am talking about the object created by ableist society.

These terms are all hopelessly embroiled in the politics of disability, or ability if you like. Given that caveat, I do nevertheless use the term 'disability' since it seems to be one that most people with disabilities use.[3] The Deaf, however, as noted above, reject this term, now seeing themselves as a linguistic subgroup like Latinos or Koreans. They feel that their culture, language, and community constitute them as a totally adequate, self-enclosed, and self-defining subnationality within the larger structure of the audist[4] state. As such, the Deaf do not regard their absence of hearing as a disability, any more than a Spanish-speaking person would regard the inability to speak English as a disability. Since most culturally Deaf people were reared in the Deaf community, went to the same residential schools, speak the same language, and participate in the same culture, they see themselves as different from other people with disabilities who, unless they take steps to become politically organized, are often isolated with their particular disability. Furthermore, the Deaf do not wish to be associated with, say, autism or schizophrenia. They see their state of being as defined not medically but rather socially and politically. Aside from self-help or social groups, people with disabilities have only relatively recently begun to think of themselves as a community. For example, if a person is born without a leg, or contracts polio or meningitis and loses the ability to walk or speak, that person is not automatically part of a culture, a language, a way of life. Such a person is, so the argument goes, just a person with a limb missing or with a speech problem. Or if a person is mentally delayed, he or she cannot be said to be part of a culture of the mentally delayed.

While I honor that argument, I still see the political benefits in linking deafness to disability. I would never say that a Deaf person and a paraplegic were the same. They are not. But to the ableist majority, they may be. In writing this book, I think I can make important parallels with other disabilities by talking about deafness. However, I am acutely aware that while one can capitalize *deaf*, one cannot capitalize *disabled*. To be culturally Deaf is a reality, to be culturally Disabled is at this point perhaps only a Utopian wish that is gaining ground. It is not my aim to insult the Deaf by saying they are people with disabilities; rather, I wish to explore how people with disabilities, at the risk of insulting everyone perhaps, can be Disabled. So when I speak of disability, I may include Deafness within that category, although I will take pains to separate the Deaf experience from that of people with other disabilities.

There is another point to be made about the notion of disability. The category itself is an extraordinarily unstable one. There is a way in which its existence is a product of the very forces that people with disabilities may wish to undo. As coded terms to signify skin color – black, African-American, Negro, colored – are largely produced by a society that fails to characterize 'white' as a hue rather than an ideal, so too the categories 'disabled,' 'handicapped,' 'impaired' are products of a society invested in denying the variability of the body. The category 'disability' begins to break down when one scrutinizes who make up the disabled. The obvious cases are seen by most observers as disabled: the blind, the Deaf, people using wheelchairs, prostheses, and so on. But when we include learning impairments, dyslexia, obesity, and then compound those categories with disease-generated disabilities – AIDS, tuberculosis, multiple sclerosis, arthritis, chronic illnesses – the instability of the category 'disabled' begins to appear. The fact is that most citizens will have some level of impairment, some degree of physical difference from others. Most humans, as they age, will find themselves less able to see, hear, walk, or think so well as they did before. One disability activist recently spoke at a convention to 'normal' people and said, 'We are 500 million strong and growing. Come back in twenty years and a lot of you will be with us!'

The term 'disabled' is often used to obscure or repress the fact that disability is not a static category but one which expands and contracts to include 'normal' people as well. In addition, while many people have rallied around the term 'disability,' much as African-Americans did around 'Black' power, the term is at base one that has been used to create rigid categories of existence: either one is disabled, or one is not. People with disabilities, rightly, have seized on the term in an attempt to control its usage; but even with that empowering move, it is necessary to remember that the term still serves at least two masters.

In discussing the double-sided nature of the disability issue, I need to add a further qualification. Many people who are not impaired in the usual sense of the word still consider themselves to be part of the disabled community. Here we come to a point I am sure many readers are asking themselves: is Lennard J. Davis a person with disabilities? And what is his disability?

One needs to understand the motive behind such a question. First, disabilities always create curiosity on the part of the observer. What is the disability? How profound is it? Can I see it, touch, know it? How did it happen? What does it interfere with? What would life be like if I had that impairment? Second, a disability produces the demand for a response, or, as I will argue, it is perhaps the response that produces the disability. (In any case, there is no disability without an implied response. A socio-political process is always at work in relation to the body. It is that relation I explore in greater detail in this work.)

The question demands an answer. I must tell you the status of at least some portion of my body. Unlike other kinds of interventions around the issues of race, class, or gender, there is a powerful policing mechanism that demands I answer your question. If I am a woman, a person of color, or even poor, my body reveals enough so that I don't have to explain why I am a woman, how I became black, or why I am poor.[5] But the disabled body must be explained, or at least tolerate the inquisitive gaze (or the averted glance) of the questioner. The question never has to be put because it is always actively in a default mode – it is always already asked.

The question is put not only by 'normal' people but also by people with disabilities. As with any movement, there is an essentialist strain, a tendency towards identity politics. Can someone without disabilities ever understand what it is to be disabled? Is there a subject position that one can occupy without being subjugated? Further, there is a concern that the discourse of disability studies should be controlled by people with disabilities, just as women's studies, for example, for the most part are run by women and queer studies tend to be organized by non-heterosexuals. The problem for people who take this stand is that since one's name does not

xvi

advertise one's disability, and print tends to be a medium in which disability does not stand out in any marked or semiological way, there is no way to 'tell' if someone who writes on the subject is disabled. How can the issue of identity be taken up at all if the quality that constitutes this special identification – an impairment or more than one impairment – cannot be identified?

But I am not answering the question, I am dodging the issue and delaying my response. That is true. My aim is to confound the question and by extension the category that the question begs. And my answer is not, and should not be, clear. If the very identity of disability studies is predicated on categories constructed by an ableist culture, then the response should be obstructive and objectionable. On the other hand, if one makes the conceptual leap to label oneself disabled – and even individuals with disabilities must make that leap, including themselves in the category for the purposes of a political movement – then the leap is the issue rather than the qualifications for the leap.

The answer to whether I am a person with disabilities or not is, as the fortune-telling Magic Eight-ball says, 'unclear.' I was born into a family with Deaf parents. My first 'word' was uttered in sign language. The word was 'milk,' a sign I made through the slats of my crib. I grew up in a Deaf world, in a Deaf culture, and with a Deaf sensibility. So in that sense, I am not deaf (hearing-impaired) but I am Deaf (culturally Deaf). I am what is now referred to as a CODA (Child of Deaf Adults), and as such I consider myself similar to people who have grown up in a bicultural family. My claim of authority to write this book is based partly on that in-between, liminal position I occupied and still occupy. This is an identity I did not take on easily. My initial response to Deafness was to define myself as hearing. My parents wanted me to be hearing, and that is what I wanted. I grew up and fled my restricted home for the greater freedom of Columbia University when I was just seventeen. I did not want to trail Deafness with me, and like many other CODAs, I did not look back.

It was not until I was in my forties that I began to make a return to my childhood culture. I attended a conference for CODAs and discovered that I had to consider myself bicultural, that I had suppressed the Deaf side of my existence. The journey of the last few years has been fascinating for me.[6] I am convinced that my participation in Deaf culture is not accidental and voyeuristic – it is a part of who I am.

So does that make me Deaf? Does that make me a person with disabilities? Perhaps the work of this book can answer that question at the right level of complexity. I also want to stand behind a position articulated in a 1994 Modern Language Association session on disability in which some people with disabilities stated that they did not want the discipline of disability studies to become ghettoized or marginalized by limiting entrance to those with recognizable impairments.

Which point brings me to a pronoun: 'them.' A colleague with disabilities expressed dismay when I showed her some work of mine. 'You use "them,"' she pointed out. I had written a line speaking of people with disabilities 'themselves.' She told me I had achieved the wrong tone and sentiment, I had created an 'us'– 'them' mentality. When I asked her what alternative I might try, she said that she herself did not like using 'us,' and she suggested avoiding 'them' altogether. The fact is that 'us' suggests that the author has an impairment. Just as whites who write about people of color cannot use 'us,' so must I avoid that term. Furthermore, 'us' is a rhetorical device that implies belonging, and a Deaf scholar might not write 'us' in speaking of people with disabilities. But though I do not feel right about using 'us,' 'them' seems to me a perfectly serviceable pronoun, and one without an equivalent. Writing may always imply an 'in' and an 'out' group. For example, I am pretty sure of who is 'in' my reading cohort and who is 'out.' I know that my academic colleagues and students might read this book; I assume that some people with disabilities might read it; and I know that the farmer down the road, the people in the neighborhood I grew up in, and most adolescents will not. Yet writers generally assume that there is a homogeneity in their audience expressed in that wonderful phrase from *Jane Eyre*, 'Reader, I married him.' Who that reader is does not matter.

The assumption is that all readers can be grouped into a large cohort. So, when I use the pronoun 'them,' I do so in the same spirit as one groups any readers or group, and with the same pitfalls and bad-faith assumptions.

I am sure that some or even many people with disabilities will feel that in acting as a theorizer of disability I am adopting a patronizing role, like those educators of the deaf who presumed to know better than the Deaf. This is a real and genuine objection. I can only respond that I am aware of the issues surrounding identity politics, and, while I can accept the existential argument that only a black person can understand blackness, I cannot accept the political implications of such an argument. To develop a working politics, one has to accept that the subject position one occupies is to some extent capable of being shared by others in parallel circumstances. From that point of view I consider myself somewhat Deaf. If I were a black person, I suppose that might be the equivalent of having biracial parents. In my growing up, I identified with the Deaf, and yet, to be completely honest, I never wanted to be deaf. I wanted to be hearing, to do what the hearing did, and in many ways I sought to leave deafness behind me. But I discovered that what I was fleeing was not deafness *per se*, but the deafness constructed by the hearing world. My parents themselves, born in 1898 and 1911, lacked coherent political explanations about the Deaf world, growing up as they did before this era's activism. Their defense was to say 'We are as good as anyone else' – the subaltern's defensive response. And they were as good as any other person in the South Bronx, which is to say that they were pretty badly off.

The work of many people in Deaf studies, but particularly Harlan Lane, himself hearing, led me to understand that deafness is a category of oppression. The capitalization of 'Deaf' and the political struggles around the 'Deaf President Now' movement at Gallaudet University symbolized for me the attempt to wrest deafness from the hearing world and back into the control of the Deaf. While many Deaf scholars and students now are comfortably in control of Deaf studies, there has been too little examination of the connection between Deafness and disability. Because many Deaf activists have strongly defined themselves as a linguistic minority and not disabled, political bonds and political activity have been discouraged between the Deaf and people with disabilities. I want to aid the dissemination of insights and the creation of intellectual categories so that deafness and disability can be seen rightly to belong with the more heavily lobbied categories of race, class, gender, sexual preference, and so on. I want to move through issues of Deafness to general statements about disability. While I understand that such a move will displease some in the Deaf community, I ask that they forbear in order to see what benefits, if any, may accrue from such a method.

There are many people to thank. I should begin with my parents Morris and Eva Davis, now both dead, who brought me into Deaf culture and shared their vision and their pains with me. I would also like to thank Randy Myers, whose letter to me engaged me in the CODA world. My appreciation and admiration also extend to Jenny Singleton, Bob Hoffmeister, and Stan Schuchman – scholars who taught me that Deafness was an academic discipline worthy of looking into; to Eliot Aheroni, who made me realize the legal consequences of being deaf; to Millie Brothers who started the organization CODA; to Simi Linton, Rosemarie Thomson, Jennifer Nelson, and Jim Swan, whose interactions have contributed to my understanding of issues; and to the many people whose autobiographical writings have enlightened me about varieties of disabilities and their special relations to society and to the body. Thanks to Binghamton University for a summer stipend and continued support to attend conferences. Thanks also to my colleague there, Constance Coiner, who has appreciated my story and offered her class to me at times to teach what I know. I also wish to thank my graduate student Dirksen Bauman, who has taught me much about American Sign Language poetry. And many thanks to Michael Sprinker for his encouragement and editorial suggestions. Finally, I would like to state my appreciation of my wife Bella Mirabella and my children Francesca and Carlo, who have all aided me in my rediscovery of Deafness, tolerated me when I sometimes felt more Deaf than hearing, and delved with feeling into a world they did not at first know they were part of.

1

Introduction: Disability, the Missing Term in the Race, Class, Gender Triad

> We are prisoners of a grammar invented at an early stage of human evolution, and it seems that, since we can think only by using language, our reason too is conditioned by the most primitive notions of reality.
>
> Friedrich Nietzsche, *The Will To Power*

I

The term 'disability,' as it is commonly and professionally used, is an absolute category without a level or threshold. One is either disabled or not. One cannot be a little disabled any more than one can be a little pregnant.

One must view with suspicion any term of such Procrustean dimensions. A concept with such a univalent stranglehold on meaning must contain within it a dark side of power, control, and fear. The aim of this book is to look into this dark side, to rend the veil from the apparently obvious object: the disabled person.[7]

For most temporarily abled people,[8] the issue of disability is a simple one. A person with a visible physical impairment (someone with an injured, nonstandard or nonfunctioning body or body part) or with a sensory or mental impairment (someone who has trouble hearing, seeing, or processing information) is considered disabled. The average, well-meaning 'normal' observer feels sorry for that disabled person, feels awkward about relating to the person, believes that the government or charity should provide special services, and gives thanks for not being disabled (as in ' I cried that I had no shoes until I met a man who had no feet').

What does not occur to many people is that disability is not a minor issue that relates to a relatively small number of unfortunate people; it is part of a historically constructed discourse, an ideology of thinking about the body under certain historical circumstances. Disability is not an object – a woman with a cane – but a social process that intimately involves everyone who has a body and lives in the world of the senses. Just as the conceptualization of race, class, and gender shapes the lives of those who are not black, poor, or female, so the concept of disability regulates the bodies of those who are 'normal.' In fact, the very concept of normalcy by which most people (by definition) shape their existence is in fact tied inexorably to the concept of disability, or rather, the concept of disability is a function of a concept of normalcy. Normalcy and disability are part of the same system.

It has been the rule that the subject of disability, until quite recently, has been written about by professionals who work with, medically treat, or study the disabled. In that discourse, people with disabilities have been an object of study, and the resulting information produced has constituted a discourse as controlling as any described by Michel Foucault. It has only been in recent years that people with disabilities have found a political voice and power and have been able to write about this experience. The previous discourse, heavily medicalized and oriented toward care and treatment, served its institutional purposes well. But it failed to understand dialectically its own position in the economy of power and control, and it failed to historicize its own assumptions and agency.

So the first task at hand is to understand and theorize the discourse of disability, to see that the object of disability studies is not the person using the wheelchair or the Deaf person but the set of social, historical, economic, and cultural processes that regulate and control the way we think about and think through the body. In addition, the presumption that disability is simply a biological fact, a universal plight of humanity throughout the ages, needs to be challenged. This study aims to show that disability, as we know the concept, is really a socially driven relation to the body that became relatively organized in the eighteenth and nineteenth centuries. This relation is propelled by economic and social factors and can be seen as part of a more general project to control and regulate the body. This analysis fits in with other aspects of the regulation of the body that we have come to call crime, sexuality, gender, disease, subalternity, and so on. Preindustrial societies tended to treat people with impairments as part of the social fabric, although admittedly not kindly, while postindustrial societies, instituting 'kindness,' ended up segregating and ostracizing such individuals through the discursivity of disability.

The category of 'disability,' while politically useful, particularly in the advantages and legal protection provided by legislation such as the Americans with Disabilities Act, is not without problems. Many Deaf people, for example, do not see themselves in the category of disabled, preferring to call themselves a linguistic minority. Indeed, the term 'physical minorities' gives more of a political sense to physical difference than the more abstract category 'disabled.' In the task of rethinking and theorizing disability, one of the first steps is to understand the relationship between a physical impairment and the political, social, even spatial environment that places that impairment in a matrix of meanings and significations.

To do this, one must begin to rethink disability so that one may consider the world-view presented by that disabled moment. I use the concept of the 'moment' in its philosophical context to allow us to think of blindness or deafness, say, as modalities not disabilities. I also want to separate the attribute from a time frame – so that blindness is not placed in a time continuity (a 'chrono-tope,' to use the literary critic Mikhail Bakhtin's term). When one speaks of disability, one always associates it with a story, places it in a narrative. A person became deaf, became blind, was born blind, became quadriplegic. The disability immediately becomes part of a chronotope, a time-sequenced narrative, embedded in a story. But by narrativizing an impairment, one tends to sentimentalize it and link it to the bourgeois sensibility of individualism and the drama of an individual story, as we have seen in so many films treating the subject of disability. So deafness, a physical fact, becomes deafness, a story, with a hero or a victim, a love story, a set of attributes (lively, hard-working, hot-headed). By using the concept of the disabled moment, I want to defamiliarize disability, denarrativize it, and in a sense debourgeoisify it. Of course, I do not intend permanently to divorce disability from people, but such a move might be necessary as an initial tactic.

As an example of the act of defamiliarization I am discussing, consider that everyone who reads this book is deaf. Even if you are not Deaf, you are deaf while you are reading. You are in a deafened modality or moment. All readers are deaf because they are defined by a process that does not require hearing or speaking (vocalizing). The sign language they are participating in is one that uses marks of ink on paper (or electrical/chemical markings on computer screens). Reading is a silent process, and although anyone can vocalize what he or she reads, the vocalization is a second-order activity. In fact, to be alive and thinking in the twentieth century implies that you have performed a lot of non-oral/aural activity of this sort. Your ideas, your thoughts, your beliefs, even your emotional, erotic life have been shaped by this nonverbal, nonauditory mode of sign language. This is a moment of disability.

I am making this point to illustrate how audist our biases are when it comes to thinking about deafness and hearing. It will be one of the aims of this book to lay bare the routine assumptions made about the 'clear' polarities of deafness and hearing, of disabled and abled. That binarism, like so many others – straight/gay, male/female, black/white, rich/poor – is part of an ideology of containment and a politics of power and fear. While many progressive intellectuals have stepped forward to decry racism, sexism, and class bias, it has not occurred to most of them that the very foundations on which their information systems are built, their very practices of reading and writing, seeing, thinking, and moving are themselves laden with assumptions about hearing, deafness, blindness, normalcy, paraplegia, and ability and disability in general. Indeed, our language is peppered with words and phrases like 'lame,' 'blind,' 'deaf and dumb,' 'deaf, dumb, and blind,' 'idiotic,' and so on that carry with them moral and ethical implications.[9]

For many years it has become a mark of commonplace courtesy and intellectual rigor to note occasions when racism, sexism, or class bias creep into discourse. The intellectual left, indeed, has been accused of being too rigorous in its insistence on calling people 'African-American', 'Ms,' 'othered' and so on. Yet there is a strange and really unaccountable silence when the issue of disability is raised (or, more to the point, never raised); the silence is stranger, too, since so much of left criticism has devoted itself to the issue of the body, of the social construction of sexuality and gender. Alternative bodies people this discourse: gay, lesbian, hermaphrodite, criminal, medical, and so on. But lurking behind these images of transgression and deviance is a much more transgressive and deviant figure: the disabled body.[10]

The disabled body is a nightmare for the fashionable discourse of theory because that discourse has been limited by the very predilection of the dominant, ableist culture. The body is seen as a site of *jouissance*, a native ground of pleasure, the scene of an excess that defies reason, that takes dominant culture and its rigid, power-laden vision of the body to task. The body of the left is an unruly body: a bad child thumbing its nose at the parent's bourgeois decorum; a rebellious daughter transgressing against the phallocentric patriarch. The nightmare of that body is one that is deformed, maimed, mutilated, broken, diseased. Observations of chimpanzees reveal that they fly in terror from a decapitated chimp; dogs, by contrast, will just sniff at the remains of a fellow dog. That image of the screaming chimpanzee facing the mutilated corpse is the image of the critic of *jouissance* contemplating the paraplegic, the disfigured, the mutilated, the deaf, the blind. Rather than face this ragged image, the critic turns to the fluids of sexuality, the gloss of lubrication, the glossary of the body as text, the heteroglossia of the intertext, the glossolalia of the schizophrenic. But almost never the body of the differently abled.

Recently, an editor at a prominent university press denied this assertion of culpability by claiming in all good faith that academics really were not exposed to many disabled people. This silence was a sin of omission rather than commission, he maintained, since how many deaf people did one run into? But this editor was simply participating in an ableist discourse – setting the limits of the argument with common sense. In some universities where diversity requirements have been instituted, there has been a struggle over including disability – which seems to some people of color to be a side current that would simply muddy the waters about the central issue of racism.

To the dominant culture, even to what can still be considered the counter-culture, by their own definitions, only a small fraction of the population appears to be disabled; these people with disabilities would be equally distributed across race, gender, and class lines. This notion must, however, be seen as ideology, not as knowledge. In the realm of the body, ableist culture still reigns supreme. However, by most calculations, about one in ten people are disabled. About the same percentage have some hearing loss, if you include late-deafened adults. But the editor maintained that such people, hard-of-hearing grandparents or cousins with bad knees or eyes, could be excluded since they were not 'really' disabled. And advocates of diversity requirements do not recognize that cohort as constituting a legitimate minority.

Did these people realize that when they encountered the work of Rosa Luxemburg (who limped), Antonio Gramsci (a crippled, dwarfed hunchback), John Milton (blind), Alexander Pope (dwarfed hunchback), George Gordon Byron (club foot), José Luis Borges, James Joyce, and James Thurber (all blind), Harriet Martineau (deaf), Toulouse-Lautrec (spinal deformity), Frida Kahlo (osteomyelitis), Virginia Woolf (lupus), they were meeting people with disabilities? Do filmgoers realize when they watch the films of John Ford, Raoul Walsh, André de Toth, Nicholas Ray, Tay Garnett and William Wyler that these directors were all physically impaired (Norden 1994, 4)? Why is it when one looks up these figures in dictionaries of biography or encyclopedias that their physical disabilities are usually not mentioned – unless the disability is seen as related to creativity, as in the case of the blind bard Milton or the deaf Beethoven? There is an ableist notion at work here that anyone who creates a canonical work must be physically able. Likewise, why do we not know that Helen Keller was a socialist, a member of the Wobblies, the International Workers of the World, and an advocate of free love? We assume that our 'official' mascots of disability are nothing else but their disability.

The problem, of course, is that the manner in which this society defines disability in fact creates the category. Able-bodied (or temporarily able-bodied) people safely wall off the severely disabled so that they cannot be seen as part of a continuum of physical differences, just as white culture isolates blackness as a skin color so as not to account for degrees of melanin production. How many people with hearing aids consider themselves deaf; how many people with knee braces consider themselves impaired?[11]

The fact is that impairment of the human body is a relatively common phenomenon. It has been estimated that there are some 500 million severely impaired people in the world, approximately one in ten among the world's population (Shirley, 1983). That statistic is repeated at the national level: in 1991 the Institute of Medicine estimated a total of 35 million disabled in the USA, one in seven people. Other federal data go as high as 43 million. But these data do not include those with AIDS or those who are HIV-positive. (Shapiro 1993, 7). A United States census estimates that 13,110,000 people aged from sixteen to sixty-four have work-related disabilities, putting 8.5 percent of all working-age females and 9.3 percent of all working-age men in this category (US Bureau of Census 1982). When we consider that about one in ten Americans lives below the poverty line, or that one in eight women will develop breast cancer, we can see that disability is by no means uncommon.

In the process of disabling people with disabilities, ableist society creates the absolute category of disability. 'Normal' people tend to think of 'the disabled' as the deaf, the blind, the orthopedically impaired, the mentally retarded. But the fact is that disability includes, according to the Rehabilitation Act of 1973, those who are regarded as having a limitation or interference with daily life activities such as hearing, speaking, seeing, walking, moving, thinking, breathing, and learning. Under this definition, one now has to include people with invisible impairments such as arthritis, diabetes, epilepsy, muscular dystrophy, cystic fibrosis, multiple sclerosis, heart and respiratory problems, cancer, developmental disabilities, dyslexia, AIDS, and so on (Fine and Asch 1988, 9). When we start conceiving of disability as a descriptive term and not as an absolute category, then we can begin to think in theoretical and political ways about this category.

Another issue to recall is that disabilities are acquired. Only 15 percent of people with disabilities are born with their impairments. Disabilities are acquired by living in the world, but also by working in factories, driving insufficiently safe cars, living in toxic environments or high-crime areas. Poor people comprise a disproportionate number of the disabled – this is borne out by comparisons both within the United States and between First and Third World countries – frequently born with low weight, succumbing to diseases that vaccines and medicines would prevent, working and living in dangerous conditions, and living with poor public hygiene. In Uganda, for example, the major causes of disabling impairments are malnutrition, communicable diseases, low quality of prenatal care, and accidents including crime-related incidents (Mallory 1993, 87). In addition, people aged over sixty-five make up one-third of those with disabilities (Shapiro 1993, 6). The longer we live, the more likely we are to be disabled. Furthermore, medical advances have kept people alive who otherwise would have died from their disabilities. This increase in the numbers of the disabled is particularly notable in the case of premature babies, those with spinal cord injuries, and older people with debilitating conditions. In sum, there are more disabled people in the USA than there are, say, African-Americans. The odds are pretty good that many 'normal' people reading these words will become disabled within twenty or thirty years, and many readers with disabilities will become people with multiple disabilities.

Why we think of disability as a totalizing category is complex. 'The label of disability carries with it such a powerful imputation of inability to perform any adult social function that there is no other descriptor needed by the public' (Gliedman and Roth 1980, cited in Fine and Asch 1988, 12). The point is that successful disabled people – the Julius Caesars, the Itzak Perlmans, the Sarah Bernhardts – have their disability erased by their success. And as for the more famous people with remembered disabilities – John Milton, Ludwig van Beethoven, Franklin Delano Roosevelt, or even Stevie Wonder – we tend to see them as people who overcame their disabilities or used them in ways we conventionally associate with the genius of creativity.

It is interesting that the historical record rarely reveals disability among figures in government, perhaps because a physical impairment was not judged important to one's ability to perform the duties of public office in the preindustrial world. It comes as a surprise, therefore, to read the following description of King James I of England by a contemporary: 'His legs were very weak, having had, as was thought, some foul play in his youth, or rather before he was born, that he was not able to stand at seven years of age – that weakness made him ever leaning on other men's shoulders' (Youngs et al. 1988, 133). Similarly, though rarely referred to in contemporary records, we know that Peter Stuyvesant, first governor of New Amsterdam, had only one leg, that Gouverneur Morris, who helped draft the Constitution and was later a senator from New York, wore a 'rough stick' to replace the leg he lost in a 1780 carriage accident. Stephen Hopkins, one of the signers of the Declaration of Independence, had cerebral palsy, which he referred to when he took the pen to sign the document saying, 'My hand trembles but my heart does not' (Shapiro 1993, 59). The fact that we do not know this history of disability, that the record has never taken note of these impairments, shows us, perhaps, that such differences were not, by definition, memorable. Or if they were memorable were not seen as impairing function.

'The crucial point is that the disabled person, as conceived by the nondisabled world, has no abilities or social functions [and] . . . those who do perform successfully are no longer viewed as disabled' (Fine and Asch 1988, 12). This erasure occurs because stereotyping requires that a person be categorized in terms of one exclusive trait. Disabled people are thought of primarily in terms of their disability, just as sexual preference, gender, or ethnicity becomes the defining factor in perceiving another person.

There is a tremendous conceptual gap between being impaired and being disabled. As soon as we use the term 'disabled' we add a political element: suddenly there is a disabler and a disabled. Claire Liachowitz makes the point forcefully:

> much of the inability to function that characterizes physically impaired people is an outcome of political and social decisions rather than medical limitations . . . an increasing number of sociological and psychological theorists regard disability as a complex of constraints that the able-bodied population imposes on the behavior of physically impaired people. (Liachowitz 1988, xi, xiii)

This conceptualization involves the idea that in an ableist society, the 'normal' people have constructed the world physically and cognitively to reward those with like abilities and handicap those with unlike abilities. For example, television had the capacity to caption broadcasts for a long time, but by not making such technology available, networks made it difficult if not impossible for deaf viewers to follow programs. Now that all televisions in America will have a decoder chip built into them, deaf viewers can have the opportunity to watch and understand any television show. Similarly, people in wheelchairs would have no problem with access to buildings or transportation if architecture and design considered accommodating them. Only in 1994 did Avis, at the prodding of the Attorney General, agree to install more hand controls for paraplegics in its cars (*New York Times*, 2 September 1994, A:20). Operas, plays, and television broadcasts have begun, on a very limited basis, to provide visual interpreters for blind people. Again, if exhibitions supposedly open to the 'public' were to accommodate the 10 percent of the population with disabilities by having interpretative facilities for the blind, the deaf, people in wheelchairs, and so on, then such people would be able to attend as if 'normal.'[12]

In fashioning some kind of theoretical approach to disability, one must consider the fact that the disabled body is not a discrete object but rather a set of social relations. In fact, the body generally, as I will discuss in Chapter 6, has been conceptualized as a simple object when it is in fact a complex focus for competing power structures. For example, if I ask you to think about the nude in art, chances are good that you will visualize a specific kind of body. Chances are remarkably good that the body will be female, white, and not visibly impaired. Few readers would imagine an Asian woman or a woman of color, even fewer a nude using a wheelchair. The reasons for such visualized assumptions are complex, involving further assumptions about beauty, about idealization, about sexuality, about gender, and so on. Intricately placed in that web of assumptions is a power move, I would call it, to fix the body as entire, intact, whole.

This process of visualization needs to be considered when one theorizes disability. Disability presents itself to 'normal' people through two main modalities – function and appearance. In the functional modality, disability is conceived of as inability to do something – walk, talk, hear, see, manipulate, and so on. This aspect of disability is of course part of a continuum of the many things that people can or cannot do. For example, I cannot do mathematical functions very well therefore I am somewhat learning-impaired. Few would consider that limitation a disability. But if I cannot walk very well with a prosthetic limb or a club foot, then I am disabled. The construction of disability is based on a deconstruction of a continuum. The functional modality has to do with standards of movement, sight, hearing and so on that have been established in a quantitative way. If my vision is less than 20/20 with glasses then I am legally blind, but if my vision is problematic but correctable, then I am not. These standards are part of a quantification of the human body begun in the nineteenth century which will be discussed in Chapter 2. And these standards are perhaps not un-related to the standardized movements of the body demanded in factory work. So the functional side seems at least to have a practical, technical, class-related side to it as well.

The question of appearance is the second major modality by which disability is constructed. The person with disabilities is visualized, brought into a field of vision, and seen as a disabled person. Here Erving Goffman's notion of 'stigma' comes into play 'since it is through our sense of sight that the stigma of others most frequently becomes evident' (Goffman 1963, 48). The body of the disabled person is seen as marked by the disability. The missing limb, blind gaze, use of sign language, wheelchair or prosthesis is seen by the 'normal' observer. Disability is a specular moment.[13] The power of the gaze to control, limit, and patrol the disabled person is brought to the fore. Accompanying the gaze are a welter of powerful emotional responses. These responses can include horror, fear, pity, compassion, and avoidance.

Several points are to be made here. The first is that attention must be paid to the violence of the response – in a way more than to the object of the response. As Freud realized, disgust or repulsion masks a secret attraction to the object; so too must one analyze the negative feelings associated with disability. The common response of 'normal' people is to say that the disabled object produces strong feelings ranging from disgust to pity in the observer. But that approach seems to be more an ideological justification than a political explanation. Rather, it would seem more appropriate to say that the disabled object is produced or constructed by the strong feelings of repulsion. A person with an impairment is turned into a disabled person by the Medusa-like gaze of the observer; paradoxically, the observer becomes disabled by his or her reaction to the disabled person. The social context becomes disabled, as one sociologist detailed the stages of this process: '. . . the familiar signs of discomfort and stickiness [of the 'normal' toward people with disabilities]: the guarded references, the common everyday words suddenly made taboo, the fixed stare

12

elsewhere, the artificial levity, the compulsive loquaciousness, the awkward solemnity' (cited in Goffman 1963, 19).

What is repulsion after all but the personal, internalized version of the desire to repel, repress, extroject, annihilate the object? Repulsion is the learned response on an individual level that is carried out on a societal level in actions such as incarceration, institutionalization, segregation, discrimination, marginalization, and so on. Thus, the 'normal,' 'natural' response to a person with disabilities is in reality a socially conditioned, politically generated response. This aspect of repulsion, its constructed side, is obvious to anyone who has grown up with family members who have disabilities or to anyone who lives with a person with disabilities. In temporarily abled people brought up in disabled families the imperative to cast out, to repulse has never been established. The person with a disability is just that – a person with some kind of limitation or difference. One student told me that her mother had no fingers on one hand. As a child she had never considered this particularly strange, and she was always surprised when strangers stared at her mother's hand. To her it was a loving, caressing hand that she might joke about, kiss, or hold. The point is not that she was habituated to what others might consider a horror, but that she had not received the instruction to cast the hand away.

This brings me to another major point. Disability exists in the realm of the senses. The disabled body is embodied through the senses. So there is a kind of reciprocal relationship between the senses and disability. A person may be impaired by the lack of a sense – sight, hearing, taste, or even touch, although touch is almost never completely gone. Yet paradoxically, it is through the senses that disability is perceived. One understands this more clearly when one thinks of cyberspace. In the space of e-mail, for example, some disabilities disappear: the Deaf, for example, or people using wheelchairs or with other physical limitations, are not disabled. In 'talking' with Deaf colleagues on e-mail, particularly those whom I have never 'seen,' I often 'forget' that my interlocutor is deaf. Recently, in planning to attend a session at the Modern Language

Association on disability, I received and sent a welter of messages on e-mail to a number of people involved. I had no way of knowing which of these people was disabled, or in which way. When speaking on the telephone with a person who uses a wheelchair, I have no way of knowing if that person is unable to walk. The sense of sight, what James Joyce called 'the ineluctable modality of the visible,' is really not that ineluctable. Many disabilities are constructed through the sense of sight and can be deconstructed in virtually real locations that do not rely on sight. Or, to take another example, the Deaf are perceived as such because one hears a different speech inflection or sees sign language. Without those sensory clues, the Deaf are embedded in the sensory grid of the 'normal' person. To a passerby on the street, the Deaf person is indistinguishable from anyone else until he or she begins to engage in communication.

The point is that the body is not only – or even primarily – a physical object. It is in fact a way of organizing through the realm of the senses the variations and modalities of physical existence as they are embodied into being through a larger social/political matrix. As Robert F. Murphy points out (1987, 133), disability 'is not just a departure from the moral code, but a distortion of conventional classification and knowing.'

Another major point is that most constructions of disability assume that the person with disabilities is in some sense damaged while the observer is undamaged. Furthermore, there is an assumption that society at large is intact, normal, setting a norm, undamaged. But the notion of an undamaged observer who is part of an undamaged society is certainly one that needs to be questioned. The social critic Theodor Adorno subtitled his work *Minima Moralia* as *Reflections from a Damaged Life*. While Adorno was not disabled in any traditional sense, he saw his life as damaged because he saw society as profoundly damaged and damaging. 'Our perspective of life passed into an ideology which conceals the fact that there is life no longer' (Adorno 1984, 15). From a materialist perspective it is difficult to construct a model that does not include the notion that contemporary life is disabled, dysfunctional, dystopic. Adorno wrote: 'The libidinal achievements demanded of an individual behaving as healthy in body and mind, are such as can be performed only at the cost of the profoundest mutilation . . . ' (ibid., 58). The attempt to make a simple relation between subject and object in which a disabled subject is linked to an able object is dialectical anathema. The process of perception is bound up in a toing and froing of interaction that makes the paradigm of the observer–observed patently simplistic.

So in thinking of disability, we have to consider the disability of thinking. Thought and modes of thought will necessarily contain within them their own disincentives to theorize disability. The problems of the ideology of language, the predisposition of philosophy and thought to contain within them reified elements of Enlightenment doctrines – doctrines that postulate the benefits of wholeness, of the ideal, of the totality of systems – will make it nearly impossible to wrest that language into the service of a new way of seeing (feeling, touching, signing). In theorizing disability, then, we must develop a different way of conceptualizing the visual field, of thinking about seeing, of perceiving thinking. In that sense, we will seek to correct the simple relation between subject and object, between subjected beings and bodies and their objecti-fication by a world that sees them, and by seeing opposes them.

II

To make the point about the repression of disability more dramatic, I would like to focus on one of the foundational ableist myths of our culture: that the norm for humans is to speak and hear, to engage in communication through speaking and hearing. In challenging this supposition, I will rely on some of the arguments put forth by Jeffrey Kittay and Wlad Godzich in *The Emergence of Prose*. In the same sense that the norm of gender was seen as masculine, and the norm of race was seen as white, and the norm of class was seen as bourgeois, the norm of signifying practice is

seen as prose. As Kittay and Godzich point out, the impression
we have is that people spoke in prose first and then in verse, while
the opposite may have been true. But still we believe that the
universal, undiacritical method of communication is prose. Their
point is that the method that a culture chooses as its main
signifying practice tells us much about that culture.

> Which kinds of messages are transmitted through which kinds of
> signifying practices? What are the differences among signifying
> practices, and why is one kind of message rather than another
> relegated to one signifying practice rather than another? . . . Is it to
> be communicated between physical, bodily presences or via inert
> signs? (Kittay and Godzich 1987, 4)

From the point of view of this chapter, the facile equation
made between speaking/hearing and writing – all seen as linked
signifying practices – is actually a much more complex set of
arrangements. If we look carefully, we can see that the aural/oral
method of communicating, itself seen as totally natural, like all
signifying practices, is not natural but based on sets of assumptions
about the body, about reality, and of course about power. For
example, Kittay and Godzich point out that the recording of verse,
the writing down of the performance of the bard, is not a simple
act of transcription; nor can we say that writing has taken over from
performance. They maintain that in the Middle Ages, such written
texts were meant not as texts *per se* but as scripts for performance,
that is, 'the text to be read is a virtuality to be actualized in
performance' (ibid., 15). As texts became more common, a switch
occurred to a consciousness of textuality that was no longer to be
performed. It is at that moment that prose arose.

Prose for them 'withholds itself from view. . . . It thus can claim
a foundational role and functions as the ground of reference, a sort
of degree-zero of language for all further formal elaboration. . . .
Prose is meant to have no place; prose does not happen. Prose is
what assigns place' (ibid., 197). In the same way that prose appears
to be a neutral, surrounding medium that invisibly embodies

thought, so too speech appears as the anterior wall onto which prose throws its grappling hook. 'But speech is not the end of the regress; speech is body-generated language; under and around speech, as in performance, is the individual *soma*' (ibid., 198). Prose points in a diexis to speech as the anterior logical ground for originary myths of signifying practice.

Kittay and Godzich alert us to beware of naturalistic explanations for signifying systems. In this world of signification, common sense makes bad sense. If we follow the commonsense explanation, humans begin in prehistory with gestures and then move to words. Rousseau puts the argument best. In his essay on the origins of language, he notes that 'speech distinguishes man among the animals' and that speech 'owes its form to natural causes alone' (1966, 5). He attributes speech to 'instinct' rather than rationality, and notes that while gesture and speech are both natural, 'the first is easier and depends less upon conventions' (ibid., 6). Rousseau moves from gesture to speech to writing as a natural progression, although he allows gesture to coexist with speech. 'It seems then that need dictated the first gestures, while the passions stimulated the first words' (ibid., 11).

What is wrong with this model? Or, more appropriately, what kind of assumptions are linked to this naturalized way of thinking about signifying practices? First, the model presumes crude gestures arose first leading to that articulated language – the aural/oral form of communication – seen as natural, common, and universal. But may we not construct another originary myth? What if a highly articulated and developed sign language like American Sign Language predated speech? Why do we always assume that crude gestures preceded speech or, as with prose, that speech preceded writing? A sign language, as is currently spoken by the Deaf throughout the world, could well have been the first signifying practice. In fact, it is impossible to ascertain whether humans spoke or signed first; or, as with the native Americans, whether they spoke and signed concurrently.

I realize I am making an extreme argument, but I am doing so to question the simplicity with which we assume that speech and prose are natural. Even Rousseau acknowledged that sign language could be highly elaborated and not composed merely of crude gestures:

> The mutes of great nobles understand each other, and understand everything that is said to them by means of signs, just as well as one can understand anything said in discourse. M. Pereyra and those like him who not only consider that mutes speak, but claim to understand what they are saying, had to learn another language, as complicated as our own, in order to understand them. (ibid., 9)

In fact, there is some evidence that sign language may well have preceded speech. Only about 250,000 years ago do we see the appearance of a human larynx similar to the one we have today. In terms of human evolution, this a very late development. If the facility for language appeared earlier, if the brain developed before the vocal chords, as it appears, then it is at least possible that sign language was the norm. The fact that the movements of the hands when people use sign language are controlled not by the motor part of the brain, which controls fine movements of the hand, but rather by the language areas in the brain called Broca's Region, indicates a somatic connection between language and signing. Researchers have recently shown us that sign language will evolve in deaf children whether or not there is a signing adult teaching them. Furthermore, research indicates that the sign language improves as the children speak with each other, even if the parent's sign language does not improve (*New York Times*, 1 September 1992, B:6). In other words, in individuals with a brain that processes language, a fully articulated sign language will develop whether or not there is a vocal capacity. Hence, a fully articulated and grammatical sign language could have been our first language, as it becomes every day when deaf children begin in the world babbling in sign.

Another point needs to be made here. In setting up the common-sense notion that language occurs in two forms and only two forms – speech or writing – we are engaging in a tautology based on an equation of language as such and reason. Steven Pinker points out that there is no inherent connection between the particular language a culture uses and language *per se*. Nor is it correct to link that language to reason or thought. In fact, as he points out, thought and grammar are human instincts, not particularly dependent on language (Pinker 1994, 85). In other words, we can think and form concepts without language, using what he calls 'mentalese.' If what we have is a grammar that is built into our brains, or had been discovered at some time in human history, the particular kind of language that emerges – spoken, signed, or whatever – does not really matter. So the idea that sign language is the radical other of speech is actually quite incorrect (ibid., 57). Speech is no better or worse than sign, and Pinker points out that writing and speech are by no means as clear forms of communication as we might think. Even the 'obviousness' or 'naturalness' of speech is called into question. For example, Pinker notes that 'all speech is an illusion' (ibid., 159) in which we do not so much listen to a speaker as try to fit that speech into preconstructed categories, so that 'we simply hallucinate word boundaries when we reach the edge of a stretch of sound that matches some entry in our mental dictionary' (ibid., 159–60). In other words, the limpid clarity of speech is itself an illusion that conceals the extent to which the receiver of speech is continually improvising to make the act of talking make sense. Likewise writing is called into question as the best possible way to record or transfer language. Pinker points out that while language is an instinct, 'written language was not' (ibid., 189). He notes that most societies have lacked written language, that alphabetic writing was only invented once in history by a particular culture and then borrowed by other cultures. 'Illiteracy . . . is the rule in much of the world, and dyslexia . . . [is] found in five to ten percent of the population' (ibid.). By conceptualizing *language* as writing and speech, or by fetishizing the aural/oral incarnation of language, we are performing in effect an act of repression against language, in the largest sense of the term.

Rather than seeing speech as a naturally occurring and inherently superior method of communicating, it might be intellectually more rigorous and less ableist to see that sign language may have been actively repressed in some cultures in favor of a hegemony of the aural/oral signifying practices and eventually in the direction of the hegemony of prose. For when sign language is repressed as a signifying practice, what is repressed is a connection with the body. The body of course will signify, and indeed linguistic studies routinely tell us that a great part, perhaps the majority, of communication is accomplished through body language.

As a signifying practice, what advantages are there to sign language? First, it is linked to the performative. As Kittay and Godzich suggest about verse, sign language does not have difficulty in pointing, in indicating. Prose must torturously defy its own constraints to indicate who is speaking, who is acting, where things are. Verse and sign language quite simply are more closely associated with a certain kind of truth of being. The signifying process associated with bard or *jongleur*, associated with verse, participates in a world whose communications are more immanent. Sign language, like verse, is a language in which 'the diexis is *implicit*' (Kittay and Godzich 1987, 21). In other words, the language indicates directly by embodying, literally, the narrative.

The myth that needs to be debunked is that speech is somehow closer to writing than is sign language. The 'natural' progression gesture–speech–writing is in fact wrong. Sign language is far closer to writing than is speech. Speech is an oral production linked to the mouth. Sign language can be seen as a form of writing done in space rather than on paper. Typing, for example, is closer to signing than it is to speech. This analogy allows me to argue, in Chapter 3, that the Deaf person becomes actualized as a cultural icon in the eighteenth century when European society began, on a mass scale, to read.

An illustration of our bias toward speech and writing, as well as toward seeing and hearing, can be found in a fascinating short story 'The Persistence of Vision' by John Varley. He envisions a Utopian society called Keller in which all the people are blind and deaf. The narrator intrudes into this society and is befriended by a young woman who is the daughter of blind–deaf parents although she, like all the offspring, can see and hear, since the adults were blind and deaf as a result of a rubella epidemic, not genetic factors. The narrator's words come to us through the medium of writing, but he discovers that the society communicates through 'bodytalk,' a variant of finger spelling. The narrator's written version cannot represent the hand gestures:

> 'That's (—) and (—),' she said, the parentheses indicating a series of hand motions against my palm. I never learned a sound word as a name for any of them . . . and I can't reproduce the bodytalk names they had. (Varley 1978, 284)

Varley has to face the dilemma of how to represent signing in a medium that authorizes the scriptable. His narrator has to conceptualize a world in which the priority of speech and prose is made irrelevant.

But in this society there is another level of communication called 'Touch,' a deeper kind of communication achieved through physical contact of naked bodies. Blindness when combined with deafness necessitates touch. Touch, as Varley makes clear, is very underutilized in an aural/oral/visual world. The line between the sexual and the nonsexual, between heterosexuality and homosexuality is erased, since all body contact is a form of talk, and everyone talks with everyone. The language Touch is itself a metalanguage, a language beyond language.

> It was a language of inventing languages. Everyone spoke their own dialect because everyone spoke with a different instrument: a different body and set of life experiences. It was modified by everything. *It would not stand still.* (ibid., 307, emphasis in original)

It is precisely in the place of deafness and blindness, so long considered to be a locus of inarticulateness, of confusion, that Varley sees the ultimate in communicative clarity. Yet the aural/oral/seeing narrator realizes he will never be able to be part of the society. 'Unless I was willing to put out my eyes and ears,

I would always be on the outside. I would be the blind and deaf one' (ibid., 312). So he leaves, only to return later and receive the gift of blindness and deafness in some real and metaphorical way at the same time.

While the short story contains some of the stereotypical hallmarks of literature about the disabled, it also manages to make some interesting points. In following the clichés of such fiction, the author gives special intuitive or compensatory powers to the blind–deaf. They are empathetic and erotic, in tune with nature and ethically upright. The story is framed by a love connection between an outsider and one of the members of the society (although in this case Pink is both of and not of the society – she is bicultural, if you like). But the main point is a strong one: that our construction of the normal world is based on a radical repression of disability, and that given certain power structures, a society of people with disabilities can and does easily survive and render 'normal' people outsiders. The aim of the rest of this book is to show how and why this is so.

2

Constructing Normalcy

> If such a thing as a psycho-analysis of today's prototypical culture
> were possible ... such an investigation would needs show the
> sickness proper to the time to consist precisely in normality.
>
> Theodor Adorno, *Minima Moralia*

We live in a world of norms. Each of us endeavors to be normal
or else deliberately tries to avoid that state. We consider what
the average person does, thinks, earns, or consumes. We rank our
intelligence, our cholesterol level, our weight, height, sex drive,
bodily dimensions along some conceptual line from subnormal to
above-average. We consume a minimum daily balance of vitamins
and nutrients based on what an average human should consume.
Our children are ranked in school and tested to determine where
they fit into a normal curve of learning, of intelligence. Doctors
measure and weigh them to see if they are above or below average
on the height and weight curves. There is probably no area of
contemporary life in which some idea of a norm, mean, or average
has not been calculated.

To understand the disabled body, one must return to the
concept of the norm, the normal body. So much of writing about
disability has focused on the disabled person as the object of study,
just as the study of race has focused on the person of color. But as
with recent scholarship on race, which has turned its attention to
whiteness, I would like to focus not so much on the construction
of disability as on the construction of normalcy. I do this because

the 'problem' is not the person with disabilities; the problem is the way that normalcy is constructed to create the 'problem' of the disabled person.

A common assumption would be that some concept of the norm must have always existed. After all, people seem to have an inherent desire to compare themselves to others. But the idea of a norm is less a condition of human nature than it is a feature of a certain kind of society. Recent work on the ancient Greeks, on preindustrial Europe, and on tribal peoples, for example, shows that disability was once regarded very differently from the way it is now. As we will see, the social process of disabling arrived with industrialization and with the set of practices and discourses that are linked to late eighteenth- and nineteenth-century notions of nationality, race, gender, criminality, sexual orientation, and so on.

I begin with the rather remarkable fact that the constellation of words describing this concept 'normal,' 'normalcy,' 'normality,' 'norm,' 'average,' 'abnormal' – all entered the European languages rather late in human history. The word 'normal' as 'constituting, conforming to, not deviating or differing from, the common type or standard, regular, usual' only enters the English language around 1840. (Previously, the word had meant 'perpendicular'; the carpenter's square, called a 'norm,' provided the root meaning.) Likewise, the word 'norm,' in the modern sense, has only been in use since around 1855, and 'normality' and 'normalcy' appeared in 1849 and 1857 respectively. If the lexicographical information is relevant, it is possible to date the coming into consciousness in English of an idea of 'the norm' over the period 1840–1860.

If we rethink our assumptions about the universality of the concept of the norm, what we might arrive at is the concept that preceded it: that of the 'ideal,' a word we find dating from the seventeenth century. Without making too simplistic a division in the historical chronotope, one can nevertheless try to imagine a world in which the hegemony of normalcy does not exist. Rather, what we have is the ideal body, as exemplified in the tradition of nude Venuses, for example. This idea presents a mytho-poetic body that is linked to that of the gods (in traditions in which the god's body is visualized). This divine body, then, this ideal body, is not attainable by a human. The notion of an ideal implies that, in this case, the human body as visualized in art or imagination must be composed from the ideal parts of living models. These models individually can never embody the ideal since an ideal, by definition, can never be found in this world. When ideal human bodies occur, they do so in mythology. So Venus or Helen of Troy, for example, would be the embodiment of female physical beauty.

The painting by François-André Vincent *Zeuxis Choosing as Models the Most Beautiful Girls of the Town of Crotona* (1789, Museé du Louvre, Paris) shows the Greek artist, as we are told by Pliny, lining up all the beautiful women of Crotona in order to select in each her ideal feature or body part and combine these into the ideal figure of Aphrodite, herself an ideal of beauty. One young woman provides a face and another her breasts. Classical painting and sculpture tend to idealize the body, evening out any particularity. The central point here is that in a culture with an ideal form of the body, all members of the population are below the ideal. No one young lady of Crotona can be the ideal. By definition, one can never have an ideal body. There is in such societies no demand that populations have bodies that conform to the ideal.

By contrast, the *grotesque* as a visual form was inversely related to the concept of the ideal and its corollary that all bodies are in some sense disabled. In that mode, the grotesque is a signifier of the people, of common life. As Bakhtin, Stallybrass and White, and others have shown, the use of the grotesque had a life-affirming, transgressive quality in its inversion of the political hierarchy. However, the grotesque was not equivalent to the disabled, since, for example, it is impossible to think of people with disabilities now being used as architectural decorations as the grotesque were on the façades of cathedrals throughout Europe. The grotesque permeated culture and signified the norm, whereas the disabled body, a later concept, was formulated as by definition excluded from culture, society, the norm.

If the concept of the norm or average enters European culture, or at least the European languages, only in the nineteenth century, one has to ask what is the cause of this conceptualization? One of the logical places to turn in trying to understand concepts like 'norm' and 'average' is that branch of knowledge known as statistics. Statistics begins in the early modern period as 'political arithmetic' – a use of data for 'promotion of sound, well-informed state policy' (Porter 1986, 18). The word *statistik* was first used in 1749 by Gottfried Achenwall, in the context of compiling information about the state. The concept migrated somewhat from the state to the body when Bisset Hawkins defined medical statistics in 1829 as 'the application of numbers to illustrate the natural history of health and disease' (cited in Porter, 1986, 24). In France, statistics were mainly used in the area of public health in the early nineteenth century. The connection between the body and industry is tellingly revealed in the fact that the leading members of the first British statistical societies formed in the 1830s and 1840s were industrialists or had close ties to industry (ibid., 32).

It was the French statistician Adolphe Quetelet (1796–1847) who contributed the most to a generalized notion of the normal as an imperative. He noticed that the 'law of error,' used by astronomers to locate a star by plotting all the sightings and then averaging the errors, could be equally applied to the distribution of human features such as height and weight. He then took a further step of formulating the concept of 'l'homme moyen' or the average man. Quetelet maintained that this abstract human was the average of all human attributes in a given country. For the average man, Quetelet wrote in 1835, 'all things will occur in conformity with the mean results obtained for a society. If one seeks to establish, in some way, the basis of a social physics, it is he whom one should consider . . .' (cited in ibid., 53). Quetelet's average man was a combination of *l'homme moyen physique* and *l'homme moyen morale*, both a physically average and a morally average construct.

The social implications of this idea are central. In formulating the idea of *l'homme moyen*, Quetelet is also providing a justification for *les classes moyens*. With bourgeois hegemony comes scientific justification for moderation and middle-class ideology. The average man, the body of the man in the middle, becomes the exemplar of the middle way of life. Quetelet was apparently influenced by the philosopher Victor Cousin in developing an analogy between the notion of an average man and the *juste milieu*. This term was associated with Louis Philippe's July monarchy – a concept that melded bourgeois hegemony with the constitutional monarchy and celebrated moderation and middleness (ibid., 101). In England too, the middle class as the middle way or mean had been searching for a scientific justification. The statement in *Robinson Crusoe* in which Robinson's father extols middle-class life as a kind of norm is a good example of this ideology:

> the middle Station had the fewest Disasters, and was not expos'd to so many Vicissitudes as the higher or lower Part of Mankind; nay, they were not subjected to so many Distempers and Uneasiness either of Body or Mind, as those were who, by vicious Living, Luxury and Extravagancies on one Hand, or by hard Labour, Want of Necessaries, and mean or insufficient Diet on the other Hand, bring Distempers upon themselves by the natural consequences of their Way of Living; That the middle Station of Life was calculated for all kinds of Vertues and all kinds of Enjoyments; that Peace and Plenty were the Hand-maids of a middle Fortune; that Temperance, Moderation, Quietness, Health, Society, all agreeable Diversions, and all desirable Pleasures, were the Blessings attending the middle Station of Life. (Defoe 1975, 6)

Statements of ideology of this kind saw the bourgeoisie as rationally placed in the mean position in the great order of things. This ideology can be seen as developing the kind of science that would then justify the notion of a norm.[14]

With such thinking, the average then becomes paradoxically a kind of ideal, a position devoutly to be wished. As Quetelet wrote, 'an individual who epitomized in himself, at a given time, all the qualities of the average man, would represent at once all the greatness, beauty and goodness of that being' (cited in Porter 1986, 102). Such an average person might indeed be a literary character like Robinson Crusoe. Furthermore, one must observe that Quetelet meant this hegemony of the middle to apply not only to moral qualities but to the body as well. He wrote: 'deviations more or less great from the mean have constituted [for artists] ugliness in body as well as vice in morals and a state of sickness with regard to the constitution' (ibid., 103). Here Zeuxis's notion of physical beauty as an exceptional ideal becomes transformed into beauty as the average.

Quetelet foresaw a kind of Utopia of the norm associated with progress, just as Marx foresaw a Utopia of the norm in so far as wealth and production is concerned.

> one of the principal acts of civilization is to compress more and more the limits within which the different elements relative to man oscillate. The more that enlightenment is propagated, the more will deviations from the mean diminish. . . . The perfectibility of the human species is derived as a necessary consequence of all our investigations. Defects and monstrosities disappear more and more from the body. (ibid., 104)

This concept of the average, as applied to the concept of the human, was used not only by statisticians but even by the likes of Marx. Marx actually cites Quetelet's notion of the average man in a discussion of the labor theory of value. We can see in retrospect that one of the most powerful ideas of Marx — the notion of labor value or average wages — in many ways is based on the idea of the worker constructed as an average worker. As Marx writes:

> Any average magnitude, however, is merely the average of a number of separate magnitudes all of one kind, but differing as to quantity. In every industry, each individual labourer, be he Peter or Paul, differs from the average labourer. These individual differences, or 'errors' as they are called in mathematics, compensate one another and vanish, whenever a certain minimum number of workmen are employed together. (Marx 1970, 323)

So for Marx one can divide the collective work day of a large number of workers and come up with 'one day of average social labor' (ibid., 323). As Quetelet had come up with an average man, so Marx postulates an average worker, and from that draws conclusions about the relationship between an average and the extremes of wealth and poverty that are found in society. Thus Marx develops his crucial concept of 'abstract labor.'

We tend not to think of progressives like Marx as tied up with a movement led by businessmen, but it is equally true that Marx is unimaginable without a tendency to contemplate average humans and think about their abstract relation to work, wages, and so on. In this sense, Marx is very much in step with the movement of normalizing the body and the individual. In addition, Marxist thought encourages us toward an enforcing of normalcy in the sense that the deviations in society, in terms of the distribution of wealth for example, must be minimized.

The concept of a norm, unlike that of an ideal, implies that the majority of the population must or should somehow be part of the norm. The norm pins down that majority of the population that falls under the arch of the standard bell-shaped curve. This curve, the graph of an exponential function, that was known variously as the astronomer's 'error law,' the 'normal distribution,' the 'Gaussian density function,' or simply 'the bell curve,' became in its own way a symbol of the tyranny of the norm (see Figure. 1, p. 34). Any bell curve will always have at its extremities those characteristics that deviate from the norm. So, with the concept of the norm comes the concept of deviations or extremes. When we think of bodies, in a society where the concept of the norm is operative, then people with disabilities will be thought of as deviants. This, as we have seen, is in contrast to societies with the concept of an ideal, in which all people have a non-ideal status.[15]

In England, there was an official and unofficial burst of interest in statistics during the 1830s. A statistical office was set up at the Board of Trade in 1832, and the General Register Office was created in 1837 to collect vital statistics. All of this interest in numbers concerning the state was a consequence of the Reform Act of 1832, the Factory Act of 1833, and the Poor Law of 1834. The country was being monitored and the poor were being surveiled. Private groups followed, and in 1833 a statistical section of the British Association for the Advancement of Science was formed in which Quetelet as well as Malthus participated. In the following year Malthus, Charles Babbage, and others founded the Statistical Society of London. The Royal London Statistical Society was founded in 1835.

The use of statistics began an important movement, and there is a telling connection for the purposes of this book between the founders of statistics and their larger intentions. The rather amazing fact is that almost all the early statisticians had one thing in common: they were eugenicists. The same is true of key figures in the movement: Sir Francis Galton, Karl Pearson, and R. A. Fisher.[16] While this coincidence seems almost too striking to be true, we must remember that there is a real connection between figuring the statistical measure of humans and then hoping to improve humans so that deviations from the norm diminish – as someone like Quetelet had suggested. Statistics is bound up with eugenics because the central insight of statistics is the idea that a population can be normed. An important consequence of the idea of the norm is that it divides the total population into standard and nonstandard subpopulations. The next step in conceiving of the population as norm and non-norm is for the state to attempt to norm the nonstandard – the aim of eugenics. Of course such an activity is profoundly paradoxical since the inviolable rule of statistics is that all phenomena will always conform to a bell curve. So norming the non-normal is an activity as problematic as untying the Gordian knot.

MacKenzie asserts that it is not so much that Galton's statistics made possible eugenics but rather that 'the needs of eugenics in large part determined the content of Galton's statistical theory' (1981, 52). In any case, a symbiotic relationship exists between statistical science and eugenic concerns. Both bring into society the concept of a norm, particularly a normal body, and thus in effect create the concept of the disabled body.

It is also worth noting the interesting triangulation of eugenicist interests. On the one hand Sir Francis Galton was cousin to Charles Darwin, whose notion of the evolutionary advantage of the fittest lays the foundation for eugenics and also for the idea of a perfectible body undergoing progressive improvement. As one scholar has put it, 'Eugenics was in reality applied biology based on the central biological theory of the day, namely the Darwinian theory of evolution' (Farrall 1985, 55). Darwin's ideas serve to place disabled people along the wayside as evolutionary defectives to be surpassed by natural selection. So, eugenics became obsessed with the elimination of 'defectives,' a category which included the 'feebleminded,' the deaf, the blind, the physically defective, and so on.

In a related discourse, Galton created the modern system of fingerprinting for personal identification. Galton's interest came out of a desire to show that certain physical traits could be inherited. As he wrote:

> one of the inducements to making these inquiries into personal identification has been to discover independent features suitable for hereditary investigation. . . . it is not improbable, and worth taking pains to inquire whether each person may not carry visibly about his body undeniable evidence of his parentage and near kinships. (cited in MacKenzie 1981, 65)

Fingerprinting was seen as a physical mark of parentage, a kind of serial number written on the body. But further, one can say that the notion of fingerprinting pushes forward the idea that the human body is standardized and contains a serial number, as it were, embedded in its corporeality. (Later technological innovations will reveal this fingerprint to be embedded at the genetic level.) Thus the body has an identity that coincides with its essence and cannot be altered by moral, artistic, or human will. This indelibility of corporeal identity only furthers the mark placed on the body by other physical qualities – intelligence, height, reaction time. By this logic, the person enters in an identical relationship with the body, the body forms the identity, and the identity is unchangeable and indelible as one's place on the normal curve. For our purposes, then, this fingerprinting of the body means that the marks of physical difference become synonymous with the identity of the person.

Finally, Galton is linked to that major figure connected with the discourse of disability in the nineteenth century – Alexander Graham Bell. In 1883, the same year that the term 'eugenics' was coined by Galton, Bell delivered his eugenicist speech *Memoir upon the Formation of a Deaf Variety of the Human Race*, warning of the 'tendency among deaf-mutes to select deaf-mutes as their partners in marriage' (1969, 19) with the dire consequence that a race of deaf people might be created. This echoing of Dr Frankenstein's fear that his monster might mate and produce a race of monsters emphasizes the terror with which the 'normal' beholds the differently abled.[17] Noting how the various interests come together in Galton, we can see evolution, fingerprinting, and the attempt to control the reproductive rights of the deaf as all pointing to a conception of the body as perfectible but only when subject to the necessary control of the eugenicists. The identity of people becomes defined by irrepressible identificatory physical qualities that can be measured. Deviance from the norm can be identified and indeed criminalized (fingerprints came to be associated with identifying deviants who wished to hide their identities).

Galton made significant changes in statistical theory that created the concept of the norm. He took what had been called 'error theory,' a technique by which astronomers attempted to show that one could locate a star by taking into account the variety of sightings. The sightings, all of which could not be correct, if plotted would fall into a bell curve, with most sightings falling into the center, that is to say, the correct location of the star. The errors would fall to the sides of the bell curve. Galton's contribution to statistics was to change the name of the curve from 'the law of frequency of error' or 'error curve,' the term used by Quetelet, to the 'normal distribution' curve (see Figure 1, p. 34).

The significance of these changes relates directly to Galton's eugenicist interests. In an 'error curve' the extremes of the curve are the most mistaken in accuracy. But if one is looking at human traits, then the extremes, particularly what Galton saw as positive extremes – tallness, high intelligence, ambitiousness, strength, fertility – would have to be seen as errors. Rather than 'errors' Galton wanted to think of the extremes as distributions of a trait. As MacKenzie notes:

> Thus there was a gradual transition from use of the term 'probable error' to the term 'standard deviation' (which is free of the implication that a deviation is in any sense an error), and from the term 'law of error' to the term 'normal distribution.' (1981, 59)

But even without the idea of error, Galton still faced the problem that in a normal distribution curve that graphed height, for example, both tallness and shortness would be seen as extremes in a continuum where average stature would be the norm. The problem for Galton was that, given his desire to perfect the human race, or at least its British segment, tallness was preferable to short-ness. How could both extremes be considered equally deviant from the norm? So Galton substituted the idea of ranking for the concept of averaging. That is, he changed the way one might look at the curve from one that used the mean to one that used the median – a significant change in thinking eugenically.

If a trait, say intelligence, is considered by its average, then the majority of people would determine what intelligence should be – and intelligence would be defined by the mediocre middle. Galton, wanting to avoid the middling of desired traits, would prefer to think of intelligence in ranked order. Although high intelligence in a normal distribution would simply be an extreme, under a ranked system it would become the highest ranked trait. Galton divided his curve into quartiles, so that he was able to emphasize ranked orders of intelligence, as we would say that someone was in the first quartile in intelligence (low intelligence) or the fourth quartile (high intelligence). Galton's work led directly to current 'intelligence quotient' (IQ) and scholastic achievement tests. In fact, Galton revised Gauss's bell curve to show the superiority of the desired trait (for example, high intelligence). He created what he

33

called an 'ogive' (see Figure 2), which is arranged in quartiles with an ascending curve that features the desired trait as 'higher' than the undesirable deviation. As Stigler notes:

> If a hundred individuals' talents were ordered, each could be assigned the numerical value corresponding to its percentile in the curve of 'deviations from an average': the middlemost (or median) talent had value 0 (representing mediocrity), an individual at the upper quartile was assigned the value 1 (representing one probable error above mediocrity), and so on. (1986, 271)

What these revisions by Galton signify is an attempt to redefine the concept of the 'ideal' in relation to the general population. First, the application of the idea of a norm to the human body creates the idea of deviance or a 'deviant' body. Second, the idea of a norm pushes the normal variation of the body through a stricter template guiding the way the body 'should' be. Third, the

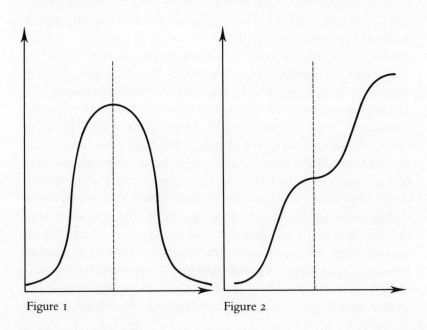

Figure 1   Figure 2

revision of the 'normal curve of distribution' into quartiles, ranked order, and so on, creates a new kind of 'ideal.' This statistical ideal is unlike the classical ideal which contains no imperative to be the ideal. The new ideal of ranked order is powered by the imperative of the norm, and then is supplemented by the notion of progress, human perfectibility, and the elimination of deviance, to create a dominating, hegemonic vision of what the human body should be.

While we tend to associate eugenics with a Nazi-like racial supremacy, it is important to realize that eugenics was not the trade of a fringe group of right-wing, fascist maniacs. Rather, it became the common practice of many, if not most, European and American citizens. While Marx used Quetelet's idea of the average in his formulation of average wage and abstract labor, socialists as well as others embraced eugenic claims, seeing in the perfectibility of the human body a Utopian hope for social improvement. Once people allowed that there were norms and ranks in human physiology, then the idea that we might want to, for example, increase the intelligence of humans, or decrease birth defects, did not seem so farfetched. These ideas were widely influential: in the ensuing years the leaders of the socialist Fabian Society, including Beatrice and Sidney Webb, George Bernard Shaw and H. G. Wells, were among the eugenicists (MacKenzie, 1981, 34). The influence of eugenicist ideas persisted well into the twentieth century, so that someone like Emma Goldman could write that unless birth control was encouraged, the state would 'legally encourage the increase of paupers, syphilitics, epileptics, dipsomaniacs, cripples, criminals, and degenerates' (Kevles 1985, 90).

The problem for people with disabilities was that eugenicists tended to group together all allegedly 'undesirable' traits. So, for example, criminals, the poor, and people with disabilities might be mentioned in the same breath. Take Karl Pearson, a leading figure in the eugenics movement, who defined the 'unfit' as follows: 'the habitual criminal, the professional tramp, the tuberculous, the insane, the mentally defective, the alcoholic, the diseased from birth or from excess' (cited in Kevles 1985, 33). In 1911, Pearson headed the Department of Applied Statistics, which included the Galton and Biometric Laboratories at University College in London. This department gathered eugenic information on the inheritance of physical and mental traits including 'scientific, commercial, and legal ability, but also hermaphroditism, hemophilia, cleft palate, harelip, tuberculosis, diabetes, deaf-mutism, polydactyly (more than five fingers) or brachydactyly (stub fingers), insanity, and mental deficiency' (ibid., 38–9). Here again one sees a strange selection of disabilities merged with other types of human variations. All of these deviations from the norm were seen in the long run as contributing to the disease of the nation. As one official in the Eugenics Record Office asserted:

> the calculus of correlations is the sole rational and effective method for attacking . . . what makes for, and what mars national fitness. . . . The only way to keep a nation strong mentally and physically is to see that each new generation is derived chiefly from the fitter members of the generation before. (ibid., 39–40)

The emphasis on nation and national fitness obviously plays into the metaphor of the body. If individual citizens are not fit, if they do not fit into the nation, then the national body will not be fit. Of course, such arguments are based on a false notion of the body politic – as if a hunchbacked citizenry would make a hunchbacked nation. Nevertheless, the eugenic notion that individual variations would accumulate into a composite national identity was a powerful one. This belief combined with an industrial mentality that saw workers as interchangeable and therefore sought to create a universal worker whose physical characteristics would be uniform, as would the result of their labors – a uniform product.

One of the central foci of eugenics was what was broadly called 'feeblemindedness.'[18] This term included low intelligence, mental illness, and even 'pauperism,' since low income was equated with 'relative inefficiency' (ibid., 46).[19] Likewise, certain ethnic groups were associated with feeblemindedness and pauperism. Charles

Davenport, an American eugenicist, thought that the influx of European immigrants would make the American population 'darker in pigmentation, smaller in stature . . . more given to crimes of larceny, assault, murder, rape, and sex-immorality' (cited in ibid., 48). In his research, Davenport scrutinized the records of 'prisons, hospitals, almshouses, and institutions for the mentally deficient, the deaf, the blind, and the insane' (ibid., 55).

The loose association between what we would now call disability and criminal activity, mental incompetence, sexual license, and so on established a legacy that people with disabilities are still having trouble living down. This equation was so strong that an American journalist writing in the early twentieth century could celebrate 'the inspiring, the wonderful, message of the new heredity' as opposed to the sorrow of bearing children who were 'diseased or crippled or depraved' (ibid., 67). The conflation of disability with depravity expressed itself in the formulation 'defective class.' As the president of the University of Wisconsin declared after World War One, 'we know enough about eugenics so that if the knowledge were applied, the defective classes would disappear within a generation' (ibid., 68). And it must be reiterated that the eugenics movement was not stocked with eccentrics. Davenport was funded by Averell Harriman's sister Mary Harriman, as well as John D. Rockefeller. Prime ministers A. J. Balfour, Neville Chamberlain, and Winston Churchill, President Theodore Roosevelt, H. G. Wells, John Maynard Keynes, and H. J. Laski, among many others, were members of eugenicist organizations. Francis Galton was knighted in 1909 for his work, and in 1910 he received the Copley Medal, the Royal Society's highest honor. A Galton Society met regularly in the American Museum of Natural History in New York City. In 1911 the Oxford University Union moved approval of the main principles behind eugenics by a vote of almost two to one. In Kansas, the 1920 state fair held a contest for 'fitter families' based on their eugenic family histories, administered intelligence tests, medical examinations, and venereal disease tests. A brochure for the contest noted about the awards, 'this trophy and medal are worth more than livestock sweepstakes. . . .

For health is wealth and a sound mind in a sound body is the most priceless of human possessions' (ibid., 62).

In England, bills were introduced in Parliament to control mentally disabled people, and in 1933 the prestigious scientific magazine *Nature* approved the Nazis' proposal of a bill for 'the avoidance of inherited diseases in posterity' by sterilizing the disabled. The magazine editorial said 'the Bill, as it reads, will command the appreciative attention of all who are interested in the controlled and deliberate improvement of human stock.' The list of disabilities for which sterilization would be appropriate were 'congenital feeblemindedness, manic depressive insanity, schizophrenia, hereditary epilepsy, hereditary St Vitus's dance, hereditary blindness and deafness, hereditary bodily malformation and habitual alcoholism' (cited in MacKenzie 1981, 44). We have largely forgotten that what Hitler did in developing a hideous policy of eugenics was just to implement the theories of the British and American eugenicists. Hitler's statement in *Mein Kampf* that 'the struggle for the daily livelihood [between species] leaves behind, in the ruck, everything that is weak or diseased or wavering' (cited in Blacker 1952, 143) is not qualitatively different from any of the many similar statements we have seen before. And even the conclusions Hitler draws are not very different from those of the likes of Galton, Bell, and others:

> In this matter, the State must assert itself as the trustee of a millennial future. . . . In order to fulfill this duty in a practical manner, the State will have to avail itself of modern medical discoveries. It must proclaim as unfit for procreation all those who are afflicted with some visible hereditary disease or are the carriers of it; and practical measures must be adopted to have such people rendered sterile. (cited in Blacker 1952, 144)

One might want to add here a set of speculations about Sigmund Freud. His work was made especially possible by the idea of the normal. It shows us that sexuality, long relegated to the trash heap of human instincts, was in fact normal, and that perversion was simply a displacement of 'normal' sexual interest. Dreams which behave in a manner 'unknown or only exceptionally permissible in normal mental life' (Freud 1977, 297) are seen as actually normal and 'the dreams of neurotics do not differ in any important respect from those of normal people' (ibid., 456). In fact, it is hard to imagine the existence of psychoanalysis without the concept of normalcy. Indeed, one of the core principles behind psychoanalysis was that we each start out with normal psychosexual development and neurotics become abnormal through a problem in that normal development. As Freud put it: 'if the *vita sexualis* is normal, there can be no neurosis' (ibid., 386). Psychoanalysis can correct that mistake and bring patients back to their normal selves. Although I cannot go into a close analysis of Freud's work here, it is instructive to think of the ways in which Freud is producing a eugenics of the mind – creating the concepts of normal sexuality, normal function, and then contrasting them with the perverse, abnormal, pathological, and even criminal. Indeed, one of the major critiques of Freud's work now centers on his assumption about what constitutes normal sexuality and sexual development for women and men.

The first depiction in literature of an attempt to norm an individual member of the population occurred in the 1850s during this development of the idea of the normal body. In Flaubert's *Madame Bovary*, Charles Bovary is influenced by Homais, the self-serving pharmacist, and Emma to perform a trendy operation that would correct the club foot of Hippolyte, the stableboy of the local inn. This corrective operation is seen as 'new' and related to 'progress' (Flaubert 1965, 125). Hippolyte is assailed with reasons why he should alter his foot. He is told, it 'must considerably interfere with the proper performance of your work' (ibid., 126). And in addition to redefining him in terms of his ability to carry out work, Homais adds: 'Think what would have happened if you had been called into the army, and had to fight under our national banner!' (ibid., 126). So national interests and again productivity are emphasized. But Hippolyte has been doing fine in his job as stableboy; his disability has not interfered with his performance in the community under traditional standards. In fact, Hippolyte seems to use his club foot to his advantage, as the narrator notes:

> But on the equine foot, wide indeed as a horse's hoof, with its horny skin, and large toes, whose black nails resembled the nails of a horse shoe, the cripple ran about like a deer from morn till night. He was constantly to be seen on the Square, jumping round the carts, thrusting his limping foot forwards. He seemed even stronger on that leg than the other. By dint of hard service it had acquired, as it were, moral qualities of patience and energy; and when he was given some heavy work to do, he would support himself on it in preference to the sound one. (ibid., 126)

Hippolyte's disability is in fact an ability, one which he relies on, and from which he gets extra horsepower, as it were. But although Hippolyte is more than capable, the operation must be performed to bring him back to the human and away from the equine, which the first syllable of his name suggests. To have a disability is to be an animal, to be part of the Other.

A newspaper article appears after the operation's apparent initial success, praising the spirit of progress. The article envisages Hippolyte's welcome back into the human community.

> Everything tends to show that his convalescence will be brief; and who knows if, at our next village festivity we shall not see our good Hippolyte appear in the midst of a bacchic dance, surrounded by a group of gay companions . . . (ibid., 128)

The article goes on to proclaim, 'Hasn't the time come to cry out that the blind shall see, the deaf hear, the lame walk?' The imperative is clear: science will eradicate disability. However, by a touch of Flaubertian irony, Hippolyte's leg becomes gangrenous and has to be amputated. The older doctor who performs the operation lectures Charles about his attempt to norm this individual.

> This is what you get from listening to the fads from Paris! . . . We are practitioners; we cure people, and we wouldn't dream of operating

on someone who is in perfect health. Straighten club feet! As if one could straighten club feet indeed! It is as if one wished to make a hunchback straight! (ibid., 131)

While Flaubert's work illustrates some of the points I have been making, it is important that we do not simply think of the novel as merely an example of how an historical development lodges within a particular text. Rather, I think there is a larger claim to be made about novels and norms.

While Flaubert may parody current ideas about normalcy in medicine, there is another sense in which the novel as a form promotes and symbolically produces normative structures. Indeed, the whole focus of *Madame Bovary* is on Emma's abnormality and Flaubert's abhorrence of normal life. If we accept that novels are a social practice that arose as part of the project of middle-class hegemony,[20] then we can see that the plot and character development of novels tend to pull toward the normative. For example, most characters in nineteenth-century novels are some-what ordinary people who are put in abnormal circumstances, as opposed to the heroic characters who represent the ideal in earlier forms such as the epic.

If disability appears in a novel, it is rarely centrally represented. It is unusual for a main character to be a person with disabilities, although minor characters, like Tiny Tim, can be deformed in ways that arouse pity. In the case of Esther Summerson who is scarred by smallpox, her scars are made virtually to disappear through the agency of love. On the other hand, as sufficient research has shown, more often than not villains tend to be physically abnormal: scarred, deformed, or mutilated.[21]

I am not saying simply that novels embody the prejudices of society toward people with disabilities. That is clearly a truism. Rather, I am asserting that the very structures on which the novel rests tend to be normative, ideologically emphasizing the universal quality of the central character whose normativity encourages us to identify with him or her.[22] Furthermore, the novel's goal is to reproduce, on some level, the semiologically normative signs

ENFORCING NORMALCY

surrounding the reader, that paradoxically help the reader to read those signs in the world as well as the text. Thus the middleness of life, the middleness of the material world, the middleness of the normal body, the middleness of a sexually gendered, ethnically middle world is created in symbolic form and then reproduced symbolically. This normativity in narrative will by definition create the abnormal, the Other, the disabled, the native, the colonized subject, and so on.

Even on the level of plot, one can see the implication of eugenic notions of normativity. The parentage of characters in novels plays a crucial role. Rather than being self-creating beings, characters in novels have deep biological debts to their forebears, even if the characters are orphans — or perhaps especially if they are orphans. The great Heliodoric plots of romance, in which lower-class characters are found actually to be noble, take a new turn in the novel. While nobility may be less important, characters nevertheless inherit bourgeois respectability, moral rectitude, and eventually money and position through their genetic connection. In the novelistic world of nature versus nurture, nature almost always wins out. Thus Oliver Twist will naturally bear the banner of bourgeois morality and linguistic normativity, even though he grows up in the workhouse. Oliver will always be normal, even in abnormal circumstances.[23]

A further development in the novel can be seen in Zola's works. Before Zola, for example in the work of Balzac, the author attempted to show how the inherently good character of a protagonist was affected by the material world. Thus we read of the journey of the soul, of everyman or everywoman, through a trying and corrupting world. But Zola's theory of the novel depends on the idea of inherited traits and biological determinism. As Zola wrote in *The Experimental Novel*:

Determinism dominates everything. It is scientific investigation, it is experimental reasoning, which combats one by one the hypotheses of the idealists, and which replaces purely imaginary novels by novels of observation and experimentation. (1964, 18)

42

In this view, the author is a kind of scientist watching how humans, with their naturally inherited dispositions, interact with each other. As Zola wrote, his intention in the Rougon-Macquart series was to show how heredity would influence a family 'making superhuman efforts but always failing because of its own nature and the influences upon it' (Zola 1993, viii). This series would be a study of the 'singular effect of heredity' (ibid.). Zola mentions the work of Darwin and links his own novels to notions of how inherited traits interact in particular environments over time and to generalizations about human behavior:

> And this is what constitutes the experimental novel: to possess a knowledge of the mechanism of the phenomena inherent in man, to show the machinery of his intellectual and sensory manifestations, under the influence of heredity and environment, such as physiology shall give them to us. (Zola 1964, 21)

Clearly stating his debt to science, Zola says that 'the experimental novel is a consequence of the scientific evolution of the century' (ibid., 23). The older novel, according to Zola, is composed of imaginary adventures while the newer novel is 'a report, nothing more' (ibid., 124). In being a report, the new novel rejects idealized characters in favor of the norm.

> These young girls so pure, these young men so loyal, represented to us in certain novels, do not belong to the earth. . . . We tell everything, we do not make a choice, neither do we idealize. (ibid., 127)

Zola's characters belong to 'the earth.' This commitment constitutes Zola's new realism, one based on the norm, the average, the inherited.

My point is that a disabilities studies consciousness can alter the way we see not just novels that have main characters who are disabled but any novel. In thinking through the issue of disability, I have come to see that almost any literary work will have some reference to the abnormal, to disability, and so on. I would explain this phenomenon as a result of the hegemony of normalcy. This normalcy must constantly be enforced in public venues (like the novel), must always be creating and bolstering its image by processing, comparing, constructing, deconstructing images of normalcy and the abnormal. In fact, once one begins to notice, there really is a rare novel that does not have some characters with disabilities – characters who are lame, tubercular, dying of AIDS, chronically ill, depressed, mentally ill, and so on.

Let me take the example of some novels by Joseph Conrad. I pick Conrad not because he is especially representative, but just because I happen to be teaching a course on Conrad. Although he is not remembered in any sense as a writer on disability, Conrad is a good test case, as it turns out, because he wrote during a period when eugenics had permeated British society and when Freud had begun to write about normal and abnormal psychology. Conrad, too, was somewhat influenced by Zola, particularly in *The Secret Agent*.

The first thing I noticed about Conrad's work is that metaphors of disability abound. Each book has numerous instances of phrases like the following selections from *Lord Jim*:

a dance of lame, blind, mute thoughts – a whirl of awful cripples. (Conrad 1986, 114)

[he] comported himself in that clatter as though he had been stone-deaf. (ibid., 183)

there was nothing of the cripple about him. (ibid., 234)

Her broken figure hovered in crippled little jumps . . . (ibid., 263)

he was made blind and deaf and without pity . . . (ibid., 300)

a blind belief in the righteousness of his will against all mankind . . . (ibid., 317)

unmoved, like a deaf man . . . (ibid., 319)

44

They were erring men whom suffering had made blind to right and wrong. (ibid., 333)

you dismal cripples, you . . . (ibid., 340)

These references are almost like tics, appearing at regular intervals. They tend to focus on deafness, blindness, dumbness, and lameness, and they tend to use these metaphors to represent limitations on normal morals, ethics, and of course language. While it is entirely possible to maintain that these figures of speech are hardly more than mere linguistic convention, I would argue that the very regularity of these occurrences speaks to a reflexive patroling function in which the author continuously checks and notes instances of normalcy and instances of disability – right down to the linguistic level.

Conrad's emphasis on exotic locations can also be seen as related to the issue of normalcy. Indeed, as I will show later, the whole conception of imperialism on which writers like Conrad depend is largely based on notions of race and ethnicity that are intricately tied up with eugenics, statistical proofs of intelligence, ability, and so on. And these in turn are part of the hegemony of normalcy. Conrad's exotic settings are highlighted in his novels for their deviance from European conceptions. The protagonists are skewed from European standards of normal behavior specifically because they have traveled from Europe to, for example, the South Seas or the Belgian Congo. And Conrad focuses on those characters who, because they are influenced by these abnormal environments, lose their 'singleness of purpose' (which he frequently defines as an English trait) and on those who do not.

The use of phrenology, too, is linked to the patroling of normalcy, through the construction of character. So, in *Heart of Darkness* for example, when Marlow is about to leave for Africa a doctor measures the dimensions of his skull to enable him to discern if any quantitative changes subsequently occur as a result of the colonial encounter. So many of the characters in novels are formed from the ableist cultural repertoire of normalized head, face, and body features that characteristically signify personal qualities. Thus in *The Secret Agent*, the corpulent, lazy body of Verloc indicates his moral sleaziness, and Stevie's large ears and head shape are explicitly seen by Ossipon as characteristic of degeneracy and criminality as described in the theories of the nineteenth-century eugenic phenologist Cesare Lombroso.

Stevie, Conrad's most obviously disabled character, is a kind of center or focus of *The Secret Agent*. In a Zolaesque moment of insight, Ossipon sees Stevie's degeneracy as linked to his sister Winnie:

> he gazed scientifically at that woman, the sister of a degenerate, a degenerate herself – of a murdering type. He gazed at her and invoked Lombroso. . . . He gazed scientifically. He gazed at her cheeks, at her nose, at her eyes, at her ears . . . Bad! . . . Fatal! (Conrad 1968, 259)

This eugenic gaze that scrutinizes Winnie and Stevie is really only a recapitulation of the novelistic gaze that sees meaning in normative and nonnormative features. In fact, every member of the Verloc family has something 'wrong' with them, including Winnie's mother who has trouble walking on her edematous legs. The moral turpitude and physical grimness of London is embodied in Verloc's inner circle. Michaelis, too, is obese and 'wheezed as if deadened and oppressed by the layer of fat on his chest' (ibid., 73). Karl Yundt is toothless, gouty, and walks with a cane. Ossipon is racially abnormal having 'crinkly yellow hair . . . a flattened nose and prominent mouth cast in the rough mould of the Negro type . . . [and] almond-shaped eyes [that] leered languidly over high cheek-bones' (ibid., 75) – all features indicating African and Asian qualities, particularly the cunning, opiated glance.

Stevie, the metaphoric central figure and sacrificial victim of the novel, is mentally delayed. His mental slowness becomes a metaphor for his radical innocence and childlike revulsion from cruelty. He is also, in his endless drawing of circles, seen as invoking 'the symbolism of a mad art attempting the inconceivable' (ibid., 76). In this sense, his vision of the world is allied with that of Conrad, who himself could easily be described as embarked on the same project. Stevie is literally taken apart, not only by Ossipon's gaze and by that of the novelist, but centrally by the bungled explosion. His fragmented body[24] becomes a kind of symbol of the fragmentation that Conrad emphasizes throughout his opus and that the Professor recommends in his high-tech view of anarchism as based on the power of explosion and conflagration. Stevie becomes sensitized to the exploitation of workers by his encounter with a coachman with a prosthetic hook for an arm, whose whipping of his horse causes Stevie anguish. The prosthetic arm appears sinister at first, particularly as a metonymic agent of the action of whipping. But the one-armed man explains: "'This ain't an easy world . . . 'Ard on 'osses, but dam' sight 'arder on poor chaps like me." he wheezed just audibly' (ibid., 165). Stevie's radical innocence is most fittingly convinced by the man's appeal to class solidarity, so Stevie ultimately is blown up for the sins of all.

In *Under Western Eyes*, the issue of normalcy is first signaled in the author's Introduction. Conrad apologizes for Razumov's being 'slightly abnormal' and explains away this deviation by citing a kind of personal sensitivity as well as a Russian temperament. In addition, Conrad says that although his characters may seem odd, 'nobody is exhibited as a monster here' (Conrad 1957, 51). The mention of exhibition of monsters immediately alerts us to the issue of nineteenth-century freak shows and raises the point that by depicting 'abnormal' people, the author might see his own work as a kind of display of freaks.[25] Finally, Conrad makes the point that all these 'abnormal' characters 'are not the product of the exceptional but of the general – of the normality of their place, and time, and race' (ibid., 51). The conjunction of race and normality also alerts us to eugenic aims. What Conrad can be seen as apologizing for is the normalizing (and abnormalizing) role of the novel that must take a group of nationals (Russians) and make them into the abnormal, non-European, nonnormal Other. Interestingly, Conrad refers to anarchists and autocrats both as 'imbecile.' The use of this word made current by eugenic testing also shows us how pervasive is the hegemony of normalcy.

Razumov's abnormality is referred to by the narrator, at one point, as being seen by a man looking at a mirror 'formulating to himself reassuring excuses for his appearance marked by the taint of some insidious hereditary disease' (ibid., 220). What makes Razumov into the cipher he is to all concerned is his lack of a recognizable identity aside from his being a Russian. So when he arrives in Geneva, Razumov says to Peter Ivanovitch, the radical political philosopher, that he will never be 'a mere blind tool' simply to be used (ibid., 231). His refusal to be a 'blind tool' ends up, ironically, in Razumov being made deaf by Necator, who deliberately bursts his eardrums with blows to the head. The world becomes for Razumov 'perfectly silent – soundless as shadows' (ibid., 339) and 'a world of mutes. Silent men, moving, unheard . . . ' (ibid., 340). For both Conrad and Razumov, deafness is the end of language, the end of discourse, the ultimate punishment that makes all the rest of the characters appear as if their words were useless anyway. As Necator says, 'He shall never be any use as spy on any one. He won't talk, because he will never hear anything in his life – not a thing' (ibid., 341). After Razumov walks into the street and is run over by a car, he is described as 'a hopeless cripple, and stone deaf with that' (ibid., 343). He dies from his disabilities, as if life were in fact impossible to survive under those conditions. Miss Haldin, in contrast, gains her meaning in life from these events and says, 'my eyes are open at last and my hands are free now' (ibid., 345). These sets of arrangements play an intimate part in the novel and show that disability looms before the writer as a *memento mori*. Normality has to protect itself by looking into the maw of disability and then recovering from that glance.

I am not claiming that this reading of some texts by Conrad is brilliant or definitive. But I do want to show that even in texts that do not appear to be about disability, the issue of normalcy is fully deployed. One can find in almost any novel, I would argue, a kind of surveying of the terrain of the body, an attention to difference – physical, mental, and national. This activity of consolidating the hegemony of normalcy is one that needs more attention, in addition to the kinds of work that have been done in locating the thematics of disability in literature.

What I have tried to show in this chapter is that the very term that permeates our contemporary life – the normal – is a configuration that arises in a particular historical moment. It is part of a notion of progress, of industrialization, and of ideological consolidation of the power of the bourgeoisie. The implications of the hegemony of normalcy are profound and extend into the very heart of cultural production. The novel form, that proliferator of ideology, is intricately connected with concepts of the norm. From the typicality of the central character, to the normalizing devices of plot to bring deviant characters back into the norms of society, to the normalizing coda of endings, the nineteenth- and twentieth-century novel promulgates and disburses notions of normalcy and by extension makes of physical differences ideological differences. Characters with disabilities are always marked with ideological meaning, as are moments of disease or accident that transform such characters. One of the tasks for a developing consciousness of disability issues is the attempt, then, to reverse the hegemony of the normal and to institute alternative ways of thinking about the abnormal.

3

Universalizing Marginality: How
Europe Became Deaf in the
Eighteenth Century

> This [sign] language is so natural to mankind that despite the help
> we get from spoken languages to express our thoughts and all their
> nuances, we still make frequent use of it, especially when we
> are moved by some passion, and we leave off using the cold and
> measured tone prescribed by our institutional training, to bring us
> closer to the tone of nature.
>
> *Synthetic Essay on the Origin and Formation of Languages*
> (author unknown, 1774)

I have discussed how normalcy became the norm during the
nineteenth century. In that century a cultural change occurred,
whose understanding will help articulate the ideas presented in
this book. But I now turn our attention back to look at the period
that preceded that change. In addition, while so far I have been
discussing disability as a general concept, now I will focus, at least
for a few chapters, on deafness.

There is more documentation on deafness in the early modern
period than on any other disability. This attention to deafness is not
simply convenient for the scholar, but also raises questions. Why
did Europe find deafness a point of fascination in the eighteenth
century? Why did deafness become a cultural activity? Not-
withstanding the objections I discussed in the Preface, I believe
that if I can look at deafness as a phenomenon, I can generalize
what I have learned to disability in general. But the usefulness of
this experiment will have to be judged after the fact.

Therefore, the point of this chapter is that deafness, far from being an epiphenomenon of eighteenth-century cultural interests, was perhaps one of its central areas of concern. I want to make a claim for the centrality of what might seem to be extremely marginal. Further, I want to make the somewhat preposterous suggestion that Europe became deaf during the eighteenth century. I hope to show how cultural deafness became one of the hallmarks of early modern ideas about public symbol and information production, and how the deaf person became an icon for complex intersections of subject, class position, and the body.

My claim to the centrality of deafness needs to be broken down into separate smaller claims. The first of these is that deafness becomes of interest to European culture in the eighteenth century; the second, related claim is that this interest is the reciprocal reaction to, or perhaps the cause of, deafness becoming visible for the first time as an articulation in a set of discursive practices.

Michel Foucault in his classic *Madness and Civilization* shows how madhouses replaced leper colonies as the dominant confining institution in Europe at the close of the Middle Ages. This switch from the confinement of defects of the body to the confinement of defects of the mind signals a switch to an age of Reason and, by extension, madness, from an age that focused on the super-ficial disease of the body. Thus madness became visible, and the treatment of madness became a discourse. I shall argue in a similar vein that deafness became visible in the Enlightenment and thus became the subject of a discourse of treatment by professionals while ironically also becoming symbolic of an aspect of the Enlightenment subject itself.

Before the late seventeenth and early eighteenth centuries, the deaf were not constructed as a group. There is almost no historical or literary record of the deaf as such. We may rarely read of a deaf person but there is no significant discourse constructed around deafness. The reason for this discursive nonexistence is that, then as now, most deaf people were born to hearing families, and therefore were isolated in their deafness. Without a sense of group solidarity and without a social category of disability, they were mainly seen as isolated deviations from a norm, as we now might consider, for example, people who are missing an arm. For these deaf, there were no schools, no teachers, no discourse, in effect, no deafness.

Likewise, the deaf themselves could not constitute themselves as a subgroup, as might other outsiders such as Jews, subalterns, even women, because they remained isolated from each other and were thus without a shared, complex language. The only deaf people who fully attained sociability were found in urban areas or in families or groupings of hereditary deafness. Here the use of sign language, as it developed over time, allowed the deaf to consider themselves a group and to communicate with each other.[26]

Of course, while deafness did not 'exist' before the eighteenth century, a number of authors had written about deafness. There are references to deafness in the Old and New Testaments and in writings by Aristotle, Augustine, Descartes, and others. But something qualitatively different happens during the eighteenth century. Consider that up to the beginning of the century no deaf schools had ever existed in England, on the European continent, or anywhere else for that matter. According to one writer, 'it was not until the middle of the eighteenth century that Britain and Europe turned to the education and training of their disabled populations.' By the end of the century deaf schools had been established in the cities of Amsterdam, Paris, Vienna, Karlsruhe, Prague, Munich, Waitzen, Fresing, Lenz, Rome, Naples, Malta, Goningen, Tarente, Madrid, and Zurich, and in Portugal, Poland, Denmark, and Sweden. By 1789 a dozen schools had been founded in Europe and by 1822 there were sixty. Clearly, these data amount to something more than a statistical blip. The beginning of what we now call 'special education' started with deafness, so that 'by the close of the eighteenth century, special education was accepted as a branch of education, albeit a minor enterprise' (Winzer 1993, 39).

Of course, one might conclude that deafness itself was not so much the central phenomenon as was education. But there had consistently been hospices for the blind in Europe since the third century.[27] The blind were historically regarded as objects of charity, if not veneration for their alleged 'second sight.' The most famous institution for the blind was the Hospice de Quinze-Vingts founded in Paris by Louis IX in 1260, where it still exists. Quinze-Vingts was established to care for three hundred knights captured and blinded during the Crusades. While it is true that systematic education for the blind began only in the eighteenth century with the founding of the Institution des Enfants Aveugles in Paris in 1784, the blind had been constituted as a group long before that point. William Paulson argues that the development of education for the blind in turn involved a desacralization of the blind and an accompanying medicalization of the disability. Deafness as a phenomenon engaged the intellectual moment of this period in a way that blindness and other disabilities did not. Deafness, after all, was about language, about the essential human quality of verbal communication. While Diderot wrote on both the blind and the deaf, he saw blindness as posing a fundamental question about the nature of perception, whereas deafness was more fundamentally about the existence and function of language. Citing Diderot, Paulson says (1987, 48):

> What the blind man lacks is *denomination*, the ability to name visible objects, to put signs and referents together. Yet without that ability he is able to manipulate the signs as well as anyone else, creating an illusion of reference that is broken only when one remembers that he is blind.

The relation to language is therefore not as vexed for the blind as it is for those who are deaf.[28]

An indication of how special a place the deaf held in the eighteenth-century imagination can be seen in the remarkable success of Jean Nicolas Bouilly's play about the Abbé de l'Epée, the founder of the first deaf school. This theatrical piece had over one hundred performances in Paris at the end of the eighteenth century, making it the second-greatest dramatic success of the era, surpassed only by Beaumarchais's *Marriage of Figaro*.[29]

The seventeenth and eighteenth centuries saw the first major publications of books relating to deafness. Among the early works published in Europe were a medical treatise by a German physician, Solomon Alberti's *Discourse on Deafness and Speechlessness* (1591); G. Bonifacio's treatise *Of The Art of Signs* (1616); and Juan Pablo Bonet's *A Method of Teaching Deaf Mutes to Speak* (1620). In England, the first books published were John Bulwer's *Philocophus* [The Deaf Man's Friend] (1648) and later his *Chirologia, or the Natural Language of the Hand* (1654). Bulwer was a member of the Royal Society, as were a number of the early writers on deafness. George Delgarno's *Art of Communication* (1680); John Wallis's *De loquela* (1653); 'A Letter to Robert Boyle Esq.' (1670); and William Holder's *Elements of Speech* (1699) were all products of Royal Society members. George Sibscota's *Deaf and Dumb Man's Discourse* (1670) and Johan Ammon's *Surdus Loquens* [The Talking Deaf Man] (1694) were other works published in the latter part of the seventeenth century. The eighteenth century witnessed Ammon's *Dissertatio de loquela* (1700); Daniel Defoe's *Duncan Campbell* (1720); the Abbé de l'Epée's *Instruction of Deaf and Dumb by Means of Methodical Signs* (1776); J. L. F. Arnoldi's *Practical Instructions for Teaching Deaf-Mute Persons to Speak and Write* (1777); and R. A. Sicard's *Theory of Signs* (1782), among others.

Starting in 1771 in Paris, the Abbé de l'Epée held public displays of the ability of deaf students every Tuesday and Friday morning from 7 a.m. until noon, but the crowds increased so dramatically that he had to add another session in the evening. In 1772 printed programs warned that 'because the assembly hall can only hold one hundred people, spectators are kindly requested not to remain more than two hours' (Lane 1984b, 47). It is hard to imagine this kind of devotion to a cause that was in effect marginal. In 1794 Sicard held performances once a month for Parisians, in addition to special demonstrations for the various emperors of Europe, the pope, and even a command performance before the British parliament. These monthly sessions began at noon and ended at 4 p.m., with three to four hundred spectators assembled. Deaf people were asked abstract questions through interpreters, like 'Why is baptism called the portal of the sacraments?' Deaf students replied in written French as well as in Latin, Italian, Spanish,

German, and English. These public demonstrations were attended by many French intellectuals, including Condillac, the philosopher Lord Monboddo, the papal nuncio, the statesman John Quincy Adams, and many others (ibid., 46–7). On a tour of the Hebrides in 1773, Dr Johnson made a special stop to visit the deaf school run by Thomas Braidwood.

What I am trying to demonstrate is that deafness was for the eighteenth century an area of cultural fascination and a compelling focus for philosophical reflection. The question is, why?

Some answers may be obvious. As Harlan Lane points out in his *Wild Boy of Aveyron*, philosophers of this period were obsessed with trying to define what made humans human. Aristotle's classic and elegant definition included upright gait, human appearance, and language. The investigation of 'savages,' orangutans, wild children, and the deaf allowed 'scientific' observation as to what 'natural man' might be like. Rousseau, Herder, Condillac, Monboddo, Locke and others argued over how language began, how reason and thought intertwined into the human essence. The wild child and the deaf person provided living examples of the mind untouched by civilization. Here questions such as the following could be put: Are there thoughts prior to language? Can a being be human without language? Condillac, in his *Treatise on Sensations*, imagined a statue brought to life in stages, illustrating the development of human from animal. How appropriate that Sicard at one of his public events found a prelingual deaf child and presented him before a crowd saying, 'I have been waiting to introduce you to a new subject, almost an infant, a little savage, a block of unchiseled marble or rather a statue, yet to be animated and endowed with intellect' (Lane 1984b, 34). Sicard went on to give the child his very first lessons in language before the eyes of the crowd, who were conscious of seeing the new natural man sought by explorers and now by philosophers. Such theatrical displays employed a controlling gaze which allowed the audience to observe the primitive emerge into language – and into deafness.

The irony, of course, is that deafness, while an area of cultural fascination, had to be contained and controlled, as it still is, by the very hearing world that was fascinated by it.[30] The panopticon created by Sicard put the deaf on display but did not allow the deaf to control their own display except by the deviousness of subaltern strategies. We can hear the somewhat sadistic probing by the hearing world and the competent but defiant response of Jean Massieu at one of these sessions.

'What is a sense?' Massieu was asked.

'An idea-carrier,' he answered.

'What is hearing?' asked some people trying to disconcert him.

'Hearing is auricular sight.'

'What is gratitude?' asked the abbé Sicard.

'Gratitude is the memory of the heart,' Massieu answered him.

'What is God?'

'The necessary Being – the sun of eternity.'

'What is eternity?' someone asked.

'A day without yesterday or tomorrow,' Massieu immediately replied. (Lane 1984a, 78–9)

In response to being at the focal point of the clinical gaze, Massieu develops an almost aerobic response to these difficult mental exertions. His deafness is anatomized by examining his language abilities, a procedure for which he creates strategies of compliance.

These types of examinations and philosophical disquisitions help us to place deafness as an emergent, constructed category. Yet I would suggest that philosophical and even medical curiosity are only epiphenomenons of another condition that brought deafness to cultural attention. The wild child/deaf person scenario is based on the idea that deaf people are without a language, unless they learn either to write or to speak the language of the hearing majority. Dr Johnson called deafness 'one of the most desperate human calamities' for that reason. Johnson voices one view of deafness as a limit to sociability, social intercourse, education, and, indeed, humanity and reason. But there is another and more powerful view of deafness woven into eighteenth-century culture. This view sees the deaf person as someone who reasons, feels, thinks, and uses language just as hearing people do, only the language used is different from that of the linguistic majority. The language is in fact the language of texts, of writing, of novels.

In *Duncan Campbell*, Daniel Defoe embodies this idea of the deaf man as textual master. Duncan Campbell is not merely equal to hearing people but is portrayed as a hyperbolically superior being, a godlike man of great intelligence, handsome looks, and supernatural powers. Far from being perceived as disabled, he is seen as enabled with the gift of second sight which allows him to write a person's name and foretell his or her future at first meeting. Although in actuality Campbell was a fraud, the fact that Defoe regards him as deaf allows us to learn something about attitudes toward the deaf, if not about Defoe's attitude to fact and fiction.[31] What is interesting about Defoe's account is that it rests on the assumption that Campbell has his own integral language. Defoe quotes extensively from John Wallis, who had published a book on educating the deaf (though he seems simply to have plagiarized the method from George Delgarno) and was, interestingly, Defoe's brother-in-law.[32] According to Defoe, Wallis had written:

> It will be convenient all along to have pen, ink, and paper, ready at hand, to write down in a word what you signify to him by signs, and cause him to write, or show how to write what he signifies by signs, which way of signifying their mind by signs deaf persons are often very good at: and we must endeavor to learn their language, if I may so call it, in order to teach them ours, by showing what words answer to their signs. (Defoe 1974, 31)

Wallis, and by extension Defoe, acknowledges that the deaf have their own pre-existing language and that language is mediated for the hearing world through writing and textuality. In Defoe's novel, when Duncan meets an old hearing friend, the author comments, 'Here the reader must understand they discoursed on their fingers, and wrote by turns' (ibid., 164).

In addition to making the point that the deaf possess a language, many writers, including Wallis, emphasize a connection between deafness and writing. For Defoe, writing seems the natural way for a deaf person to communicate, as natural as sign language. Defoe names other famous deaf people, including Sir John Gawdy, Sir Thomas Knotcliff, Sir Henry Lydall, and Mr Richard Lyns of Oxford who 'were all of this number, and yet men eminent in their several capacities, for understanding many authors, and expressing themselves in writing with wonderful facility' (ibid., 32). Here, being deaf leads naturally to writing. This correlation is made clearly by trope when Duncan must tell a beautiful young woman that she will be disfigured by smallpox and then die: '. . . he begged to be excused, and that his pen might remain as dumb and silent as his tongue on that affair.' The metonymy of pen and tongue again connects writing to deafness. This link is made more explicit when Duncan 'tells' a long story to a group of friars by writing it down:

> so taking up another piece of paper, Fathers, said he, shall I entertain you with a story of what passed upon this head, between two religious fathers, as all of you are, and a prince of Germany. . . . The story is somewhat long, but very much to the purpose and entertaining; I remember it perfectly by heart, and if you will have patience while I am writing it, I do not doubt but that I shall not only satisfy you, but please you and oblige you with the relation. (ibid., 131)

In this moment Duncan acts as a novelist, translating experiential reality into textual signs, and his deafness melts away into the matrix of writing. It is no coincidence, then, that one of Duncan's favorite activities is walking in graveyards: 'one would imagine he takes delight to stalk along by himself on that dumb silent ground, where the characters of the persons are only to be known, as his own meaning is, by writing and inscriptions on the marble' (ibid., 154). The character of the dead and the ground, considered 'dumb' and 'silent,' is given language in the graphic trace on the tombstones, and Duncan can read them as can any novel reader who, of course, must get at character through decoding a cluster of signs.

What I am saying is that given a written text, there is little difference between a hearing person and a deaf one in the reading or writing process. The deaf can read and write – they only have to translate from sign language to the signs of written language. This point of connection, which may be thought fanciful, was recognized by at least one eighteenth-century reader, who wrote to the *Spectator* (No. 474, 3 September 1712) seeking the whereabouts of Duncan Campbell:

> now hearing you are a dumb man too, I thought you might correspond and be able to tell me something.

This reader sees the narrative persona of 'the *Spectator*' as 'dumb' specifically because he cannot speak except through writing! Authors are mute *because* of typography.

Writing is in effect sign language, a language of mute signs. Sicard emphasized this connection when he said 'written language . . . alone can replace speech' (Lane 1984b, 37). Saboureux de Fontenay, a deaf man writing in 1764, describes finger spelling as a language in which 'the hand is used like a pen' (Lane 1984a, 26), and the Abbé l'Epée described sign language as a type of 'writing in the air' (cited in Mirzoeff 1992, 581). Rousseau acknowledges that both writing and gesture are forms of sign language virtually equal to speech. He says if humans could not speak:

> we would have been able to establish societies little different from those we have, or such as would have been better able to achieve their goals. We would have been able to institute laws, to choose leaders, to invent arts, to establish commerce, and to do, in a word, almost as many things as we do with the help of speech. (1966, 9)

Rousseau's theory is echoed in a statement attributed to the Abbé Sicard:

> May there not exist in some corner of the world an entire people of deaf-mutes? Well suppose these individuals were so degraded, do you think that they would remain without communication and without intelligence? They would have, without any manner of doubt, a language of signs, and possibly more rich than our own; it would be, certainly unequivocal, always the faithful portrait of the affections of the soul; and then what should hinder them from being civilized? Why should they not have laws, a government, a police, very probably less involved in obscurity than our own? (cited in Kitto 1852, 107)

Herder, too, acknowledges that speech is not necessary for language, and he notes that 'the savage, the hermit living alone in the forest, would have had to invent language for himself . . . without the help of a mouth and without the presence of a society' (1966, 118). Diderot in his *Letter on the Deaf and Dumb* says that speech itself is just a representation of the state of the soul: 'Ah sir, how much our apprehension is modified by the signs we use! And how cold a copy is even the most vivid speech of what takes place within us' (1966, 34). All of these philosophers point to the notion that any sign system can be language.

So intertwined were the issues of writing and language with the issue of deafness that they seemed inseparable. Tellingly, Sicard's career was deeply interwoven with textual language. In 1795 he was appointed to the section on grammar in the French Institute, which later became the French Academy. He helped lay the groundwork for the academy's dictionary of the French language and was also a member of the Grammatical Society. Another dictionary maker, Dr Johnson, is described by Boswell during a visit to Braidwell's school for the deaf in a 'circumstance . . . which was truly characteristic of our great Lexicographer. "Pray," said he, "can they pronounce any *long words*?" Mr Braidwood informed him they could. Upon which Dr Johnson wrote one of his *sesquipedalia verba*, which was pronounced by the scholars, and he was satisfied' (Boswell 1936, 389). Johnson saw his visit to the deaf as, among other things, an opportunity for a lexicographical exhibition.

Why then was deafness such an area of focused activity and philosophical reflection in Europe during the eighteenth century? Why the obsessive connection between deafness and writing? We need to recall that it was during this period that reading became consolidated as an activity. J. Paul Hunter points to data suggesting that 'literacy in the English-speaking world grew rapidly between 1600 and 1800 so that by the latter date a vast majority of adult males could read and write, whereas two centuries earlier only a select minority could do so' (1990, 65). Debates ensued during the period as to whether written or spoken language was the primary form of linguistic communication. David Bartine details the transition from an oral culture to a culture of silent reading in his *Early English Reading Theory: Origins of Current Debates*. These debates imagine the possibility that written language was the primary form of linguistic enterprise. Benjamin Smart, for example, 'asserted more emphatically than his predecessors that writing is the original and primary language for all forms of reading. Even for an oral reader the nature of written language is the *first* consideration' (Bartine 1989, 133). If this is the case, then the deaf are living examples of the ideology of the written text at work. As Oliver Sacks notes (1989, 6, note 13):

> The congenitally deaf, it should be added, may have the richest appreciation of (say) written English, of Shakespeare, even though it does not 'speak' to them in an auditory way. It speaks to them, one must suppose, in an entirely visual way – they do not hear, they *see*, the 'voice' of the words.

As if chosen by Roland Barthes, the deaf experience the text at the degree zero of writing, as a text first and foremost. That is, to be deaf is to experience the written text in its most readerly incarnation. The text would not then be transformed into an auditory translation but would be seen as language itself. It is probably no coincidence that John Kitto, who wrote an autobiography about becoming deaf called *Lost Senses*, ends his opening chapter with a history of his reading. Kitto has to apologize for his emphasis on reading by saying, 'These facts, although they may seem at first to bear more upon my literary biography than upon my deafness, which is my proper theme, are necessarily introduced here' (1852, 18–19). The fact is that Kitto more or less intuitively senses a connection between deafness and textuality.

This point can also be turned around. Because the eighteenth century was a period in which readers on a large scale first began to experience reality through texts,[33] they may be said to have had a different relation to reality and to texts. Part of that difference has to do with the fact that in order to become readers, people in the eighteenth century had to become deaf, at least culturally so. That is, to read requires muteness and attention to nonverbal signs. Writing and reading became the dominant forms of using sign language, the language of printed signs, and thus hearing readers and deaf readers could merge as those who see the voice of the words. Elizabeth Eisenstein points out that the political world changed through the advent of print. 'Printed materials encouraged silent adherence to causes whose advocates could not be located in any one parish and who addressed an invisible public from afar' (1968, 42). The very nature of political assent, through the silent decoding of reading, became a newly 'deafened' process that did not require adherents to gather in a public place, that did not rely on a vocal response to a rallying cry. As the hearing person became deaf, the deaf person became the totemic representation of the new reading public.

One can see this attention to deafness as part of a general transition from a society that based its cultural production on performances to one that focused its cultural attention on texts. In a text-based society, the physical presence of an auditor or an audience is no longer necessary, as it would be in a world based on performances. The cultural narrowness of a society in which spoken language is paramount expands to include all users of language, spoken or not.[34]

This point may seem strange, but the fact that you are reading this essay without my physical presence proves that it is irrelevant whether or not you are deaf, at least insofar as receiving and understanding my meaning are concerned. Further, if you consider that most of the knowledge you have about academic discursive matters is almost entirely derived from nonhearing knowledge acquisition, then you can understand the import of this widespread shift from performance to text-based knowledge.[35] As Foucault and others have noticed, knowledge *per se* since the classical period is embedded in discursive structures, and for the past three hundred years such discursive forms as described by Foucault are mainly of the type that are recorded in texts and make up the ensemble of texts that constitute the archive.

In opposition to this archival knowledge, the eighteenth century's fascination with conversation can be seen as a kind of cultural nostalgia for a form that was in the process of becoming anachronistic.[36] It is of course most telling that such accounts of conversation, particularly the obsessive compiling of Johnson's conversation by Boswell and the splenetic compendium of conversational abuse by Swift in his *Polite Conversation*, are themselves only known in their typographic incarnation. The deaf then, seen as readers and writers *par excellence*, as fellow creatures who existed first and foremost in semiology, were the first totemic citizens in the new age of textuality.

Yet, as with any good totem, the deaf person was both universalized and marginalized, held up as an object of admiration and patronized as an object of pity. Like contemporary African-Americans and Chicanos, who are celebrated in an era of putative multiculturality and made visible as such by the media, but who are in reality reviled and oppressed by an economic system that relies on their impoverishment, so the deaf in the eighteenth century had this polysemous interpretation imposed on them. Their subject positions were, in this sense, overdetermined. Here the issue of class comes into syncretic combination with the issues of otherness and of disability. As is still the case, unless a deaf person happened to be born into a wealthy or noble family, he or she would occupy the lowest economic rungs of society. In families in which deafness is hereditary, that economic position will be passed along to the next generation as well. So the majority of deaf in the eighteenth century had jobs as menial workers. They may therefore be described as necessarily part of a working class, and their disability is made complex and multifaceted by its connection with issues of class, as well as linguistic domination.

The testimony of Pierre Desloges, a student of the Abbé de l'Epée, may illustrate some of the themes I have been describing in this chapter. Fittingly, most of what we know about Desloges comes from a pamphlet he wrote in 1779 entitled *Observations d'un sourd et muet sur 'Un Cours élémentaire d'éducation des sourds et muets' publié en 1779 par M. l'abbé Deschamps.*[37] His marginality, like that of the majority of deaf people in his moment, is universalized through print, which articulates him as part of an official discursive practice, removing him from the marginality of the streets. He becomes a representation of a group, yet, as Ernesto Laclau and Chantal Mouffe point out, 'every relation of representation is founded on a fiction: that of the presence at a certain level of something which is absent from it' (Laclau and Mouffe 1989, 119). In this sense, what is absent from any account by Desloges is the physical presence of his deafness. Ironically, that feature of his existence is under erasure because of the very existence of print and Desloges's writerly existence.[38]

These are the facts of his life presented by the writer. Desloges was born in 1747 in the town of Le Grand-Pressigny in the Loire valley. After an attack of childhood smallpox, he became deaf and mute. His education ended with his disability, but he had acquired some skills in reading and writing. At the age of twenty-one he went to Paris and took up the trades of bookbinding and paperhanging. Only at the age of twenty-seven did he learn the sign language used by the Paris deaf community.

The first significant aspect of his pamphlet is its very existence. Had there not been an interest in deafness, it is hard to imagine that an obscure paperhanger in Paris could have been launched into print. Moreover, his purpose in writing is not mainly auto-biographical but rather an attempt to defend deaf education based on sign language, as practiced by the Abbé de l'Epée, against the attack made by Deschamps, who in turn was influenced by the first 'oralist,' Jacob Pereire. That a publisher was willing to print a commentary on this debate indicates the cultural relevance of the subject.

Desloges's marginality is signaled initially by the hearing editor, who first highlights the dubious status of the work by insisting on its not being a fiction. By now, such assertions of factuality only serve to fictionalize a work.[39] Further, the editor stresses that the writing is authentic:

[I] corrected the young man's quite faulty spelling. I pruned some repetitions and softened a few words that could have given offense. Aside from these minor emendations, the essay is entirely the work of the deaf Desloges. (Lane 1984a, 29)

These words immediately contextualize the otherness of Desloges, who must be linguistically sanitized and standardized. His deafness is seen as a mark of difference that separates him from normal readers whose spelling does not have to be corrected and whose usage will not offend. Yet, at the same time, the entrance of the deaf consciousness into the realm of the textual is celebrated: 'I felt the chief interest of this essay would come from its author, that perhaps for the first time a deaf-mute had the honor of being published' (ibid., 29). This doubleness of attitude toward Desloges's marginality will play out in much more complex ways, as I will show.

Desloges begins his essay constructing a subject position from his own marginality. He notes immediately that he is of the lower classes, saying, 'My line of work obliges me to go into many homes.' He adds that 'the whole of my subsistence comes from my daily work, while my writing must be done during the time I have for sleeping' (ibid., 30). He is speaking both as a deaf man and, in some sense more tellingly, as a working man. His writing is seen as occupying a time other than that which a man of letters devotes to it; writing time is in fact stolen from a very full workday. Although there certainly was a tradition of working-class characters in fiction, it was much rarer to have an actual member of that class appear in print. The otherness of Desloges's deafness permits the class element to be overridden and permitted through the gate of print. Body always effaces class in the sphere of bourgeois narrative, as in Richardson's novel Pamela's body erases her class lines.

Desloges is writing out of a profound marginalization. His contact with the hearing world is based on misunderstanding; through writing, that is, using the non-hearing text, he is hoping to eliminate such miscommunication: 'I am invariably questioned about the deaf. But most often the questions are laughable as they are absurd; they merely prove that almost everyone has gotten the falsest possible ideas about us' (ibid., 30). Here too we see that he is not simply questioned about being deaf, but about 'the deaf,' a clear indication that the category of deafness has emerged as an area of cultural curiosity. Furthermore, he notes that he is writing this work to correct the public's errors, particularly 'the last straw' (ibid., 30) of misunderstanding accomplished by Deschamps's book against the use of sign language as an instructional medium. One of the advantages of a text-based society is that individual voices and minority opinions can be more easily heard, if they are permitted access, and Desloges recognizes this empowerment provided by print. In the same way that print culture was involved in the development of nationalism,[40] print also created some version of solidarity for marginalized groups. So Desloges can write:

> As would a Frenchman seeing his language disparaged by a German who knew at most a few words of French, I too felt obliged to defend my own language from the false charges leveled against it by Deschamps. (ibid., 30)

Here we can see that perhaps some aspect of the emergence of the deaf is linked to their defining themselves as a linguistic subgroup. Like races, nationalities, ethnic groups, and nations, their redefinition as a political entity is linked to larger issues about the growth of nationalism in the eighteenth and nineteenth centuries.

Like other writers translating from a foreign language, Desloges will have problems explaining the subtleties of his own language. He can write in French, but to try to convey the sense of sign language may be an insurmountable problem. A single sign 'made in the twinkling of an eye would require entire pages' to describe, and such detail would 'soon become boring to the delicate ears accustomed to the winsome sounds of speech.' Desloges is looking across a cultural divide between speech and sign language. The fact that Desloges sees this transaction as audible rather than textual, referring to the reader's 'ears' rather than eyes as the recipient of his text, points to a curious structuring of languages. Sign language for Desloges is actually a text, but one performed rather than printed. Speech is a 'winsome sound,' more ethereal and less text-based, less semiological than sign. At the same time, the performative nature of sign gives it 'so much strength and energy' that it can only lose its muscular verve when translated into written language. Here we see the mediating role of sign language as a middle term between speech and writing.

For Desloges, spoken language has a double impossibility. Most deaf people are mute only because they cannot hear, but Desloges has an additional impairment he attributes to smallpox but which is clearly part of a larger neurological problem. When he developed smallpox at seven years of age, he remained ill for two years with complications that caused him to lose all his teeth and develop a strokelike dysfunction of his lips, so that they 'became so slack that I can close them only with great effort or the assistance of my hand. . . . One can reproduce my speech fairly accurately by trying to speak with the mouth open, without closing lips or teeth' (ibid., 31). This double impossibility, being both deaf and physiologically mute, makes speech seem quite arbitrary to Desloges. He feels acutely that spoken language is privileged over textual language. This privileging of one sense over another is not natural, as Rousseau argued, but arbitrary. As Desloges writes, sign language is the 'most natural means for leading the deaf to an understanding of langues, nature having given them this language to substitute for the other languages of which they are deprived.' Some of the cognitive dissonance one experiences in reading Desloges's work may arise from the fact that he is writing about his deafness and mutism in the most logical, coherent, and elegant language. The arbitrary privileging of hearing language over nonspoken language, and the consequent marginalization of those who do not participate in that linguistic majority, emerges as a fact of power.

Desloges gains the strength to overcome this linguistic domination by chance when he is twenty-seven years old. At this point, he gains the power of sign language – a power linked to seeing himself as belonging to an oppressed group, the deaf. Before this period, 'for as long as I was living apart from other deaf people, my only resource for self-expression was writing or my poor pronunciation' (ibid., 32). But it is only through contact with the other deaf people in Paris, who are themselves working class, that Desloges finds power in his marginal status. Fatefully, he meets a deaf, 'illiterate' Italian servant who teaches him signing. The fact that the man is described as illiterate makes us realize how strong the association between letters and literacy is. This servant was certainly 'literate' in sign language, but that kind of literacy is discounted, even by Desloges.

At this point in the book, frustratingly Desloges abruptly announces, 'I think this is enough about me and that a longer treatment of such a minor subject would try my readers' patience' (ibid.). One can speculate that Desloges's entrance into sign language leads him to the subject of the Abbé de l'Epée, in whose defense he spends the rest of the book. Truly marginalizing himself, confining his own story to the margins of the text, Desloges only exists insofar as he is a successful example of a teaching method. But, like subalterns and slaves, Desloges is able to exist by tactics of submission that are in fact defensive. He does, after all, narrate his own life, and present a textual representation of his language and therefore of himself.

Without mentioning his own life story again, Desloges inserts his deaf existence and working-class perspective into the text. He attacks indirectly the power of the hearing world over the deaf when he notes that 'deaf people who are abandoned in asylums or isolated somewhere in the provinces' (ibid., 16) do not learn sign language. When deaf people are united, as they are in major urban areas like Paris, they can organize linguistic power. He gives himself as an example of someone whose signs had been 'unordered and unconnected' before coming into contact with 'deaf people more highly educated' than himself. When this synergistic meeting occurs, language happens through the regulation of a subaltern community.

This critical mass of deaf people is uniquely both deaf and underclass. In Desloges' tones, one can hear a will to power that perhaps reflects republican sentiments of the time.

> There are congenitally deaf people, Parisian laborers, who are illiterate and who have never attended the abbé de l'Epée's lessons, who have been found so well instructed about their religion, simply by means of signs, that they have been judged worthy of admittance to the holy sacraments, even those of the eucharist and marriage [which had been previously denied to the deaf]. No event – in Paris, in France, or in the four corners of the world – lies outside the scope of our discussion. We express ourselves on all subjects with as much order, precision, and rapidity as if we enjoyed the faculty of speech and hearing. (ibid., 36)

The matter of class and the matter of deafness merge into a kind of empowerment founded on community and communication. In fact, Desloges makes the argument that deafness and sign actually reconfigure the Deaf into the category of people with special abilities: '. . . our ideas concentrated in ourselves, so to speak, necessarily incline us toward reflectiveness and meditation' (ibid., 37). That is, ideas seem not to need a semiology; the deaf experience ideas in themselves. To bolster this point further, Desloges echoes Hobbes's lament that modern languages have fallen away from original ideas when he says that sign language is 'a faithful image of the object expressed.' The metonymic nature of sign anchors the deaf to the signified rather than the signifier. As such, sign can better express emotions and sentiments, and Desloges goes so far as to claim that 'no other language is more appropriate for conveying great and strong emotion' (ibid.). But the romantic aspirations for sign language as a physical form of poetry are balanced by an Enlightenment concern for rationality. Desloges thus claims that sign is more efficient than speech: 'The phrase *le mos [sic] qui vient* contains four words; nevertheless I use only two signs for it, one for the month and one for the future' (ibid., 38).

Sign language, as a language of the underclass, is replete with class markers. In Desloges's words: '. . . when necessity or expressive clarity demands, we always mention the social class of the person we are speaking about or wish to introduce' (ibid., 41). To designate a close acquaintance one needs only three signs: gender, then class, then profession. In designating nobility, there are signs for upper and lower nobility, which are followed by occupation, coat of arms, or livery. Manufacturers are distinguished from tradesmen 'for the deaf have the good sense not to confuse these two occupations.' The sensitivity of the deaf as constituting a marginalized underclass is reflected in their minute gradations of class. So the sign for trades-man is made as follows: 'with the thumb and index finger, we take the hem of a garment or some other object and present it the way a tradesman offers his merchandise; we then make the movement for counting money with our hands, and cross our arms like some-one resting.' This gestural rebus combines the ideas of capital, trade, money, and leisure, painting the very essence of the bourgeois cash nexus. The same subtlety of class analysis is included in the sign for 'working' that applies to 'manufacturers, artisans, and laborers.' But an additional sign is added to indicate who is doing the supervising and who is doing the obeying. 'We raise the index finger and lower it in a commanding way – that is the sign common to all supervisors' (ibid., 41). The same sign distinguishes a shopkeeper from a street vendor.

The point here is that sign language renders visible in linguistic form the nuances of class power. This language is most universally a language of the laboring classes. It contains within its very structure the strategies and tactics of conformity and transgressivity typical of a subaltern group. Yet at the same time sign language offers, by virtue of its marginality, a kind of universality, as Desloges notes:

several famous scholars have worn themselves out in the vain search
for the elements of a universal language as a point of unification for all
the people of the world. How did they fail to perceive that it had
already been discovered, that it existed naturally as sign language?

Citing Condillac and Court de Gébelin, who praised sign language
as a kind of universal language, Desloges goes on to observe:

> I cannot understand how a language like sign language – the richest
> in expressions, the most energetic, the most incalculably advantageous
> in its universal intelligibility – is still so neglected and that only the
> deaf speak it. (ibid., 45–6)

The fact that Desloges would even consider recommending that
sign language be used by the hearing world indicates the very
great extent to which universal language schemes, and the notion
of internationality, were a part of the revolutionary period
at the end of the eighteenth century. Yet his idea is not so wild.
In many ways, sign language provides us with a language that
opens many doors. In one sense, critically, its existence as a third
term mediating between text and speech opens the possibility
for mediating that theoretically troubling divide. The age-old
and currently lively debates between those who see literature
as primarily a text and those who see it primarily as an expression
of the body, of reality, can perhaps find a complex intersection by
admitting the 'literature' of sign language into the discussions.

But precisely because sign language will never actually become a
universal language, we must stop and consider how truly hegemonic
and controlling a concept is the notion of writing and speech
as a 'hearing' phenomenon. The argument I have tried to make
is that the deafness of textuality is one of the best-kept secrets of
the Enlightenment and beyond. It is not so much that convention
has ruled here, but that there has been an active suppression of
the insights I have proposed in this chapter. After all, the body is
political. Its form and function have been the site of powerful
control and management. An able body is the body of a citizen;

deformed, deafened, amputated, obese, female, perverse, crippled, maimed, blinded bodies do not make up the body politic. Utterances must all be able ones produced by conformed, ideal forms of humanity. In effect, there cannot be a complete analysis of early modern, modern and postmodern culture without bringing the disabled body and the disabled utterance into line.

4

Nationalism and Deafness:

The Nineteenth Century

It is true that deaf-mutes of every country have no mother tongue.
John Kitto, *The Lost Senses* (1845)

Up to this point, I have been arguing that disability is less of an object than it is a social process. And as a process, it is part of a hegemonic way of thinking about the body and about the insertion of the body into the body politic. Just as with issues of race and gender, the normal body is defined in a way that makes a distinction between the body *an sich* and the body *für sich*. The body *as such* is probably a Utopian idea, a vision of a pristine, univalent communication based on body language alone. The body *for* a purpose is certainly the rule in the early modern world.

Marx saw the body as essentially reified by the processes that came about as a result of the accumulation of capital in the eighteenth century. The nostalgic retro-fit vision presented by Marx in the *Economic and Philosophical Manuscripts of 1844* was of an earlier period in which the body existed in sensuous relation to the world, inserted into that world and creating that world through labor. This vision, however romantic, seems to point to a kind of labor that was not easily distinguished from 'life.' The parameters of the body and its activities were seen as aspects of nature linked to the processes of natural activities and seasons.

One could go so far as to say that disability, in our sense of the word, did not exist in such a world. Of course, impairments existed, but the impaired body was part of a lived experience, and

73

in that sense functioned. It was not defined strictly by its relation to means of production or a productive economy. But by the mid-nineteenth century, the body *an sich* had become the body *für sich* and the impaired body had become disabled – unable to be part of the productive economy, confined to institutions, shaped to contours defined by a society at large.

In this regard, it is possible to see the way that the disabled body came to be included in larger constructions like that of the nation. We have only to consider the cliché that a nation is made up of 'able-bodied' workers, all contributing to the mutual welfare of the members of that nation.

In order to discuss how the concept of nationality fits into a concept of disability, it is first necessary to say what we mean when we speak of nations. It is commonplace to think of a nation as equivalent to various state or governmental groupings. But the question of nation has become vexed in recent years. As one political scientist puts it (Connor 1992, 48):

> Where today is the study of nationalism? In this Alice-in-Wonderland world in which nation usually means state, in which nation-state usually means multination state, and in which ethnicity, primordialism, pluralism, tribalism, regionalism, communalism, parochialism and sub-nationalism usually means loyalty to the nation . . .

As opposed to a governmental entity, Walker Connor suggests that *nation* should be defined as 'a group of people whose members believe they are ancestrally related' (ibid., 48). This definition allows us to rethink nation as something perhaps divorced from a self-evident entity represented by a flag (for which it stands), an anthem, a collective will. The simplicity with which Edmund Burke speaks of 'the men of England' (1980, 200) or says 'The people of England know how little influence the teachers of religion are likely to have with the wealthy and powerful of long standing' (ibid., 201–2) shows us how powerful and homogenizing is the idea of national hegemony, eliding as it does in this case the particularity of the Scots, the Welsh, the Cornish, the Irish.

The idea of a nation as a governmental entity is further refined by contemporary scholars such as Benedict Anderson, Immanuel Wallerstein, Etienne Balibar, Hayden White and Homi Bhabha, among others, who propose alternative ways of thinking about nationality. Anderson thinks of the nation as a manifestation of print culture. For him, the gradual honing of a group of people into readers of a common language creates the idea of a homogeneous organization. So it was readers 'connected through print, [who] formed, in their secular, particular, visible invisibility, the embryo for the nationally imagined community' (Anderson 1983, 47). Likewise, Homi Bhabha deconstructs nation and narrative, while Hayden White writes of histories as forms of fictive metanarrative that novelize a nation to itself. Wallerstein prefers to down-play national entities, seeing them as aspects of a world capitalistic system, whilst Balibar sees nationalism as a self-constructing, destructive set of ideologies, always in a state of flux, but always defining power structures.

This reassessment of nationalism changes the discussion so that groups of people who see themselves bound by a common language, culture, and narrative are defined as nations or nationalities. This redefinition allows for ethnic and religious minorities to claim national identity, and gender even comes into play, as Sylvia Walby notes, since women must be seen as a distinct nationality within a nation.

Perhaps one of the most concise definitions of nationality is to be found in a somewhat unlikely source – the writings of Joseph Stalin. His 1913 pamphlet entitled *Marxism and the National Question* outlines five features necessary for a group to consider itself a nationality: (1) a common language; (2) a stable community; (3) a territory; (4) economic cohesion; (5) a collective psychology and character. Stalin stresses that nationality should not be thought of as something tribal or racial in nature, as something essentialist, but as constructed through history. And inextricably connected to that construction is language.[41]

But a nationality alone does not constitute a nation, as we can see in the struggles now taking place in Eastern Europe and the former Soviet Union. Nationality needs a political dimension. 'A nation,' Stalin refines, 'is not merely a historical category but a historical category belonging to a definite epoch, the epoch of rising capitalism. The process of elimination of feudalism and the development of capitalism was at the same time a process of amalgamation of people into nations' (Stalin 1934, 13). It is this historical development of the agglutinizing of heterogeneous peoples into the modern nation-state that took place in the eighteenth century as part of the process of increasing bourgeois hegemony that consolidated the idea of nation and the ideology of nationality.

As Benedict Anderson, among others, points out, the consolidation of national interests was very much involved with the enforcement of a common language on a heteroglossic group of peoples. 'Nothing served to "assemble" related vernaculars more than capitalism, which within the limits imposed by grammars and syntaxes, created mechanically-reproduced print-languages, capable of dissemination through the market' (Anderson 1983, 47). The novel, according to Anderson, was one step in the formation of national entities, yoking as it did images of national character, national language, and progress through structured time. Moreover, Edward Said has taken pains to show how novels help to construct national identities through normalizing imperialist attitudes toward 'others' into narrative form.

In this chapter, I want to observe some of the features of this discourse of nationalism as it impacts on what I might call the nationality of Deafness, and by extension disability. As I have tried to show, the modern and postmodern redefinition of nation allows for groups of people claiming a community, a language, a common history and culture to assert themselves as nationalities.[42]

At first blush, it might seem that deafness should be regarded as a social/medical phenomenon and as such would have little to do with the issues of nation and nationality. However, the issue of a common language is intricately involved in the way the Deaf were treated in the eighteenth and nineteenth centuries, and parallels can be drawn between that experience and the experience of other linguistically divergent groups in colonial settings. Instead of calling the Deaf a nationality, one might consider them as occupying the place of an ethnic group. In fact, Connor notes that the term '"ethnic" is derived from the closest equivalent to *nationem* in ancient Greek, *ethnos*' and as such is quite close in meaning to 'nation' (1992, 55, note 1). Paul Brass places ethnicity within the realm of nationality, and defines an ethnic group as 'any group of people dissimilar from other peoples in terms of objective cultural criteria [language or dialect, distinctive dress or diet or customs, religion or race] and containing within its membership . . . the elements for a complete division of labor and for reproduction' (1991, 19). Brass notes that 'ethnic identity is itself a variable, rather than a fixed or "given" disposition' (ibid.,13). By these criteria, the Deaf can be defined as an ethnic group or a nationality.[43] If an *ethnos* is defined as a culturally similar group sharing a common language, then the Deaf conceivably fit that category.

The issue is by no means a simple one because the relationship between language and ethnicity is not monolithic. As Etienne Balibar points out, ethnicity is derived from two sources: language and race. 'Most often the two operate together, for only their complementarity makes it possible for the "people" to be represented as an absolutely autonomous unit' (Balibar and Wallerstein 1991, 96). However, language is also the first ethnic trait to go by the board, since second-generation immigrants typically no longer bear the traces of their parents' accents or even their original language. In the United States now, second- and third-generation Italian-Americans, Jews, or Germans, for example, rarely speak their 'native' tongues, although in the past Jews, for example, might have.

In the case of the Deaf, the issue of language presents itself as a defining structure of consciousness in quite a different way from the issues surrounding other disabilities. Unlike blindness or physical impairment, deafness is in some sense an invisible disability. Only when the Deaf person begins to engage in language does the disability become visible. The deaf can be thought of as a population whose different ability is the necessary use of a language system that does not require oral/aural communication.

Within a nation, they represent a linguistic minority. There are certainly other disabilities that involve a difficulty or inability to communicate (aphasia, autism), but none of these impairments imply the necessity for another language. While the blind have Braille, Braille is not a language, but merely a way of transcribing whatever language the blind person may know. No one would claim that the blind have a language other than that of their mother tongue. As such, the deaf can be thought of as a group defined by language difference.

This point perhaps needs some further elaboration. It is commonly thought that deafness involves the inability to use language properly. If only deaf citizens could speak and understand English, there would be no problem for them or the larger community. Thus, deaf people are schooled arduously in lip reading, speech therapy, and the activities associated with the oral/aural form of communication. However, it is precisely this focusing on the dysfunctionality of the deaf that constitutes a privileging of the aural/oral system of communication. As Balibar writes, 'the production of ethnicity is also the racialization of language and the verbalization of race' (Balibar and Wallerstein 1991, 104). Because people are interpellated as subjects by language, because language itself is a congealed set of social practices, the actual dysfunctionality of the Deaf is to have another language system. That system challenges the majority assumption about the function of language, about the coherence of language and culture. Consequently, the Deaf are, in a sense, racialized through their use of sign language as a system of communication. They are seen as outside the citizenry created by a community of language users,[44] and therefore ghettoized as outsiders.

But unlike other people with disabilities, also ostracized if not ghettoized, the Deaf have a community, a history, a culture; moreover, the Deaf tend to intermarry, thus perpetuating that culture. There is within the Deaf world a body of 'literature' including written as well as signed works, a theatrical/choreographic tradition, academic discursive practices, pedagogic/ideological institutions, and so on. In this sense, the Deaf have created their own 'nationalism' as a resistance to audist culture.[45] This level of social organization, community and resistance has not generally been achieved by other physically impaired peoples, although political consciousness and organizing have increased in recent years, and a body of literature is beginning to develop around the area of disability studies.

Ethnicity is, one can say, produced by a dialectical process in which a dominant group singles out a minority and ethnicizes its members; but reciprocally, minorities can ethnicize themselves in the course of trying to claim privileges and status from social elites. As de Vos says, ethnic identity is the 'subjective, symbolic or emblematic use [by] a group of people . . . of any aspect of culture, in order to differentiate themselves from other groups' (1975, 16). If any aspect of culture can form the seed around which an ethnic community can coalesce, certainly the Deaf can be regarded as such. Furthermore, the formation of a group identity is both imposed from outside ('You are disabled: You are Deaf.') and from within ('We are Deaf!' 'Deaf Power!'). So the site of ethnicity, as it were, is a contested one in a struggle for who will define the ethnicity of the group, who will construct it.

It is also possible to think of the Deaf as a race, that is, as a group carrying genetic information that affects physical traits and that can be passed down from generation to generation. One could argue that the concept of 'race' is itself a product of imperialism, that to consider a people to be a race on the basis of some inherited trait was something that arose when it became necessary to think of humanity as divided into races. To think of the Deaf as a race is clearly to follow a dubious line of reasoning, but it is worth considering at least for the sake of argument. There are two senses in which the issue of racism can come into play here. The first would fit in with Colette Guillaumin's insistence on a 'broad definition of racism' that would include exclusion based not just on ethnic groupings but on grounds of gender, class, sexual preference, and disability. The second would posit Deaf people themselves as constituting a race on the basis of inherited traits.

In relation to the latter, one must consider that there are two causes of deafness: one is inherited traits and the other is impairment caused by disease or accident. If we focus on the former, we can trace lines of inherited deafness, as does Nora Ellen Groce in her study of deafness on Martha's Vineyard. Since the trait for hereditary deafness is a recessive one, the idea of a deaf race is a bit farfetched. But many genetic traits, such as those for hair color, eye color, skin color, are considered racial traits because segregation or geographical isolation has forced those traits to remain within a specific population. As Immanuel Wallerstein suggests, 'it makes little difference whether we define pastness in terms of genetically continuous groups (races), historical socio-political groups (nations) or cultural groups (ethnic groups). They are all peoplehood constructs, all inventions of pastness, all contemporary political phenomena' (Balibar and Wallerstein 1991, 78–9).

Discussions of race have to take into account the historical determinants of race. In other words, the very concept of race is historically determined and can be considered the product of a particular historical period of development. As Wallerstein points out, '*race* was a primary category of the colonial world, accounting for political rights, occupational allocation and income' (ibid., 189). Theories of race became elaborated during the period of greatest imperialism; indeed it is hard to imagine a justification for imperialism without a theory of race. It is no coincidence that the eugenics movement impacted directly on deaf people at this time.

Eugenics only further emphasizes the connection between disability and racism. As Etienne Balibar notes, 'the phantasm of prophylaxis or segregation (the need to purify the social body, to preserve "one's own" or "our" identity from all forms of mixing, interbreeding or invasion) . . . are articulated around stigmata of otherness (name, skin colour, religious practices)' (ibid., 18). The stigma of disability, of physical (and, in the case of deafness, inherited) traits, creates the icon of the other body – the disabled figure – an icon that needs to be excluded in a similar way to the body marked as differently pigmented or gendered.

This tendency toward prophylaxis, of course, is reciprocally one of the processes by which an ethnic group forms its own existence.

Logically, as the Deaf were constructed into a group, institutional-ized, and regulated, they perceived themselves to be such a group and acted as such. The very structures that are the equivalent to what Althusser identified as the ideological state apparatus – educational institutions, associations, newspapers, language – and even the desire of Deaf people to form their own state were pinpointed by the eugenicist Alexander Graham Bell as causes for alarm. He foresaw the development of these ideological apparatuses as leading to 'the production of a defective race of human beings [which] would be a great calamity to the world' (Bell 1969, 41). Fearing the emergence of a 'deaf variety' of humans and therefore seeking to discourage intermarriage among deaf people, Bell proposed that residential schools should be abolished, education through the medium of sign language should be forbidden, and the Deaf should be prohibited from teaching the deaf.[46] These steps are reminiscent of the measures frequently implemented by colonial powers seeking to dismantle the culture of a nonnational or indigenous people.

It may be worth noting here that while a biological stigma must be part of an anti-disability discourse, it is necessary to consider the signification of physical traits. There may well be allegorical mean-ings ascribed to deafness, blindness, lameness, and so on. As Balibar says, 'bodily stigmata play a great role in [racism's] phantasmatics, but they do so more as signs of a deep psychology, as signs of a spiritual inheritance rather than a biological heredity' (Balibar and Wallerstein 1991, 24). Here, Balibar is speaking of the Jews, whose physical differences from non-Jews can often be indiscernible, yet paradoxically the more invisible the physicality of the Jew, the more dangerous the infiltration. The mark of circumcision, for example, is one of the most hidden of 'disabilities,' particularly during the periods when general circumcision of the male public was not the rule. To be a Jew then meant more symbolically than physically, although the symbolic and the physical were joined at the hip. Likewise, the deaf represent, among other things, the idea of moral and spiritual deafness, an inability to hear the word of God, an inability to participate in reason, and in life. Likewise, the blind are morally blind, and the lame inept. The body illustrates those moral precepts to be avoided in the culture. If, as Balibar suggests, much of modern racism derives from early anthropology's tendency to classify with an aim of making distinctions between humanity and animality (ibid., 56–7), then the deaf and the blind, as well as the mentally impaired and some of the physically deformed, will be seen as more animal, less human, than the norm. Animals are 'dumb'; they cannot hear language; they are morally deaf and blind. Thus the 'normal' majority can, through this classificatory grid, see itself as most properly human. In studying disability, we must keep in mind the significations of body, the language of deformity as it is encoded by the 'normal' majority.

In order to continue the argument that the Deaf constitute a threat to ideas of nation, wholeness, moral rectitude and good citizenship, I must develop the material significance of the point made in Chapter 3, that deafness as a discourse first appears in the eighteenth century. Before the eighteenth century there were individual deaf people and families of the deaf, and in urban areas even loose associations of the deaf, but there was no discourse about deafness, no public policy on deafness, no educational institutions – and therefore the deaf were not constructed as a group. Since most deaf people are born to hearing families, the deaf themselves did not see themselves as part of a community unless they were part of an urban assemblage of the Deaf. It was only by attending the residential schools created in the eighteenth century that the deaf became a community. The dramatic rise in the number of deaf schools in Europe – there were none at the beginning of the century and close to sixty by the end – indicates the groundswell that made this new ethnic group self-aware.

Moreover, by the beginning of the nineteenth century there had developed a more or less standardized language of the deaf that was transnational. That is, sign language had regional variations but was basically a universal language. This language was disseminated through the deaf schools, and the teachers in these schools were themselves deaf. So an educational system evolved that consolidated the deaf into a community.

Thus, the Deaf became a new subgroup within each state throughout Europe; like Jews and gypsies, they were an ethnic group in the midst of the nation. Though their numbers were small, they still amounted to a linguistic subgroup that increasingly perceived itself as a community with its own history and culture. By Stalin's criteria, all the Deaf lacked to claim nationhood were a territory and economic cohesion. One might indeed make a comparison with, for example, the Russian Jews who were excluded from Stalin's definition of nationality because they lacked a territory, although the Bund claimed national status for them.

Douglas Baynton shows us that by the nineteenth century, the Deaf were regarded as foreigners living within the United States, a kind of fifth column in society resisting nationalization. Baynton quotes from the oralist publication the *American Annals of the Deaf and Dumb* which in 1847 described the deaf not as afflicted individuals but as a 'strongly marked class of human beings' with 'a history peculiar to themselves' (Baynton 1992, 221). Baynton concludes that 'deaf people were not so much handicapped *individuals* as they were a collectivity, a people – albeit, as we shall see, an inferior one' (ibid.). While the audist establishment initially constructed the deaf person as a model inhabitant of the Enlightenment, a citizen in the world of print culture, it came to see deaf people, particularly those using the 'foreign' sign language, as an ethnic minority with its own history and language that must be incorporated into the state and the nation. Educators were concerned that if deaf people 'are to exercise intelligently the rights of citizenship, then they must be made people of our language.' They insisted that 'the English language must be made the vernacular of the deaf if they are not to become a class unto themselves – foreigners among their own countrymen' (ibid., 229). This was part of a larger argument for the suppression of sign language because it 'isolated people from the national community' (ibid., 217).

Pierre Desloges in writing his book defending sign language is actually defending his nationality, if you like, from the hegemonic attempt to take away the native language of the Deaf. As we have seen, Desloges made an immediate equation between his deafness, his language, and his nationality:

> As would a Frenchman seeing his language disparaged by a German who knew at most a few words of French, I too felt obliged to defend my own language from the false charges leveled against it by Deschamps. (Lane 1984a, 30)

The debate between oralism and sign is often seen as one that pits the hearing community against deaf standards, but I think the issue is sharpened if we think of it as involving a political attempt to erase an ethnic group. Like the ethnic groups who have lost their language and thus their existence as nationalities (the Cornish in the United Kingdom, the Frisians in the Netherlands, the Sorbs and Wends of eastern and central Europe), the Deaf were in danger of being wiped out as a linguistically marked community.

The Deaf were not unique in waging such a struggle. The Romanians had to establish their own press and print a grammar in 1780 to keep from being erased by the Transylvanians; the Bulgarians resisting the dominance of Greek Orthodox clerics in the eighteenth century took similar steps. (Brass 1991, 30). Moreover, in dominant nation-states foreigners and minorities, as well as the lower classes in general, were denigrated in cultural forms of symbolic production as a way of establishing national solidarity. One has only to think of the hundreds of examples of French people being ridiculed in English literature of the period (particularly Captain Mirvan's excoriation of all aspects of Madame Duval's Frenchness in *Evelina*), or of Cimarosa's ridicule of an English suitor's accent and, tellingly, of a deaf father in the Italian opera *The Secret Marriage*. Class accents would not do either, as a nation attempts to create a standard, printed, representation of the official language.[47]

The nexus of deafness, class and nationality achieved its most extreme form when Jane Elizabeth Groom proposed in the 1880s that the deaf should leave England and found a deaf state in Canada. Groom's reasoning was particularly related to class. She advocated founding a deaf state because the deaf in England were poor and could not compete with hearing people in a tight labor market. The answer could be not revolution, but secession. There was, in America, another movement to found a deaf state in the West.

The fact that some Deaf people wanted to found a separate state is a strong enough argument for seeing them as a nationality or an ethnic group. It is more than possible to consider the flexibility of the concept of nationality and to see the way in which the nation-state, in its formation in the eighteenth and nineteenth centuries, elided various groups not normally thought of as national minorities – women, gays and lesbian, linguistic subgroups – in an attempt to make one nation out of many.

Having used the Deaf as a particular example to discuss the relationship of impairment to nationhood, now I would like to muddy the waters somewhat by introducing the idea of class. As Desloges's book emphasized, a strong connection exists between Deaf culture and working-class culture. Furthermore, there is a very deep relationship between disability in general and class. Mike Oliver in *The Politics of Disablement: A Sociological Approach* makes the point that 'just as we know that poverty is not randomly distributed internationally or nationally . . . neither is impairment' (1990, 13). One expert notes that in the Third World 'not only does disability usually guarantee the poverty of the victim but, most importantly, poverty is itself a major cause of disability' (Doyal 1983, 7).

If it is the case that disability causes poverty, and that poverty likewise causes disability, since poor people are more likely to get infectious diseases, more likely to lack genetic counseling, more likely to be injured in factory-related jobs and in wars, and generally more likely to have a dangerous work environment, then we have to see disability as intricately linked to capitalism and imperialism, or the latter-day version of imperialism that shifts factory work to Third World countries and creates poor and rich nations to facilitate a division of labor. The distinction some might want to make between disability and poverty collapses at some level.

For example, David Rothman in his account of the development of the asylum in the United States notes that in the colonial period the mentally ill were primarily seen as a category of the indigent. 'The lunatic came to public attention not as someone afflicted with delusions or fears, but as someone suffering from poverty' (Rothman 1971, 4). Later, the first almshouses sheltered not so much the poor as the disabled poor. In the first such institution built in New York City, about half the population was composed of people with physical or mental disabilities, including those with age-related impairments (ibid., 39).

Class is not absent even in the broad classification of disability. For example, in the case of people who use wheelchairs, the paraplegic or quadriplegic, we need to consider that among the approximately 1 million Americans in this category, class and race figure largely. Injury to the spinal cord through accident is one of the most common causes of paralysis, and this type of injury occurs disproportionately among young, working-class men (Murphy 1990, 139). Particularly among the baby boom generation, those wounded veterans who returned from Vietnam make up a great number of wheelchair users, and they were largely drawn from the working class. The chief cause of traumatic paraplegia and quadriplegia in American cities now is injuries sustained from gunshot wounds – and most of the people so injured are drawn from the lower classes, particularly from people of color. Contact sports, job injuries, and automobile accidents still tend to draw their victims largely from young, working-class males (ibid., 139). So even 'chance' and 'accidents' fit a pattern involving class and race.

Industrialization re-created the category of work, and in so doing re-created the category of worker. The very idea of citizenship came to be ideologically associated with this kind of work, and various kinds of inclusions and exclusions in the category of nation were associated with work and work-related issues. Thus we see women initially bracketed out of the workforce and into the domestic sphere in middle-class life, while proletarian families were redistributed into the factory orbit. In effect, the imperatives of industrialism and capitalism redefined the body. 'Able-bodied workers' were those who could operate machines, and the human body came to be seen as an extension of the factory machinery. Ironically, this reciprocity between human and machine led to a conception of the mechanical perfection of the human body. The eighteenth-century notion that the human body was a divinely crafted machine led to a much more industrial interpretation of that insight so that the factory worker became a mere cog in the machinery. Likewise, the increasing mechanization of the body led to an increase of destructive acts against the human body in the form of factory-related mutilations. The machine, like a latter-day Moloch, demanded human bodies and transformed them into disabled instruments of the factory process.

Friedrich Engels, in *The Condition of the Working Class in England*, describes this necessary chain of transformation. 'A number of cripples gave evidence before the Commission, and it was obvious that their physical condition was due to their long hours of work. Deformity of this type generally affects the spine and legs' (Engels 1968, 171). He cites a report by a Leeds physician, one Francis Sharp, who wrote as follows:

> During my practice at the hospital, where I have seen about 35,000 patients, I have observed the peculiar twisting of the ends of the lower part of the thigh bone. This affection I had never seen before I came to Leeds, and I have remarked that it principally afflicted children from 8 to 14 years of age. At first I considered it might be rickets, but from the numbers which presented themselves particularly at an age beyond the time when rickets attack children, and finding that they were of a recent date, and had commenced since they began work at the factory, I soon began to change my opinion. I now . . . can most decidedly state they were the result of too much labour. So far as I know they all belong to factories, and acquired this knock-kneed appearance from the very long hours the children worked in the mills. (ibid., 171)

The report mentions varicose veins, spinal distortions, and deformities of the limbs. Engels himself corroborates these observations. 'It is easy to identify such cripples at a glance, because their deformities are all exactly the same. They are knock-kneed and deformed and the spinal column is bent either forwards or sideways' (ibid., 173). Miners are described as 'either bandy-legged or knock-kneed and suffer from splayed feet, spinal deformities and other physical defects. This is due to the fact that their constitutions have been weakened and they are nearly always forced to work in a cramped position' (ibid., 280). Factory accidents contributed to this nineteenth-century, negative version of body sculpting. As Engels writes, 'In Manchester, one sees not only numerous cripples, but also plenty of workers who have lost the whole or part of an arm, leg, or foot' (ibid., 185). Engels records that there were 962 machine-related injuries in Manchester in 1842 alone.

If Engels's work gives us an insight into the way the body was perceived in the nineteenth century, it becomes clear that industrialization was seen as a palpable force in quite literally reshaping the bodies of the body politic. Even the mind was seen as subject to the ills of a capitalist society. In 1854 Edward Jarvis attempted to explain to a Massachusetts medical society how the tensions of the free market led to mental illness.

> In this country, where no son is necessarily confined to the work or employment of his father, but all the fields of labor . . . are open to whomsoever will put on the harness . . . their mental powers are strained to their utmost tension; they labor in agitation . . . their minds stagger under the disproportionate burden. (cited in Rothman 1971, 115)

Jarvis notes that in precapitalist countries 'these causes of insanity cannot operate' (cited in ibid.).

Repeated references to diminished physical size, lack of robustness, delayed puberty, mental illness, endemic disease, and physical deformity led to a collective realization that the nation was in peril as a result of industrial practice. The symbol of this problem was the deformed worker. Likewise, the technical solution to this problem was the breeding of a better, more robust national stock. The eugenics movement came into existence as a way of repairing the declining stock of England and America, a decline that was the result, as the eugenicists saw it, of a rapidly multiplying lower class and an influx of 'foreign' peoples with lower intelligence, less physical strength, and greater licentiousness than the natives.[48]

The relationship between disability and industrialization is a complex one. The argument has been made that in a preindustrialized society, people with impairments might more easily be part of the social fabric. In an unpublished dissertation, Martha L. Edwards argues that disability in ancient Greece did not limit the ability of men to fight or engage in wars. While no Utopia for the disabled, ancient Greek society provided 'an acknowledgement of human physical variety. There was a wide variety of physical variation, and one did what one could given one's ability.'

In a similar vein, J. Gwaltney (1970) shows that blindness was not perceived as a disability in a Mexican village. Other works describe how deaf people were fully included in societies on Martha's Vineyard and in the Amazon in which most hearing members of the community could also sign (Groce 1985; Farb 1975). Thus the communal life and pace of rural society may not have constructed the disabled body in the way that industrialized societies did.

> The blind and the deaf growing up in slowly changing scattered rural communities had more easily been absorbed into the work and life of those societies without the need for special provision. Deafness, while working alone at agricultural tasks that all children learned by observation with little formal schooling, did not limit the capacity for employment too severely. Blindness was less of a hazard in uncongested familiar rural surroundings, and routine tasks involving repetitive tactile skills could be learned and practised by many of the blind without special training. The environment of an industrial society was, however, different. (Topliss 1979, 11)

The demands of a factory system require another version of the body and another version of time:

> The speed of factory work, the enforced discipline, the time-keeping and production norms – all these were a highly unfavourable change

from the slower, more self-determined and flexible methods of work into which many handicapped people had been integrated. (Ryan and Thomas 1980, 101)

Another seemingly unlikely area in which we may connect disability with national identity and class was in the freak shows that began in the middle of the nineteenth century. Robert Bogdan in his book *Freak Show: Presenting Human Oddities for Amusement and Profit* (1988) makes a rather interesting connection between physical disability and race when he notes that not only were the obviously disabled – the mentally delayed, the physically different – exhibited at freak shows, but also physically normal native peoples of colonized countries were exhibited grouped under the heading of 'freaks.' As one press agent for the amusement world noted, 'The Borneo aborigines, the head-hunters, the Ubangis, and the Somalis were all classified as freaks. From the point of the showman the fact that they were different put them in the category of human oddities' (Bogdan 1988, 177). These people came from Oceania, Asia, Africa, Australia, South America and the Arctic, and the notion of racial difference put them in the same category as the disabled. As Bogdan says, 'showmen took people who were culturally and ancestrally non-Western and made them freaks by casting them as bizarre and exotic: cannibals, savages, barbarians' (ibid.).

Some of those put on display in the United States were actually residents of the countries they were said to come from,[49] but more often than not they were American-born individuals whose relatives had earlier come from those foreign locations. In 1872, for example, P. T. Barnum announced the appearance of four Fiji natives who were cannibals, including a princess. As it turned out, the three men had been brought up since childhood as Christians and lived in California, and the woman was African-American, a native of Virginia (ibid., 183). In such strange arrangements, people of color, disabled by society in so many ways, were transformed into non-Western natives who would then be seen as 'freaks' and commodified as such.

The equation between people with disabilities and the non-Western worked both ways. Bogdan points out that beginning in 1850 and continuing through the 1940s, a 'pattern' can be discerned in which 'showmen constructed exhibits using people we would now call mentally retarded by casting them in an extreme form of the exotic mode' (ibid., 119). Such people were made to seem as if they were representative of other races or 'missing links' in evolution. Two severely mentally impaired, microcephalic siblings from Circleville, Ohio, were exhibited as 'Wild Australian Children' and said to be 'neither idiots, lusus naturae, nor any other abortion of humanity, but belonged to a distinct race hitherto unknown to civilization' (ibid., 120). Hiram and Barney Davis, each approximately three feet tall and mentally impaired, were billed as 'The Astonishing Wild Men, From the Island of Borneo.' Maximo and Bartola, two microcephalic children bought from their parents in Central America were hawked as 'The Last of the Ancient Aztecs of Mexico.' Other microcephalics were exhibited as Aztecs because of their small heads and facial features. In the case of William Henry Johnson, an African-American microcephalic, the publicity projected this mentally impaired man as the 'missing link' found in Gambia. Johnson, described as 'What is It? or The Man-Monkey,' was said to have been found in Africa '"in a perfectly nude state" roving through the trees like the monkey and the orangutan.' His 'keeper' is quoted as saying that 'the formation of the head and face combines both that of the native African and the Orang Outang . . . he has been examined by some of the most scientific men we have, and pronounced by them to be a *CONNECTING LINK BETWEEN THE WILD NATIVE AFRICAN AND THE BRUTE CREATION*' (ibid., 137).

What is most interesting about this strange phenomenon is that the category of disability defines itself through an appeal to nationalism. The disabled person is not of this nation, is not a citizen, in the same sense as the able-bodied. That the freak show begins in the same period as we have seen statistics and eugenics begin indicates a change in the way people thought about the physically different. In addition, discussions of disability always slide into discussions of race. The connections we have discovered between non-Western people and disabled people – both in the simple sense of non-Western culture being seen as 'freakish' and in the glib elisions made between microcephalics, non-humans, and the colonized world – show dramatically how similarly race, nation, and physical identity are defined. We might also add that the people who tended to make up the freaks, hoaxes or not, were drawn exclusively from the lower classes.

I want to end this discussion of nationality by looking at another disabled person, perhaps a kind of freak in this sense, who became a national symbol of identity. I am speaking of Franklin Delano Roosevelt.

A president of the United States has become more than a simple physical entity; he has become an icon of the power and vigor of the country. Much public relations time and effort is spent on making the man in office seem physically perfect and devoid of illness or disability. Countless photographs of a president golfing, jogging, romping on the beach emphasize his robustness and *joie de vivre*. Yet moments slip through the veil of well-being surrounding the president, and these moments are memorable in a disconcerting way. Who does not recall Carter collapsing during a running race or Bush vomiting into the lap of the Japanese prime minister? Johnson's revealing of his surgical scar was an unwanted reminder of his mortality. More profoundly, Eisenhower's heart attack and a series of assassinations and assassination attempts are reminders of the physical vulnerability of the person in office.[50] When Reagan survived an assassination attempt, the White House publicists covered up the extent of the President's injuries and the pain of his quite lengthy recovery. The unwillingness to show the public the autopsy photographs of Kennedy stems from, among other possibly conspiratorial reasons, an impulse to prevent the nation from visualizing the President as having a wounded, mutilated body or being physically damaged.

In fact, Kennedy had what we could certainly call a disability: Addison's disease. This debilitating and possibly life-threatening dysfunction of the adrenal glands was consistently managed by those who controlled public relations around Kennedy. The back pain was romanticized as stemming from war wounds received when Kennedy was the captain of *PT 109*. The President's rocking chair, used to alleviate the pain of his illness, was transformed into a rather evocative symbol associated with New England, the presidency, and the battle story. The fact that Kennedy was constantly medicated with painkillers was erased, and even the telltale puffiness of Kennedy's face, a side effect of long-term cortisone use, was forgotten.

But none of these attempts at management come close to the efforts that surrounded Roosevelt's disability. Roosevelt himself was made into a symbol of the triumph over physical disability, and his own story was seen as paralleling the USA's recovery and triumph from the Depression. Roosevelt's erect posture, his upturned face and jauntily held cigarette holder together were a symbol for America of hope, possibility, and recovery. Roosevelt's case is so interesting because he was the first president to be truly 'mechanically reproduced,' to use Walter Benjamin's term. His was truly the first media presidency, and his time in office spanned the heydays of photography, photojournalism, radio, and television. Although radio was in a sense the primary medium, Roosevelt had to control the medium of photography and film as no president before had needed to. In this sense, Roosevelt forged the visual image and aural identity of the presidency for the modern media.

Of the hundreds of thousands of photographs and films of Roosevelt, documented the period from 1928, when he became Governor of New York, until 1945, when he died in office, there are only two photos extant showing Roosevelt using a wheelchair. This archival evidence confirms the popular notion of Roosevelt – that he contracted polio, went to Warm Springs to recover, and then went on to become president. As Hugh Gallagher notes:

> Roosevelt's biographers have tended to treat his paralysis as an episode – with a beginning, a middle, and an end. By their accounts, Roosevelt gets polio, struggles through his rehabilitation, and then overcomes his adversity. End of chapter. The handicap is

not mentioned again. It is viewed only as one of the stages through which FDR passes in preparation for the presidency. (Gallagher 1985, 210)

The USA never had the facts about Roosevelt's polio. These, according to Gallagher's meticulously documented study *FDR's Splendid Deception*, were that Roosevelt became, as a result of polio, a paraplegic who after his illness never was able to move his legs or stand without assistance. This fact was well known to Roosevelt's family and friends. One visitor to Hyde Park wrote of Roosevelt in 1921:

> He's had a brilliant career as Assistant of the Navy under Wilson, and then a few brief weeks of crowded glory and excitement when nominated by the Democrats for the Vice Presidency. Now he is a cripple – will he ever be anything else? (ibid., 28)

The writer of this letter expresses a common assumption – that the disability will become the person.

Roosevelt was determined that people should not define him in this stigmatized role, and he managed the reception of his image so that he would not be, in our terms, a disruption in the visual field. According to Gallagher, 'from the very first, Roosevelt was determined not to be seen in a wheelchair unless absolutely necessary, and not to be lifted up stairs in view of the public.' This desire not to be seen as visibly disabled connects us once again to the realm of the senses – the visual sense in particular. We might link up this notion of the visibility of disability with the notion of the invisibility of nationalism. As Balibar points out, there is an assumption that true nationalism is invisible, a degree zero of existence, but that false nationalism can be seen. Thus we have 'the alleged, quasi-hallucinatory visibility of the "false nationals"': the Jews, "wogs", immigrants, Blacks. . . . racism thus inevitably becomes involved in the obsessional quest for a "core" of authenticity that cannot be found, shrinks the category of nationality and de-stabilizes the historical nation' (Balibar and Wallerstein 1991,

60). So, in this way, the visibility of the President's disability goes to the 'core' of his national identity. Roosevelt saw that to be visibly disabled was to lose one's full nationality, which should be an invisibility, a neutrality, a degree zero of citizenly existence.

When Roosevelt addressed the Democratic Convention to place Al Smith's name on the ballot in 1924, he formulated a plan later used consistently.

> He and [his son] James arrived early each day in order to get to their seats before the arrival of the other delegates. James would take his father by the wheelchair to the hall entrance closest to the seats of the New York delegation. At the door, Roosevelt's [leg] braces would be locked, and he would be pulled to a standing position. With James on one arm and a crutch under the other, he would slowly make his way down the aisle. At times he gripped James's arm so tightly that James had to concentrate to keep from crying out in pain. . . . [Roosevelt] did not leave the hall until the session had ended and the hall had cleared. (Gallagher 1985, 60)

Four years later at Houston, Roosevelt determined not to be seen with crutches. Eleanor wrote to him, 'I'm telling everyone you are going to Houston without crutches, so mind you stick to it' (ibid., 63). Roosevelt solved the crutch problem by developing a new technique which he practiced for a month with his eighteen-year-old son Elliot.

> Elliot would stand, holding his right arm flexed at a ninety-degree angle, his forearm rigid as a parallel bar. Roosevelt would stand beside Elliot, tightly gripping his son's arm. In his right hand Roosevelt held a cane. His right arm was straight and held rigid with his index finger pressed firmly straight down along the line of the cane. In this posture he could 'walk,' although in a curious toddling manner, hitching up first one leg with the aid of the muscles along the side of his trunk, then placing his weight upon that leg, then using the muscles along his other side, and hitching the other leg forward. . . . He was able to do this because his arms served him in precisely the same manner as crutches. (ibid., 65)

Roosevelt's system for walking was, according to Gallagher, 'treacherous, slow, and awkward.' Indeed, crutches would have been more sensible and safer. But Roosevelt wanted above all to be seen as a 'cured cripple.' In a rare reference to his own condition, Roosevelt mentioned his paralysis in a campaign speech during the 1928 race for governor of New York: 'Seven years ago . . . I came down with infantile paralysis. . . . By personal good fortune I was able to get the best kind of care and the result of having the best kind of care is that today I am on my feet' (ibid., 66). But he was on his feet only in the sense that he wore metal braces that could be locked into an upright position.

Roosevelt succeeded in convincing the world that he had beaten his disability. Will Durant's description of Roosevelt at the Democratic Convention in 1928, written for the *New York World*, makes us see an upright Roosevelt. 'On the stage is Franklin Roosevelt, beyond comparison the finest man that has appeared at either convention. . . . A figure tall and proud even in suffering' (ibid., 67).

Rumors that Roosevelt was paraplegic did surface in the press. During his run for president, a *Time* magazine article quoted an observer as saying 'This candidate, while mentally qualified for the presidency, is utterly unfit physically' (ibid., 84). An 'objective' writer was hired by Roosevelt to say that Roosevelt's health was superb, and then thousands of reprints of the report were sent to each Democratic Party county chairperson in the country as well as to prominent Democrats everywhere. Georgia's governor, Gene Talmadge, brought the subject up again in 1935, saying, 'The greatest calamity to this country is that the president can't walk around and hunt up people to talk to. . . . The only voice to reach his wheelchair were . . . cries of the "gimme crowd"' (ibid., 96). Despite this rare mention of Roosevelt's disability, the President's visual presentation was so thoroughly controlled that the image that remained was the cigarette holder and not the wheelchair.

As president, Roosevelt used his wheelchair a good deal of the day. But he did not want the public to know this, and he lied in response to direct questions, as he did to one reporter who charged that Roosevelt was still 'wheelchair bound.'

As a matter of fact, I don't use a wheelchair at all except a little kitchen chair on wheels to get about my room while dressing . . . and solely for the purpose of saving time. (ibid., 92)

That little kitchen chair was in fact Roosevelt's own design for a wheelchair that would be streamlined, small, and unobtrusive, as opposed to the rather large sanitorium wicker chairs then currently in use. The Secret Service now became the agency that concealed Roosevelt's disability, and Washington became a ramped city. As Gallagher writes:

The White House imposed certain rules, which were always obeyed. For example, the president was never lifted in public. If it was necessary to lift him in or out of the car, this was done in the privacy of a garage or behind a temporary plywood screen constructed for the purpose. He was never seen in public seated in a wheelchair. Either he appeared standing, leaning on the arm of an aide, or he was seated in an ordinary chair. (ibid., 93)

The rule was that lecterns had to be bolted to the floor. At least once this was not done, however, and Roosevelt crashed to the floor. Although reporters were present, no one filmed the event or took pictures. On another occasion, when Roosevelt was being lifted out of a car, some newsreel cameramen were filming the event and Roosevelt said, 'No movies of me getting out of the machine, boys' (ibid., 94). The Secret Service would intervene if any photographers attempted to take such photos, and they would seize and expose the film. This was official governmental action to erase any visual trace of the President's disability.

Roosevelt's car went everywhere up ramps constructed by the Secret Service. When he had to get into or out of his car, he was carried by two strong men. This carrying was the most disconcerting scene for many. John Gunther recalled: 'The shock was greatest of all when he was carried; he seemed, for one thing, very small' (ibid.).

I have taken a bit of time to detail the extraordinary steps that Roosevelt and governmental agencies took to have the President seen as ambulatory. This deception was a two-way street, since neither Roosevelt nor the public wanted to see him as a 'cripple.' And the film industry, deeply implicated in the national sense of the body, after the end of the Second World War even made a film entitled *Till the End of Time* in which a mother encourages her disabled veteran son to identify with FDR. The identification works so well that the son renounces his wheelchair and hides his prosthesis under his pants legs, just like FDR (Norden 1994, 320).

The sense of national identity associated with the President, and with the almost sacred nature of his body and physical presence, was paramount. If in the post-Depression USA every citizen had to get to work and build a better future, if the model of the able-bodied citizen was to be writ large on every Work Projects Administration mural, then the President had to embody normalcy, even if the efforts taken to create this illusion were Herculean. Since the disabled are a kind of minority group within the nation, it would hardly do for the President to be a representative of that minority group. In the perverse logic that marks the political imagination of the United States, only an aristocratic WASP could embody the aspirations of the working classes; only a physically intact man could represent those who were crippled by the ravages of an economic disaster.

The contested battle of Roosevelt's disabled body continues. In 1995 a controversy has arisen over the construction of a memorial to FDR (*New York Times*, 10 April 1995, A:10). Disability-rights activists are appalled that none of the memorial's three sculptures and bas-reliefs will show the former President with the wheelchair, crutches, braces, or canes that he used. The members of the memorial commission, headed by Senators Mark O. Hatfield and Daniel K. Inouye, and including members of Roosevelt's family, oppose any such representation, arguing that Roosevelt's elaborate avoidance of public representations of his disability indicate his wish to be seen as intact and normal. What resounds through this argument is the tenacity with which national images and identities are tied to notions of the body. More than half a century after Roosevelt's death, the specter of his 'abnormal' body still needs to be exorcized so it will not haunt the nation's sense of its own wholeness and integrity.

5

Deafness and Insight:

Disability and Theory

Now the Sirens have a still more fatal weapon than their song, namely their silence. And though admittedly such a thing has never happened, still it is conceivable that someone might possibly have escaped from their singing; but from their silence certainly never.

Franz Kafka, *Parables*

The Deafened Moment

In this chapter, I shall speak of deafness as a critical modality. Of course, to 'speak of deafness' is, strictly, not what I shall do, since I do not speak at all but write. The act of writing is falsely given the qualities of sonic duration. That very paradox goes to the heart of this book, since so many of our assumptions about writing, about language, about communication are based on the premiss that language is in fact sonic, audible, vocalized.

When I say (write) that deafness is a critical modality, I want to make a distinction between the Deaf, the deaf, and the deafened moment. The Deaf is that community of deaf people who share language, cultural values, history, and social life. The deaf are simply those who do not hear. But the deafened moment is one that does not rely on either the Deaf or the deaf. While the deaf moment does not rely on the Deaf, it exists in a dynamic relationship with that group. By the deafened moment, I am speaking (writing) of a contextual position, a dialectical moment in the reading/critical process, that is defined by the acknowledgement on the part of the reader/writer/critic that he or she is part of a process that does not involve speaking or hearing. I address this position because reading/writing has been unproblematically thought of as a process that involves hearing and vocalizing. But, as I have said, such a way of thinking is truly undialectical. As Theodor Adorno points out (1967, 33), 'the less the dialectical method can today presuppose the Hegelian identity of subject and object, the more it is obliged to be mindful of the duality of the moments.' Since we postmoderns can no longer assume an identity between reader and text (or reader and reader), we must pay more attention to the duality of the deaf and hearing moments. In this case, the deafened moment, long suppressed, must now see (signify) the light of day. When we illuminate (write) this moment, we acknowledge the political oppression involved in denying that this major form of language interaction has in fact implied the ostracism of those who are differently abled linguistically. Further, we highlight the buried assumptions of the process of reading/writing.

In this context, I will be looking at (writing about) the deafened moment as it dialectically approaches the critic, the reader, and the text. I would say that each of these three entities has a deafened moment that has been historically suppressed.

In *Blindness and Insight*, Paul de Man made the point that 'critics' moments of greatest blindness with regard to their own critical assumptions are also the moments in which those critics achieve their greatest insight' (1971, 109). Making this connection between criticism and the body, de Man spun out a metaphoric relation between sight and insight. In doing so, he followed a long tradition of somatizing moral and ethical issues. Tiresias was among the first in Western civilization to embody the idea that blindness leads to insight, and Oedipus's blindness becomes a metaphor and an enabling affliction that leads to his insightful recognition, first in Thebes and later at Colonus. Shakespeare links blindness and insight in *King Lear*, while in *Madame Bovary* Flaubert perverts the tradition by giving a blind, syphilitic beggar the final word that leads to Emma's anti-beatific insight at the horrifying end of her life. In fact, there exists a rather strong tradition connecting blindness to insight, starting with the ancient Greeks. Martha Edwards points out that in ancient Greek texts 'there are literally thousands of references to the most common term for blindness in the literary material, [but] there are only a few hundred instances of the common term for deafness.' Edwards draws the conclusion that in the ancient world 'blind people – at least in literature – were beloved, even revered. There is no literary equivalent for deaf people, who were considered slow at best, sub-human at worst' (Edwards n.d., 1).

Despite the well-worn connection between blindness and insight, de Man nevertheless manages to use blindness as a metaphor for intellectual denseness that then is transcended by insight, saying that critics who are 'blind' are 'deluded' (de Man 1971, 104), 'within error' (ibid., 103) 'mistaken' (ibid., 110), or 'aberrant' (ibid.,111). Thus, while endorsing the cultural continuity that sees blindness as leading to inner vision, de Man nevertheless also endorses the notion that blindness is a metaphor for unwillingness or inability to investigate a point or idea. Thus blindness is only partially enabling.[51]

However, once one raises the issue of disability, which is concealed by de Man's ambivalent attitude to blindness, then another question arises. Why blindness in particular? Perhaps the simplest answer is that blindness implies sight as its opposite, and reading requires sight.[52] But, as Jacques Derrida points out in his essay on Rousseau in *De la grammatologie* (1967), Western civilization has privileged the oral form of discourse as the essence of language, writing being only a trace of the spoken word. Thus the essential form of critical insight, according to that logic, should be deafness, not blindness. Blindness only puts a bar between the reader and the text. But deafness seems to place a barrier between the subject and oral language – that is, language as it is privileged by Western culture.

This discussion may alert us to the audist assumptions that readers tend to make about texts. The conflict may not be between a conception of language as oral versus written. Rather, these assumptions of Western culture may be related to the originary point of language – the mouth or the hand – and the receptive point of language – the ear or the eye. The mouth is hypostatized as the font of poetic language, oratory, conversation, while the hand is made special as the locus for writing, scholarship, the essay. But these are only assumptions; just as much assumptions as that the ear is the receptive site of music, of speech, of language – while the eye is the receiver of the artistic, of written knowledge. These assumptions remind us of the extent to which an economy of the body is involved in our own metaphors about language and knowledge. Blindness, insight, enlightenment, illumination, darkness, obscurity – these terms constitute a system of metaphors supporting the illusion of the ideal body. When the tables are turned and conversation is received through the eye and generated by the hand, as is the case in sign language, most people assume we are no longer dealing with language as such.

Derrida in *Marges de la philosophie* (1972, i–xxv) ends up privileging the ear as the means of receiving knowledge by metaphorizing the eardrum and inserting it as a term into a philosophical process. Although Derrida may want to break with Western prejudice, it is ironic that ultimately he ends up making a binary distinction between forms of language seen as normative, rather than between locations of language as produced by various parts of the body.

Even Derrida's assumption presumes that if a norm is not followed, then what follows cannot be normative behavior. So language is defined as normative, and its eccentric occurrences do not seem to be part of language – language being seen as only either of the voice or of writing. A similar analogy might be to say that sex is defined as only that which is associated with the penis or the vagina, and any other thing is not normal sex, therefore not sex. We may recognize the falsity of that argument, but still cling to notions of a normative linguistic modality.

This bias goes so far as to postulate a binarism of 'sight' and insight. If insight is gained, as de Man claims, by the moment of critical blindness, then what would be the equivalent term in an equation in which deafness replaces blindness? 'Invoice' or 'inhearing' does not quite seem right. We might try deafness and 'communication' or deafness and 'knowledge,' but these pairs fail to clinch the voice in language as insight clinches the lost sight in blindness. A better way of thinking this problem through is to place deafness next to 'textuality.' I suggest this move since, if blindness is opposed to, yet leads to, insight, what deafness is thought to be opposed to is language. But this analogy leads us ultimately to the text in its most general form – the text of language.

As de Man notes, speech in Rousseau and in Western civilization in general is conceptualized as presence, while writing is thought of as absence or negativity. This disjunction would appear to be the case since speech is the most common occasion of language, and writing seems to be separated from, a distance apart from, speech; this prejudice is linked to the body, which is seen as by definition present, immanent in the world, while writing is perceived as distanced from that body, hence negativity, hence nonbeing. Writing is seen, in this sense, as fictional transcription; orality is real testimony or enunciation. Thus, if we speak of a critic being blinded, using the hegemonic terms of Western civilization, we are saying the critic is cut off from culture, from discourse, representation, and from the technology of writing, printing, reading; the blinded critic is severed from the world of system, logocentrism, phallocentrism. Insight, in these terms, would be reintegration into that systematic – perhaps in a new or reordered way, but still nevertheless into that systematic – which is the system of symbolic production.

On the other hand, if we say that the critic is deafened, if we highlight the critical moment of deafness, we imply that the critic is severed not from the world of the symbolic, the systematic, but from the experiential, from the body. Thus the 'context' gained from the return from critical deafness would be a reconnection or a reconfiguration with the body, with immanence, with the contingent.[53]

Up to this point, I have been exploring the implications of deafness versus blindness, using the hegemonic categories of speech versus writing. These categories are not self-evident, but they are in effect enforced by mechanisms of cultural production. Derrida and de Man claim there is a preference in Western civilization that privileges speech over writing. I am not assuming that their position is true or false, at this point, but am merely exploring the possibilities for criticism if these categories are seen as merely normative. In so doing, nevertheless, I am attempting to show that even given this false dichotomy, it would be counter-hegemonic to argue for deafness rather than blindness as a critical modality. The metaphor of blindness, only too happily used in the Western tradition as a metaphor for insight, serves to reinscribe the critic into the normalizing systematic, whereas deafness has the potential to reassign the critic away from the cultural construction of system to a more transgressive role, toward the imperative of Cixous and Trinh to 'write through the body' (see page 111).

Another reason for a preference, at least strategically, for deafness over blindness is, as I have indicated, that deafness itself has been a more excluded term than blindness. The blindness/insight paradigm is a well-established part of the meaning system. Deafness has been more excluded precisely because it seems to be outside of meaning. Blind people are never considered outside of language, while deafness is conventionally seen as such. A nineteenth-century director and physician of the Institution for the Blind in Paris, Dr Guillée, encourages the point of view that the deaf were worse off than the blind:

> an insurmountable barrier separates them from the rest of men; they are alone in the midst of us, unless we know that artificial language [sign language]. . . . More favored than these melancholy children of silence, the blind enjoy all the means of conversation with other men; no obstacle hinders them from hearing or being heard, since the ear, which has been so philosophically defined as the vestibule of the soul, is always open for them. (cited in Kitto 1845, 179–80)

This common view of deafness only emphasizes the exclusion and marginalization of the deaf. The difficulty in finding a parallel term, in the deaf track, for 'insight' only confirms this point.

In speaking in this way, I hope I am not understood to be making a judgment on the merits or demerits of the disability of blindness over deafness. People who are blind and people who are deaf are physical minorities, and not many people would dare to judge which disability is the more disabling. Rather, in this chapter, I am speaking about the cultural resonances of such disabilities as they appear in metaphors about the process of knowing, as moments in an epistemological dialectic. In this case, I am saying that blindness turns out to be a loaded metaphor for the critic because it implies that texts are visual phenomenona, that they are inseparable from their typographical incarnation.[54] Furthermore, for complex reasons, blindness has been adopted by Western culture as a metaphor for insight, while deafness has been a signifier for the absence of language. I seek to redress this banishment of deafness by inscribing it into the critical syntax.

Connecting blindness with insight, as so many writers have done, or connecting deafness with muteness, only reinforces a tendency in our culture to denigrate disability. By denigration, I include the process by which people with disabilities are portrayed as 'noble,' 'heroic,' and 'special.' Privileging the inherent powers of the blind or the deaf is a form of patronizing. In the same way that women were seen as the moral center of European culture, their moral space carved out on the body of their oppression, or the subaltern was seen as the cynosure of mystical and erotic forces, so too does the attempt to redress the disability by attributing higher powers to it actually attempt to erase the difference by dressing it in moral raiment. Derrida's point that written language (*écriture*) is repressed by Western civilization may itself be part of that very prejudice by simply valorizing the other half of the repressed paradigm: If not written then oral. De Man carries this prejudice along with his blindness metaphor.

If one can avoid this prejudice, one can begin to ask objectively what is the deaf moment in the text versus the blind moment? Here, I move from considering the critic as the site of investigation to considering the text and the reader. The blind moment arrives with the inability to decipher a readable, scriptable object with its attendant graphic presentation, typography, verticality, horizontality, and visual encoding. These in effect are the micro- and macro-technical aspects of the text. I am not speaking merely of deciphering writing, although that issue comes into play, but of consuming the cultural product, the circulating, technological commodity with exchange and use value – the text.

The deaf moment, on the other hand, overtly presents itself as the inability to follow the text's sonic presence, silence, duration in time, breath, voice, and ideologically ratified forms of conversation (that is, oral exchange of semantic units). The blind moment, then, overtly seems to bar technology in the largest sense of the term, and the deaf moment overtly bars the sonic residues of the body moving through time. The blind moment is considered to bar, in the largest sense, textuality, while the deaf moment is thought to bar narrative as defined in an oral/aural culture. In this sense, deafness is set up in opposition to the oral culture of pre-eighteenth-century Europe, and blindness would appear to create an opposition to print culture.[55]

Given these alignments, it makes sense that Homer's putative blindness is linked inextricably to the narrative tradition. Homer, in the largest onomastic sense, signifies a bardic tradition, often of blind, wandering poets. The point is that the blindness is no bar to creating oral narrative. Blindness may in fact be synonymous with storytelling in an oral culture, while deafness would be the opposite of such a tradition. It is hard to imagine Homer as a deaf bard.

What I am saying is that certain senses, or lack of senses, may in fact characterize certain periods of human development. Basing himself on Walter Ong's postulation of the existence of four such periods – oral, script, print, and electronic – Donald M. Lowe makes this point in his *The History of Bourgeois Perception* (1982, 7):

> the communications media in each period, whether oral, chirographic [written], typographic, or electronic, emphasize different senses or combinations of them, to support a different hierarchical organization of sensing. And change in the culture of communications media ultimately leads to change in the hierarchy of sensing.

For Lowe, 'in an oral culture, hearing surpasses seeing as the most important of the five senses' (ibid.). And even in the thousand-year period between the invention of writing and the advent of print, 'chirography never succeeded in overcoming the oral connection between the speaker and the content of knowledge' (ibid., 6). Only the widespread dispersion of print led to a change in the hierarchy of senses, with sight becoming paramount. Martin Jay makes a similar point in his *Downcast Eyes* (1993).

The novel and print technology permitted the deaf, for the first time, to be part of the collective narrative tradition, thus reversing the overt interpretation of deafness. The first published works by deaf people appeared in the eighteenth century, and the 'deaf' Duncan Campbell was one of the first characters to appear in the work of that quite early novelist Daniel Defoe. Defoe's protagonists all explore aspects of society by occupying the place of the Other – a man deprived of all society, a criminal, a prostitute, and, logically then, a deaf man. Through the deaf man, Defoe can explore the very textuality that permits him to exist as a writer. Such texts, alongside developments in the same century which saw the construction, for the first time, of deafness as a disability, in fact as the primary disability, and the beginning and rapid expansion of institutions to 'teach' the deaf, I believe should be seen as the construction of deafness as the other of print culture.

An Excursion into the Heart of Silence

One way to understand the difference of deafness is to examine the role of silence in narrative. If one can think of a text as a kind of palimpsest of both the visual and the aural, then the textual equivalence of silence is blankness or empty space. There is a difference between the blank text and the silent text that is indicative of the difference between orality and writing. Western culture is organized to discourage silence (Jaworski 1993, 7). Silence is the repressed other of speech. A brief scan of the *Oxford English Dictionary* reveals the metaphorical use of 'silence' to stand for death, night, or incomprehensible nature. Silence in its global form is seen as unmediated absence, and in its particular form it is a break in narrative, a rupture of words, a pause or hesitation. At the end of James Joyce's short story 'A Painful Case,' for example, the main character experiences an existential silence that indicates the absence of God or any form of meaning:

> He could hear nothing: the night was perfectly silent. He listened again: perfectly silent. He felt that he was alone. (Joyce 1964, 117)

Joyce uses silence as a proleptic signal of the end of the narrative. The silence is both the immanence of nothingness and the immanent end of the short story. Silence equals death, absence, meaninglessness. Silence becomes the modernist's answer to words, to narrativity.

Likewise, in Joseph Conrad's work, silence is always seen as the border of language. In *Youth*, the narrator's version of Marlow's oral storytelling ultimately ends up confronting the silence of 'the East,' described as 'silent like death' (Conrad 1924b, 38). When Marlow comes ashore he 'faced the silence of the East . . . the silence was as complete as though it had never been broken' and he is confronted by 'beings [who] stared without a murmur, without a sigh' (ibid., 40). His sleeping companions are seen by 'the East [that] looked on them without a sound' (ibid., 41). In essence, the East is a sonic heart of darkness. But Africa too is silent. In 'An Outpost of Progress,' the terrain is seen as 'dumb solitude' (Conrad 1924a, 107) and 'the great silence of the surrounding wilderness . . . [seemed] to draw them gently, to look upon them, to envelop them with a solicitude irresistible, familiar, and disgusting' (ibid., 108). This silence is the opposite of Marlow's loquaciousness and the text's attempt to put impressions into words. Silence is the location of the mysterious, colonized Other, bereft of language and therefore of humanity.

We also speak of silence as a form of political repression. We say that women's voices have been silenced, and we correct that condition by calling for women to speak. Silence is seen as the prison-house whose guards are language. The inhabitants of silence must break their bonds and let their words echo forth in freedom.

Generally, silence is to be avoided at all costs, unless there are other events that demand silence. For example, an audience must remain silent so that actors can speak or musicians can play. Silence has to be created by rules, by force, or by agreement. As some linguists have put it, 'it only takes one person to produce speech, but it requires the cooperation of all to produce silence, (Pittenger et al. 1960, 88). The first definition of silence in the *Oxford English Dictionary* is 'to refrain from speech,' and almost all the examples it gives are ones of a ruling male silencing subordinates. Silence is the strongest enforced form of Lacan's Law of the Name of the Father because silence represents the space that permits the Law only and no other law. The response to God is reverential silence. The law produces a human silence, enforces a silence. Silence can be punitive or transgressive. We say that people who are silent are unfriendly, hostile, or passively aggressive,[56] although silence can signal intimacy, but only because intimacy removes the public ban on silence.[57]

Silence is golden because of its often transgressive nature. The familiar story of King Midas recalls this conjunction. Granted the wish that everything he touches will turn to gold, Midas finds that his food, his home, and his daughter are all thus transmuted. The silence of gold is in fact the silence of death, of the body turned to object. The tension between the power to rule, the creation of wealth, and the rule of golden silence becomes clearer. By turning his daughter to gold, he transforms the feminine into a silent object of male desire. The silence is enforced by wealth and position. The second part of the story is also linked to silence. Midas, dissenting from the river god Tmolus's decision to award Apollo the highest prize in a musical contest, is punished by having his ears turned into those of an ass. His barber, or in another version of the story his wife, discovers the shameful secret that Midas had wished to conceal and is sworn to silence. Unable to bear the enforced silence, the barber (or the wife) digs a hole and whispers into it 'King Midas has ass's ears!' The hole is then filled up, but a reed sprouts from the hole and whispers the secret to all who pass. Midas's ears call attention to the issue of sound, as does the musical contest. Midas turns the shame of his ears into the enforced silence of his wife or his barber; and they violate the Name of the Father by speaking. The silence he wishes has the aim of erasing narrative, the story of the king's ears. Power wishes to eliminate transgressive, nonapproved narration, but nature, in the form of the reed, maintains a *basso continuo* of sound, of story. The narrative Midas wishes to suppress is one about the body. Just as his wish for golden silence suppresses the body – the instincts – his wish for narrative silence stills the flow of plots, of explanations, of digressions about the body – his body.

Another parallel to the Midas story in Greek myth is the story of Odysseus's encounter with the Sirens. Odysseus's enforcement of a rule to silence is exempted in the case of his own body, although his men must obey the rule. He orders them to block their ears with wax so that they will not hear the luring song of the Sirens. As king, he has the power to enforce silence. While Adorno and Horkheimer in *The Dialectic of Enlightenment* (1972) see this myth as one that foretells the wish of enlightenment thinking to suppress the senses in the service of production, I think we can add to that reading by seeing the role of enforced silence or deafness as, again, a form of cutting off the body from the flow of narrative. Odysseus's story of the Sirens will be complete because of his political power, while he is able to enforce his masculine will on the men to deprive them of the erotic allure of the Sirens. Here, as in the Midas story, deafness and silence bar the individual from the body; thus the insight attained by the return from deafness connects Odysseus himself back to the body.

In this sense, silence is of the body. It is an immanent state of the body in which the body can be present, but verbal communication is absent. This is why Cixous can write that 'women must write through their bodies . . . get beyond the ultimate reserve-discourse, including the one that laughs at the very idea of pronouncing the word "silence"' (Marks and de Courtivron, eds 1980, 256).

Silence is located at the intersection of the instincts; sex, violence, bodily functions can occur in silence. But the spatial concept of emptiness bans the body; and the body bans emptiness. By definition, there cannot be an empty space if a body is present, even a dead one.

Empty space tends toward being an absolute negativity. It is not possible to have a little emptiness. Silence, however, is local, it is particular, not systematic or totalizing. A short silence can follow a long bout of sound. Silence is intermittent, never permanent. But a little emptiness cannot follow presence.

What does this distinction between emptiness and silence mean for narrative? Narrative in some sense is constructed to avoid silence, yet silence is an intimate part of narrative. George Steiner has shown that silence is a logical consequence of poetry, a way of transcending the word. Poets like Hölderlin and Rimbaud, rather than ending their career by silence, complete it. 'Hölderlin's silence has been read not as a negation of his poetry but as, in some sense, its unfolding and its sovereign logic' (Steiner 1967, 47). In an oral conversation, people can fall silent, although usually they do not do so for long, but in a printed text, silence can only be indicated by language. One can say, 'They fell silent.' Paradoxically, in sign language, as in written or printed text, there is no silence. There can be stillness in sign language or in print there can be blank space. In writing one can insert an ellipsis to indicate a momentary lapse in expression. Ironies abound here. First, most written and printed texts are read in silence, at least since the end of the Middle Ages. So print narratives are actually surrounded by silence. Second, within a text a 'silence' is only made possible by the noise of language. To make a true silence, one would have to present an emptiness – as Laurence Sterne does in *Tristram Shandy* when he 'prints' a blank page.[58] Yet that blank page shows us in extreme form the inherent prejudice that print is a sighted medium, that what we are getting in print is a verification that our cultural model has become one in which print replaces, stands in for, displaces orality. Sterne's silence is spatial, typographic – not based on the presence or absence of sound.

Deafness in Literature

When I say (write) that the social practices of reading and writing naturalize the visual nature of print, I am saying that there was in the eighteenth century, and still is, an inherent prejudice in the growing body of readers, the reading public, to valorize sight over hearing. This valorization in effect stands on its head the traditional notion that blindness leads to insight and deafness leads to an absence of language. In the new world of print and reading, the deaf can read texts, while the blind (before the wide promulgation of Braille, or more recently computer scanners) cannot. Relatively suddenly, the whole metaphorics of the body have to be rearranged. In this new world, the cultural icon for the reader of print culture becomes the deaf person. The deaf person becomes the case in point for the reader incarnate.

Yet, while the deaf person was the icon for the reader in the eighteenth century, a deeply ambivalent attitude existed toward the Deaf. By the nineteenth century the Deaf began to be perceived as foreign, alien, other – as Douglas Baynton's work has shown. If nations generally needed to neutralize the deaf, the literature of particular nations further carries out this function by creating within texts representations of deafness that serve an ostracizing function. Although sighted people may feel some hesitation in communicating with the blind, hearing people are more than usually intimidated by speaking with the deaf. While on the one hand the deaf person might stand for the ideal reader, on the other deafness retains its traditional sense of absence of language. The point here is that when deafness is hypostatized as a textual phenomenon, as a cultural area of inquiry and exhibition, it can be regarded as a part of the process of textuality. But when a deaf person appears in literature, the deafness no longer functions in this theoretical and abstract way. Now deafness reverts to its old sense of absence of language. And since language is seen as human, as 'us,' the deaf are seen as 'not us.' For this reason deafness is often portrayed comically in literature and drama, especially if the deaf character is incidental to the storyline. The deaf character is the butt of many 'eh-what??' jokes. For example, the loquacious Miss Bates in Austen's *Emma* is paired with her deaf mother; both are objects of derision, as when Miss Bates explains:

> My mother's deafness is very trifling you see – just nothing at all. By only raising my voice, and saying anything two or three times over, she is sure to hear; but then she is used to my voice. (1985, 172)

Of course she is, as are we. And of course, when Miss Bates is insulted at Box Hill, it is her loquaciousness that Emma finds offensive. Miss Bates's response is 'Ah! – well – to be sure. Yes, I see what she means, and I will try to hold my tongue.' Loquaciousness needs to be tempered with dumbness; likewise loquaciousness is often paired with deafness, as in the old saying quoted by Coleridge: 'The most happy marriage I can picture or imagine to myself would be the union of a deaf man to a blind woman.'[59] The implication is that the wife talks too much. As Peter Stallybrass points out, in the Renaissance silence was enforced on women by men who fear their production of speech. 'Silence,' he notes, 'the closed mouth, is made a sign of chastity. And silence and chastity are, in turn, homologous to woman's enclosure within the house' (Stallybrass 1987, 127).

Both garrulousness and deafness are linked threats to novelistic language, to patriarchal structures; as such they must be ridiculed. The loquacious female pops up throughout literature: we have Midas's wife, Juliet's nurse, Mrs Bennett in *Pride and Prejudice*, Flora in *Little Dorrit*, Dora in *David Copperfield*, the Woman of Shamlegh in *Kim*, and the granny in D. H. Lawrence's *The Virgin and the Gypsy*.[60] The latter is an illustration that even age does not dull loquaciousness. Lawrence writes thus:

> She was hibernating in her oldness, her agedness. But in a minute her mouth would open, her mind would flicker awake, and with her insatiable greed for life, other people's life, she would start on her quest for every detail. She was like an old toad. (1984, 29–30)

The voracious sexual mouth becomes the voracious speaking mouth, transformed by negative gender implications into a toad snatching flies.

Both the deaf person and the loquacious woman violate the rules of 'speech' in the novel. One violates through silence, the other by excessive verbiage – in either case, proper language is sabotaged. Dickens sees Flora's speech as 'running on with astonishing speed, and pointing her conversation with nothing but commas, and very few of them' (*Little Dorrit* 1884, 161). She violates the grammar of written language, but she also violates the norms of conversation. In this transgression, she represents the danger that language can become gibberish, a stream of schizophrenic associations like those that make up Lucky's discourse in Samuel Beckett's *Waiting for Godot*. For authors, both the silence of the text and its pure verbiage must be repressed through the ostracism of the deafened moment, the ridiculing of inability to hear, and thus be part of the novel's aural/oral representation. This ostracism coincides with women's subjection since, as Jane Gallop says (1988, 71), 'in the ideology of our culture women are objects described, not speaking subjects.' Deafness, in effect, is a reminder of the 'hearingness' of narrative. It is the aporetic black hole that leads to a new kind of deconstruction of narrativity. In Victor Hugo's *Notre-Dame of Paris*, Quasimodo is a deaf, lame, half-blind hunchback whose body, signified as grotesque, is a reference to the implied grotesqueness of his deafness. He is paired with the gypsy Esmeralda, the foreign female marked as the erotic subject. Both block or challenge the narrative in a very concrete way. As the novel opens, a crowd is expectantly awaiting the performance of a mystery play written by Pierre Gringoire. Gringoire too is expecting to see his narrative performed, but ultimately it is upstaged first by a leprous beggar who distracts the crowd, then by the arrival of dignitaries, then by Quasimodo's grotesque appearance in a gurning contest, and finally by the crowd running off to see the gypsy dancing girl. The play is never performed, stopped in its conventional tracks by the metaphoric appearance of class, disease, deafness, and gender.

Quasimodo himself is constructed as having many disabilities.

He is not a person *with* disabilities but the icon of the disabled person. But his deafness is made to be his 'worst' impairment:

> 'Alas!' he said, as if doubtful whether to finish, 'it's because I'm deaf.'
> 'Poor man!' exclaimed the gypsy, with an expression of kindly compassion.
> He began to smile ruefully. 'You think that's the last straw, don't you? Yes, I'm deaf. That's the way I'm made. It's truly horrible, isn't it? . . . ' (Hugo 1978, 368)

Quasimodo's body, his ugliness, is a physical mark of his deafness, which finally makes him ultimately Other. When he is born, two nuns look at his physical features and decide that he is 'an animal fathered by a Jew on a sow' (ibid., 156). What could be worse than this metonymic miscegenation crossing all boundaries, including the obvious dietary prohibitions.

A Return to Silence

For the writer, garrulousness and silence both empty meaning from language. Meaning is the surplus value of the text's production. Or, in another modality, meaning is the symptom of the neurosis of textuality. Loquaciousness and silence reveal the symptomatic nature of meaning, and therefore are constant reminders of the deconstructive threat hovering around the text. Loquaciousness, too, in an overdetermined way, also represents the transgressive sublimation of female power. If women could legitimately give voice to their complaints, they would not need the subaltern tactics of unruly domestic linguistic infringement.

As a form, the novel mediates between silence and sound. Novels begin not with words but with silence. Silence precedes the text and supersedes the text. The text is wrapped in silence. The first words of the text are there to break the silence: 'I am born . . . ' 'It is a truth universally acknowledged . . . ' 'Call me Ishmael . . . '

'Riverrun . . . ' '*Longtemps je me suis couché* . . . ' all leading back to the founding narrative of Western culture 'In the beginning. . . . ' All these initiate by postulating an earlier silence and then introjecting that silence into the beginning words. The words begin the narrative, but the words defer to the earlier silence. The text itself is neither silent nor auditory. It is a phantasm of sound, an insubstantial echo. It is a go-between linking the silence that surrounds it to the auditory world. Writers write in silence; readers read in silence. What they write and read they hallucinate into sound. But the sound is a silent sound.[61] The Zen riddle about textuality would be: What is the sound of one person reading?

Silence is in the text. It is between each word, and in some sense, it accounts for meaning; it frames articulation. On an auditory level, each utterance erupts from silence, a fact that can be seen in voice-prints of sound production. On a graphic level, those silences are represented by space, the space between the letters and between words. Here the palimpsest of space and silence comes together in the interstices of textual language.[62]

Sign language occupies the interstice where space and silence come together; sign language is the locus where the body meets language. Like the novel, another mediator between two worlds, the language of the deaf mediates between speech and silence. However, the novel mediates by feint, by creating the illusion of materiality, by diegesis. The novel relies on naturalizing effects to make words seem to be things, characters, places, by appearing to point, to indicate direction and place. Sign language, however, is not a feint but a bodily presence. The materiality of the sign is there in the sense that it is made by using the body's gestural repertoire. But sign language is composed not of graphic traces, pictograms (though here we should bear in mind that Ezra Pound's insistence that Chinese words were actually pictures of things is a fallacy that fails to understand how signs become arbitrary, even if they are mimetic), but of movement of the body through space. Language works in general by pointing to a deferred bodily presence. When Keats writes 'This living hand, now warm and capable' and says 'see here it is – I hold it towards you,' he is using writing to indicate a deferred bodily presence. But signing the same poem would have a completely different effect. The hand would not be indicated but would be part of the signifying mechanism.

Another distinction needs to be made. The word 'silence' can define at least two states. First it is the absence of sound; second it is the absence of voice. In the first, a space can be silent, as in 'the silence of night' or 'the silence of nature.' The second state, however, indicates that a person either does not or cannot make sound. The first state is related to deafness, the second to 'dumbness.'[63] The Deaf have always resented the term 'dumb' because of its double connotation of 'mute' and 'stupid.' In fact, the double meaning of the word reveals the audist bias that to be without spoken language is to be without intelligence, like a 'dumb' animal. This Enlightenment *idée fixe*, the need to create and to deploy continually the distinction between man and animal, as Baudrillard points out, which is a symptom of the capitalist/Marxist binary, is also mimed or aped in the dumb/dumb binary (Baudrillard 1975, 22). In reality, when audist culture speaks of someone who is 'deaf and dumb,' it is confusing two issues – the reception of signs and the production of signs. Since it is assumed that the dominant sign production will be oral and sign reception will be aural,[64] then the deaf are seen as bereft of language, hence humanity. The term 'animal' or 'animalistic' is the most frequently used to indicate a life without spoken language.[65] But if sign production is seen as written or printed, and if sign reception is seen as reading or signing, then the deaf are fully capable of fitting into that world.[66]

Like deafness, dumbness represents a threat to language. Deafness may be a constant reminder to writers of the aporetic silence kept at bay by narrative; dumbness serves to remind us all that spoken language is in fact an arbitrary form of communication. A chance of biological or cultural evolution has given the majority this particular means of expression. Carol Padden and Tom Humphries point out in *Deaf In America* (1988, 92) that 'sound' is 'an organization of meaning around a variation in the physical world.' Douglas C. Baynton adds to this point (1992, 226):

To be deaf is *not* to not hear for most profoundly deaf people, but a social relation. . . . What the deaf person sees in these other [hearing and deaf] people is not the presence or absence of hearing, not their soundfulness or their silence, but their mode of communication – they sign, or they move their lips.

Baynton adds the philosophical point that silence is a meaningless concept to anyone who is born deaf. Silence is a relational concept, not an absolute category. Consequently, dumbness reveals the arbitrariness of voice communication.

In the animal kingdom, sound is not the main form of communication but rather it augments gesture, as when a growl accompanies aggressive body posture. Like animals, humans employ gesture in a rather profound sense. We know, for example, that body language is still the main form of communication between humans, with 90 percent of our attention paid to the nonverbal part of face-to-face discourse (Meyrowitz 1985, 103). Writing depends upon the chance (and then enforced) relation between orality and script. Writing that aimed to transcribe the grammar of gesture would indeed be quite different from standard written language. Dumbness is a living reminder of the arbitrariness and the materiality of the sign.[67]

Worse, dumbness is the nightmare of the writer; it is the succubus that drains the writer's words from the body. Dumbness disables the writer. By a false chain of metonymy, the writing process comes to reside in the throat and mouth. Here the words are generated, and poets are said to sing, as in 'Sing muse' or 'Arms and the man I sing.' The nightingale, traditional symbol of the poet, derives its symbolic place from the story of Philomel, who was raped by Tereus. Attracted by her beautiful voice, Tereus subsequently cut out her tongue to prevent her telling anyone about his crime. But she revealed his guilt by weaving the tale into a tapestry. The gods changed Philomel into the nightingale, symbol of poetry. The story is worth analysis because of the connection it makes between poetry, dumbness, and writing. Philomel's beautiful voice is paired with her subsequent disability. Her silencing is a graphic representation of disability, rape, the disfigurement of the female by the dominant male. Her dumbness forces her to write in the female mode of weaving. Writing becomes the inscription on the female body, as a just counter to the right of the male ruler to mark the bride's body as his through the exercise of sexual domination.[68] The recourse to feminized writing is seen as a logical continuation of Philomel's dumbness, or as a counter to it. Thus, poetry issues from the throat of the nightingale – the repressed other of dumbness.[69]

The Moses of the Pentateuch, while not dumb, has a speech impediment: 'I am not eloquent . . . but I am slow of speech, and of a slow tongue' (Exodus 4:10). Because his dysfunction prevents him from speaking in public, his brother Aaron must be his spokesperson. Moses, the law-giver, is paradoxically dumb, and must be paired with his speaking brother. The law must then be written, inscribed in stone, as the Name of the Father. In both these cases, there is a seemingly logical movement from blocked speech to writing. But the notion of silence and dumbness here becomes more complex because Moses is not allowed to say the name of God or to write it. Jewish practice forbids the naming of Yahweh, and so at the center of the tale of Moses receiving the Law is the aporia of the unnamed name – the deafened moment that gives meaning to the written law. Hesitant speech becomes speech with a built-in hesitation, and so Moses's dumbness becomes representative of the injunction against speaking the name of God.

In Shakespeare's *Titus Andronicus*, Titus's daughter Lavinia is raped, has her hands cut off, and her tongue cut out. Her rapists do this to prevent her from communicating their deed, saying:

> So, now go tell, an if thy tongue can speak,
> Who 'twas that cut thy tongue and ravished thee . . .
> Write down thy mind, bewray thy meaning so,
> An if thy stumps will let thee play the scribe.
>
> (II.iv., 1–4)

Her body, like Philomel's, is both sexually violated and made dumb, doubly so because she is deprived not only of speech but also of writing. Like Philomel's voice, her lost speech is equated with singing and birds, in effect poetry:

> O, that delightful engine of her thoughts
> That bid them with such pleasing eloquence
> Is torn from forth that pretty hollow cage,
> Where like a sweet melodious bird it sung
> Sweet varied notes, enchanting every ear.
>
> (III.i., 82–6)

Shakespeare, as the bard who sings 'with such pleasing eloquence' himself, has Lavinia stand for the repressed aporia – speechlessness and the inability to write. Yet he treats her as a signifying force because the supposed absence of signifying must be kept at bay. So, when Titus sees her, he allows her features to signify, saying, 'Thou map of woe, that thus does talk in signs' (III.ii., 12). Titus considers the possibility that he and his family might

> . . . bite our tongues, and in dumb shows
> Pass the remainder of our hateful days.
>
> (III.i., 131–2)

We may recall here that in *Hamlet* the 'dumb show' that precedes the play-within-a-play signals a kind of purely gestural theater that, while possible, is antithetical to Shakespeare's own theatrical form. Lavinia's dumbness inevitably progresses away from silence to signifying, as when Titus says, 'I can interpret all her martyred signs' (III.ii., 36). As if the pure uninterpretability of Lavinia were too much of a negation, Shakespeare nudges her dumbness toward language. Titus says that he will interpret her gestures so that

> . . . I of these will wrest an alphabet
> And by still practice learn to know thy meaning.
>
> (III.ii., 43–5)

The almost violent necessity to 'wrest' an alphabet out of dumbness demonstrates the vigor with which Shakespeare must banish the nonbeing of nonlanguage. This move toward the alphabet and writing is dramatized further when Lavinia is asked to name her assailants. She finally manages to signify by grunts and facial expression that she wants them to look at Ovid's *Metamorphosis*, and calls attention, with her stumps, to none other than the story of Philomel and Tereus. Having made her auditors understand, through reading the story in the book, what happened to her, she then writes the names of her assailants in the sand with a staff held in her mouth and guided by her stumps. The move from dumbness to gesture, then to writing and books seems inevitable, since the gaping emptiness of dumbness and the disfigurement of her writing hands are too great an antithesis to signification. Shakespeare will not, cannot allow dumbness to remain in its primary form as a sign of zero-degree significance, and writing wins out. Tellingly, Shakespeare seems to involve himself with a pun. Lavinia writes with a staff in the sand: here is the oft-noted shaky-spear or false staff, a private reference to the writer himself, feminized and writing in the symbolic shifting sands. Shakespeare creates a visual trajectory from the mouth to the pen as Lavinia clutches the latter in the former; and perhaps this is then the trajectory formed when, in *The Tempest*, Prospero breaks his staff in what many consider Shakespeare's farewell to writing:

> . . . I'll break my staff,
> Bury it certain fadoms in the earth,
> And deeper than did ever plummet sound
> I'll drown my book.
>
> (V.i., 56–9)

Shakespeare connects the staff and the book, and separates these unequivocally from sound. Thus he breaks the flow from sound to pen to book, resisting the imperative that powers writing in his work. But such a disjunction is also the end of writing – so unimaginable is it to think of writing as separated from sound.

It has become a kind of critical cliché to talk about how various forms of ideological control have 'silenced' minorities. Particularly in the case of women, the silence of power has been enforced. In looking at the archetypes of Philomel and Lavinia, it is possible to see a larger archetype. These women are literally silenced through mutilation by male power. The silence of the dumb is doubled by the gender issues, since both women are not only silenced as women but marginalized as incapable of speech. This action is all the more pertinent because both women threatened to speak too much – to become the male's nightmare/joke of the loquacious woman. These birds threaten to sing, and so they are caged in silence. Likewise, the 'deaf and dumb' person stands in as a silenced, feminized reminder of the power relations in an audist discourse.

If dumbness cannot be tolerated in writing, gesture seems to be the next step away from the nothingness of nonspeech. Gesture was historically thought of as the forerunner of speech. Thus some authors, rather than ban gesture, include this repressed other of writing. Often one will see novelists replace language with gesture, as Dickens does in *Great Expectations* when Pip is taken home by Wemmick to meet the Aged Parent, who is deaf. The Aged P is a charming character, but his deafness is nevertheless a bar to communication. Pip is told: 'Nod away at him, Mr Pip; that's what he likes. Nod away at him, if you please, like winking' (Dickens 1975, 230). The Aged P responds to almost any communication by saying 'All right, John, all right.' Ironically, the Aged P derives great pleasure from reading the news aloud. Thus in one character Dickens combines both loquaciousness and deafness. The Aged P's deafened loquaciousness is tolerated by Wemmick's filial love, as he says to Pip: 'I won't offer an apology . . . for he isn't capable of many pleasures. . . . Only tip him a nod every now and then when he looks off his paper . . . and he'll be happy as a king' (ibid., 315–16). Pip's nodding gestures are the simplest form of communication possible – affirmation.

The gesture, rooted in the body, acts as a way of interpellating silence into narration, of presenting a seemingly unmediated form of communication. Such a nonlinguistic signifying, the very undoing of Dickens's own literary loquaciousness, becomes at the end of the novel a very powerful form of connection between Pip and his benefactor Provis. As the convict is dying, Pip says, 'Sometimes he was almost, or quite unable to speak; then, he would answer me with slight pressures on my hand, and I grew to understand his meaning very well' (ibid., 469).

In these moments, gesture becomes the ground for 'true meaning.' Its apparently unmediated presence, its unsignifiable meaning whose meaning is transcendent to Pip once he understands it 'very well,' operates at the level of the instinct, of the body. The meaning of the pressure is erotic; it signifies love. Gesture defies and undoes the text, yet Dickens places it at the text's center – silent gesture becomes the truth of the text.

What I have been trying to work through in this chapter is the notion that a consideration of deafness (or of any disability) in literature can amount to more than a compilation of the ways in which deaf characters are treated in literary works. It is interesting that when I have casually spoken about my plan to write this book, the most frequent assumption has been that I am writing a book about characters with disabilities in literature. When I have responded that such was not my intention, most people seemed confused about what if anything I would then write about. The phase of raising awareness about the treatment of disabled characters in literature has been ably carried through and continues to be studied, but finally there is a limit to what can be said – that disabled characters are usually villains or outcasts, but that when they are not they are glorified as testaments to the human spirit.

The consideration of disability in relation to social process and cultural production can actually be a somewhat more fruitful endeavor by beginning to lay bare the cultural assumptions at the very base of artifacts such as plays, novels, poems and so on. Moreover, the notion of disability reveals the epistemological bases and dialectical relations inherent in any notion of aesthetics. One might even say that the consideration of disability in this context, rather than being a marginal and eccentric focus of study, goes to the very heart of issues about representation, communication, language, ideology, and so on. In fact, those who pay attention to art and cultural production have really thought very little about the way in which such endeavors are based on normative practices that imply a normative body and normative communication. This chapter, it is hoped, is a prolegomenon of sorts to a future study of the complex interactions between the body, the text, and the world.

6

Visualizing the Disabled Body:

The Classical Nude and the

Fragmented Torso

A human being who is first of all an invalid is *all* body, therein lies his inhumanity and his debasement. In most cases he is little better than a carcass — .

> Thomas Mann, *The Magic Mountain*

. . . the female is as it were a deformed male.

> Aristotle, *Generation of Animals*

When I begin to wish I were crippled – even though I am perfectly healthy – or rather that I would have been better off crippled, that is the first step towards *butoh*.

> Tatsumi Hijikata, co-founder of the Japanese
> performance art/dance form *butoh*.

She has no arms or hands, although the stump of her upper right arm extends just to her breast. Her left foot has been severed, and her face is badly scarred, with her nose torn at the tip, and her lower lip gouged out. Fortunately, her facial mutilations have been treated and are barely visible, except for minor scarring visible only up close. The big toe of her right foot has been cut off, and her torso is covered with scars, including a particularly large one between her shoulder blades, one that covers her shoulder, and one covering the tip of her breast where her left nipple was torn out.

Yet she is considered one of the most beautiful female figures in the world. When the romantic poet Heinrich Heine saw her he called her 'Notre-Dame de la Beauté.'

He was referring to the Venus de Milo.

Consider too Pam Herbert, a quadriplegic with muscular dystrophy, writing her memoir by pressing her tongue on a computer keyboard, who describes herself at twenty-eight years old:

> I weigh about 130 pounds; I'm about four feet tall. It's pretty hard to get an accurate measurement on me because both of my knees are permanently bent and my spine is curved, so 4′ is an estimate. I wear size two tennis shoes and strong glasses; my hair is dishwater blonde and shoulder length. (Browne et al., eds, 1985, 147)

In this memoir, she describes her wedding night:

> We got to the room and Mark laid me down on the bed because I was so tired from sitting all day. Anyway, I hadn't gone to the bathroom all day so Mark had to catheterize me. I had been having trouble going to the bathroom for many years, so it was nothing new to Mark, he had done it lots of times before.
>
> It was time for the biggest moment of my life, making love. Of course, I was a little nervous and scared. Mark was very gentle with me. He started undressing me and kissing me. We tried making love in the normal fashion with Mark on top and me on the bottom. Well, that position didn't work at all, so then we tried laying on our sides coming in from behind. That was a little better. Anyway, we went to sleep that night a little discouraged because we didn't have a very good lovemaking session. You would have thought that it would be great, but sometimes things don't always go the way we want them to. We didn't get the hang of making love for about two months. It hurt for a long time. (ibid., 155)

I take the liberty of bringing these two women's bodies together. Both have disabilities. The statue is considered the ideal of Western beauty and eroticism, although it is armless and disfigured. The living woman might be considered by many 'normal' people to be physically repulsive, and certainly without erotic allure. The question I wish to ask is why does the impairment of the Venus de Milo in no way prevent 'normal' people from considering her beauty, while Pam Herbert's disability becomes the focal point for horror and pity?

In asking this question, I am really raising a complex issue. On a social level, the question has to do with how people with disabilities are seen and why, by and large, they are de-eroticized. If, as I mentioned earlier, disability is a cultural phenomenon rooted in the senses, one needs to inquire how a disability occupies a field of vision, of touch, of hearing; and how that disruption or distress in the sensory field translates into psycho-dynamic representations. This is more a question about the nature of the subject than about the qualities of the object, more about the observer than the observed. The 'problem' of the disabled has been put at the feet of people with disabilities for too long.

Normalcy, rather than being a degree zero of existence, is more accurately a location of bio-power, as Foucault would use the term. The 'normal' person (clinging to that title) has a network of traditional ableist assumptions and social supports that empowers the gaze and interaction. The person with disabilities, until fairly recently, had only his or her own individual force or will. Classically, the encounter has been, and remains, an uneven one. Anne Finger describes it in strikingly visual terms by relating an imagined meeting between Rosa Luxemburg and Antonio Gramsci, each of whom was a person with disabilities, although Rosa is given the temporary power of the abled gaze:

> We can measure Rosa's startled reaction as she glimpses him the misshapen dwarf limping towards her in a second-hand black suit so worn that the cuffs are frayed and the fabric is turning green with age, her eye immediately drawn to this disruption in the visual field; the unconscious flinch; the realization that she is staring at him, and the too-rapid turning away of the head. And then, the moment after, the consciousness that the quick aversion of the gaze was as much of an insult as the stare, so she turns her head back but tries to make her focus general, not a sharp gape. Comrade Rosa, would you have felt a slight flicker of embarrassment? shame? revulsion? dread? of a feeling that can have no name?

In this encounter what is suppressed, at least in this moment, is the fact that Rosa Luxemburg herself is physically impaired (she walked with a limp for her whole life). The emphasis then shifts from the cultural norm to the deviation; Luxemburg, now the gazing subject, places herself in the empowered position of the norm, even if that position is not warranted.

Disability, in this and other encounters, is a disruption in the visual, auditory, or perceptual field as it relates to the power of the gaze. As such, the disruption, the rebellion of the visual, must be regulated, rationalized, contained. Why the modern binary – normal/abnormal – must be maintained is a complex question. But we can begin by accounting for the desire to split bodies into two immutable categories: whole and incomplete, abled and disabled, normal and abnormal, functional and dysfunctional.

In the most general sense, cultures perform an act of splitting (*Spaltung*, to use Freud's term). These violent cleavages of consciousness are as primitive as our thought processes can be. The young infant splits the good parent from the bad parent – although the parent is the same entity. When the child is satisfied by the parent, the parent is the good parent; when the child is not satisfied, the parent is bad. As a child grows out of the earliest phases of infancy, she learns to combine those split images into a single parent who is sometimes good and sometimes not. The residue of *Spaltung* remains in our inner life, personal and collective, to produce monsters and evil stepmothers as well as noble princes and fairy godmothers.

In this same primitive vein, culture tends to split bodies into good and bad parts. Some cultural norms are considered good and others bad. Everyone is familiar with the 'bad' body: too short or tall, too fat or thin, not masculine or feminine enough, not enough or too much hair on the head or other parts of the body, penis or breasts too small or (excepting the penis) too big. Furthermore, each individual assigns good and bad labels to body parts – good: hair, face, lips, eyes, hands; bad: sexual organs, excretory organs, underarms.

The psychological explanation may provide a reason why it is imperative for society at large to engage in *Spaltung*. The divisions whole/incomplete, able/disabled neatly cover up the frightening writing on the wall that reminds the hallucinated whole being that its wholeness is in fact a hallucination, a developmental fiction. *Spaltung* creates the absolute categories of abled and disabled, with concomitant defenses against the repressed fragmented body.

But a psychological explanation alone is finally insufficient. Historical specificity makes us understand that disability is a social process with an origin. So, why certain disabilities are labeled negatively while others have a less negative connotation is a question tied to complex social forces (some of which I have tried to lay out in earlier chapters). It is fair to say, in general, that disabilities would be most dysfunctional in postindustrial countries, where the ability to perambulate or manipulate is so concretely tied to productivity, which in itself is tied to production. The body of the average worker, as we have seen, becomes the new measure of man and woman. Michael Oliver, citing Ryan and Thomas (1980), notes:

> With the rise of the factory . . . [during industrialization] many more disabled people were excluded from the production process for 'The speed of factory work, the enforced discipline, the time-keeping and production norms – all these were a highly unfavourable change from the slower, more self-determined and flexible methods of work into which many handicapped people had been integrated.' (1990, 27)

Both industrial production and the concomitant standardization of the human body have had a profound impact on how we split up bodies.

We tend to group impairments into the categories either of 'disabling' (bad) or just 'limiting' (good). For example, wearing a hearing aid is seen as much more disabling than wearing glasses, although both serve to amplify a deficient sense. But loss of hearing is associated with aging in a way that nearsightedness is not. Breast removal is seen as an impairment of femininity and sexuality, whereas the removal of a foreskin is not seen as a diminution of masculinity. The coding of body parts and the importance attached to their selective function or dysfunction is part of a much larger system of signs and meanings in society, and is constructed as such.

'Splitting' may help us to understand one way in which disability is seen as part of a system in which value is attributed to body parts. The disabling of the body part or function is then part of a removal of value. The gradations of value are socially determined, but what is striking is the way that rather than being incremental or graduated, the assignment of the term 'disabled,' and the consequent devaluation are total. That is, the concept of disabled seems to be an absolute rather than a gradient one. One is either disabled or not. Value is tied to the ability to earn money. If one's body is productive, it is not disabled. People with disabilities continue to earn less than 'normal' people and, even after the passage of the Americans with Disabilities Act, 69 percent of Americans with disabilities were unemployed (*New York Times*, 27 October 1994, A:22). Women and men with disabilites are seen as less attractive, less able to marry and be involved in domestic production.

The ideology of the assigning of value to the body goes back to preindustrial times. Myths of beauty and ugliness have laid the foundations for normalcy. In particular, the Venus myth is one that is dialectically linked to another. This embodiment of beauty and desire is tied to the story of the embodiment of ugliness and repulsion. So the appropriate mythological character to compare the armless Venus with is Medusa.[70] Medusa was once a beautiful sea goddess who, because she had sexual intercourse with Poseidon at one of Athene's temples, was turned by Athene into a winged monster with glaring eyes, huge teeth, protruding tongue, brazen claws, and writhing snakes for hair. Her hideous appearance has the power to turn people into stone, and Athene eventually completes her revenge by having Perseus kill Medusa. He finds Medusa by stealing the one eye and one tooth shared by the Graiae until they agree to help him. Perseus then kills Medusa by decapitating her while looking into his brightly polished shield, which neutralizes the power of her appearance; he then puts her head into a magic wallet that shields onlookers from its effects. When Athene receives the booty, she uses Medusa's head and skin to fashion her own shield.

In the Venus tradition, Medusa is a poignant double. She is the necessary counter in the dialectic of beauty and ugliness, desire and repulsion, wholeness and fragmentation. Medusa is the disabled woman to Venus's perfect body. The story is a kind of allegory of a 'normal' person's intersection with the disabled body. This intersection is marked by the power of the visual. The 'normal' person sees the disabled person and is turned to stone, in some sense, by the visual interaction. In this moment, the normal person suddenly feels self-conscious, rigid, unable to look but equally drawn to look. The visual field becomes problematic, dangerous, treacherous. The disability becomes a power derived from its otherness, its monstrosity, in the eyes of the 'normal' person. The disability must be decapitated and then contained in a variety of magic wallets. Rationality, for which Athene stands, is one of the devices for containing, controlling, and reforming the disabled body so that it no longer has the power to terrorize. And the issue of mutilation comes up as well because the disabled body is always the reminder of the whole body about to come apart at the seams. It provides a vision of, a caution about, the body as a construct held together willfully, always threatening to become its individual parts – cells, organs, limbs, perceptions – like the fragmented, shared eye and tooth that Perseus ransoms back to the Graiae.

In order to understand better how normalcy is bred into ways of viewing the body, it might be productive to think about the body as it appears in art, photography, and the other visual media. There has been a powerful tradition in Western art of representing the body in a way that serves to solidify, rather early on in history, a preferred mode of envisioning the body. This tradition, identified by Kenneth Clark, has been most clearly articulated in the 'nude.' The nude, as Clark makes clear, is not a literal depiction of the human body but rather a set of conventions about the body: 'the nude is not the subject of art, but a form of art' (1956, 5). Or, as he says, the nude is 'the body re-formed' (ibid., 3). If that is the case, then the nude is really part of the development of a set of idealized conventions about the way the body is supposed to look.

While some nudes may be male, when people talk about 'the nude' they most often mean the female nude. Lynda Nead, in a feminist correction of Clark, points out that 'more than any other subject, the female nude connotes "Art"' (1992, 1). And in that tradition, the Venus becomes the vortex for thinking about the female body. The Venus is, rather than a subject, a masculine way of fashioning the female body, or of remaking it into a conceptual whole.

I emphasize the word 'whole,' because the irony of the Venus tradition is that virtually no Venuses have been preserved intact from antiquity. Indeed, one of the reasons for the popularity of the Venus de Milo was that from the time it was discovered in 1820 until 1893 when Furtwangler's scholarship revealed otherwise, the statue was, according to Clark, 'believed to be an original of the fifth century and the only free-standing figure of a woman that had come down from the great period with the advantage of a head' (1964, 89).

The mutilation of the statues is made more ironic by the fact that their headless and armless state is usually overlooked by art historians – barely referred to at all by Clark, for example, in the entirety of his book. The art historian does not *see* the absence and so fills the absence with a presence. This compensation leads us to understand that in the discourse of the nude, one is dealing not simply with art history but with the reception of disability, the way that the 'normal' observer compensates or defends against the presence of difference. This is a 'way of seeing' not often discussed in art criticism. Of course, one can consider that art historians are really just making the best of a bad situation, but it is possible to make a number of further observations.

First of all, the headlessness and armlessness of Venuses link them, structurally, with the Medusa tradition. Many of these Venuses have in effect been decapitated. There seems to be a reciprocal relationship between the decapitations of Medusa in myth and of Venus in reality. It seems that the Venus is really only made possible in coordination with the Medusa – that Aphrodite can romp because Medusa can kill. So it is a fitting dialectic that Medusa's beheading is contained within every broken Venus. The speechlessness of the art historian about the mutilation of his objects of beauty and desire is the effect of his metaphoric transformation to stone. This lapsus in speech is really an avoidance, a wish to avoid the castrating, terrifying vision of Medusa – the disabled, the monster, who is also the disabler. In a larger sense, as Nead suggests (1992, 17–18), all visions of the female nude, particularly in the Venus tradition, are attempts by male artists and critics to gird themselves against the irrationality and chaos of the body – particularly the female body:

> It begins to speak of a deep-seated fear and disgust of the female body and of femininity within patriarchal culture and of a construction of masculinity around the related fear of the contamination and dissolution of the male ego.

In thinking about disability, one can extend this argument and say that the fear of the unwhole body, of the altered body, is kept at bay by depictions of whole, systematized bodies – the nudes of Western art. The unwhole body is the unholy body. Or as Kaja Silverman points out (1990, 14) about images of the body in film, society creates a 'protective shield' that insulates it against the possibility of mutilation, fragmentation, castration.

Indeed, the systematization of the body by artist and critic suggests a linearity, a regularity, a completeness that belie the fragmentary, explosive way the body is constitutively experienced. Clark exemplifies this systematic approach in discussing the Esquiline Venus of the fifth century, the first embodiment of these conventions.

> But she is solidly desirable, compact, proportionate; and, in fact, her proportions have been calculated on a simple mathematical scale. The unit of measurement is her head. She is seven heads tall; there is the length of one head between her breasts, one from breast to navel, and one from the navel to the division of the legs . . . fundamentally

this is the architecture of the body that will control the observations of classically minded artists till the end of the nineteenth century. (Clark 1964, 75)

The amnesia of art historians to the subject of mutilation and decapitation (the Esquiline Venus has no head) is not accidental. The most we get from Clark in his entire book is one wistful mention of a Greco-Roman depiction of the three graces as 'a relief in the Louvre, headless, alas' (ibid., 91). The 'alas' speaks volumes. This amnesia, this looking away from incompleteness, an averting of the attention, a sigh, is the tip of a defensive mechanism that allows the art historian still to see the statue as an object of desire. So the critic's aim is to restore the damage, bring back the limbs, through an act of imagination.[71] This phenomenon is not unlike the experience of 'phantom limb,' the paradoxical effect that amputees experience of sensing their missing limb. In the case of the art historian, the statue is seen as complete with phantom limbs and head. The art historian does not see the lack, the presence of an impairment, but rather mentally reforms the outline of the Venus so that the historian can return the damaged woman in stone to a pristine origin of wholeness. His is an act of reformation of the visual field, a sanitizing of the disruption in perception.

This is the same act of imagination, or one might say control, that bans from the nude the representation of normal biological processes. For example, there are no pregnant Venuses, there are no paintings of Venuses who are menstruating, micturating, defecating – lactating and lacrimating being the only recognized activities of idealized women. There are no old Venuses (with the exception of a Diana by Rembrandt). One might think of a pregnant Venus as a temporarily disabled woman, and as such banned from the reconstruction of the body we call 'the nude.' Clark distinguishes between prehistoric fertility goddesses, like the Willendorf Venus, images of fertility and pregnancy, and the differently ideal Grecian versions which are never pregnant. As Nead notes (1992, 19), 'Clark alludes to this image of the female body [the Willendorf Venus] as undisciplined, out of control; it is excluded from the proper concerns of art in favour of the smooth, uninterrupted line of the Cycladic [Greek] figure.' As artists and art historians shun the fluids and changes in shape that are incompatible with the process of forming the 'regular' body, the evidentiary record of mutilated Venuses must be repressed by a similar process.

A cautionary word must be said on the decapitated and armless Venuses. While it is true that male statues equally are truncated, the incompleteness of the female statues suggests another obvious point that has been repressed for so long – violence. Did all these statues lose their arms and heads by sheer accident, were the structurally fragile head and limbs more likely to deteriorate than the torso, were there random acts of vandalism, or was a particular kind of symbolic brutality committed on these stone women? Did vandals, warriors, and adolescent males amuse themselves by committing focused acts of violence, of sexual bravado and mockery on these embodiments of desire? An armless woman is a symbol of sexual allure without the ability to resist, a headless nude captures a certain kind of male fantasy of submission without the complication of the individuality and the authority granted by a face, even an idealized one. We do not know and will probably never know what happened to these statues, although the destruction of the Parthenon figures has been documented as done by occupying soldiers. The point is that the violence against the body, the acts of hacking, mutilation and so on, have to be put in the context we have been discussing. An act of violence against a female statue is constitutively different from that against a male statue – and these are acts that can be placed in a range of terrorist acts against women during war. Such acts create disabled people, and so, in a sense, these Venuses are the disabled women of art. To forget that is again to commit acts of omission of a rather damning nature.

Of course, a statue is not a person. But as representations of women, the Venus statues carry a powerful cultural signification. The reaction to such statues, both by critics and other viewers, tells much about the way in which we consider the body both as a whole and as incomplete. One point to note is that the art historian, like Clark, tends to perform a complex double act.

On the one hand, the critic sees the incomplete statue as whole, imagines the phantom limbs in order to defend against incompleteness, castration, the chaotic or 'grotesque body,' as Peter Stallybrass and Allon White (1987) have, using Bakhtinian terminology, called it. On the other hand (if indeed our standard is *two* hands), the critic and the artist are constantly faced with the fragmentary nature of the body, analyzing parts, facing the gaze of the missing part that must be argued into existence.

The model for the fragmentary nature of the nude is best illustrated by the famous story of Zeuxis, as told by Pliny. When Zeuxis painted his version of Aphrodite, he constructed her from the parts of five beautiful young women of his town of Kroton. His vision of the wholeness of Aphrodite was really an assemblage of unrelated parts. Likewise, the critic in regarding the whole nude must always be speaking of parts: 'their torsos have grown so long that the distance from the breasts to the division of the legs is three units instead of two, the pelvis is wide, the thighs are absurdly short' (Clark 1964, 91). The whole can only be known by the sum of its parts – even when those parts are missing. John Barrell has detailed the reactions of eighteenth-century men to the Venus dei Medici, and noted how they tended to examine every detail of the statue. Edward Wright, for example, tells observers to 'strictly examine every part' and a typical account read thus:

> One might very well insist on the beauty of the breasts. . . . They are small, distinct, and delicate to the highest degree; with an idea of softness. . . . And yet with all that softness, they have a firmness too. . . . From her breasts, her shape begins to diminish gradually down to her waist; . . . Her legs are neat and slender; the small of them is finely rounded; and her feet are little, white, and pretty. (Barrell 1989, 127)

Another carped:

> The head is something too little for the Body, especially for the Hips and Thighs; the Fingers excessively long and taper, and no match for the Knuckles, except for the little Finger of the Right-Hand. (ibid.)

These analyses perform a juggling act between the fragmentation of the body and its reunification into an hallucinated erotic whole.[72] In imagining the broken statues, the critic must mentally replace the arms and the head, then criticize any other restoration, as does Clark in attacking the reconstruction of the Venus of Arles: 'the sculptor Girardon . . . not only added the arms and changed the angle of the head, but smoothed down the whole body, since the King was offended by the sight of ribs and muscles' (Clark 1964, 87). The point here is that the attempt of the critic to keep the body in some systematic whole is really based on a repression of the fragmentary nature of the body.

One might also want to recall that for the Greeks these statues, while certainly works of art, were also to be venerated, since they were representations of deities. For the Greeks, Aphrodite was not a myth; she was a goddess whose domain was desire. It somehow seems appropriate that the ritualistic or reverential attitude toward these statues, pointed out by Walter Benjamin (1969, 223–4), indeed their very appearance in stone (which Page Dubois sees as a cultic representation of the bones of the female spirits), has been reproduced in the attitude of that most secular of worshippers, the art critic. For the Venus has a double function: she is both a physical and a spiritual incarnation of desire. In that double sense, the critic must emphasize her spiritual existence by going beyond her physical incarnation in fallible stone, and her mutilations, to the essential body, the body of Desire, the body of the Other.

We can put this paradox in Lacanian terms. For Lacan, the most primitive, the earliest experience of the body is actually of the fragmented body (*corps morcelé*).[73] The infant experiences his or her body as separate parts or pieces, as 'turbulent movements' (Lacan 1977, 2). For the infant, rather than a whole, the body is an assemblage of arms, legs, surfaces. These representations/images of fragmented body parts Lacan calls *imagos* because they are 'constituted for the "instincts" themselves' (ibid., 11).

Among these *imagos* are some that represent the elective vectors of aggressive intentions, which they provide with an efficacity that might be called magical. These are the images of castration, mutilation, dismemberment, dislocation, evisceration, devouring, bursting open of the body, in short, the *imagos* that I have grouped together under the apparently structural term of *imagos of the fragmented body*. (ibid., 11)

The process that builds a self involves the enforced unifying of these fragments through the hallucination of a whole body, 'a Gestalt, that is to say, in an exteriority' (ibid., 2), as Lacan has pointed out. The process 'extends from a fragmented body-image to a form of its totality . . . and, lastly, to the assumption of the armour of an alienating identity' (ibid., 4). When the child points to an image in the mirror − at that stage Lacan calls 'the mirror phase' − the child recognizes (actually misrecognizes) that unified image as his or her self. That identification is really the donning of an identity, an 'armor' against the chaotic or fragmentary body.

In this sense, the disabled body is a direct *imago* of the repressed fragmented body. The disabled body causes a kind of hallucination of the mirror phase gone wrong. The subject looks at the disabled body and has a moment of cognitive dissonance, or should we say a moment of cognitive resonance with the earlier state of fragmentation. Rather than seeing the whole body in the mirror, the subject sees the repressed fragmented body; rather than seeing the object of desire, as controlled by the Other, the subject sees the true self of the fragmented body. For Lacan, because the child first saw its body as a 'collection of discrete part-objects, adults can never perceive their bodies in a complete fashion in later life' (Ragland-Sullivan 1987, 21). This repressed truth of self-perception revolves around a prohibited central, specular moment − of seeing the disabled body − in which the 'normal' person views the Medusa image, in which the Venus-nude cannot be sustained as a viable armor. In Lacanian terms, the *moi* is threatened with a breaking-up, literally, of its structure, is threatened with a reminder of its incompleteness. In a specular, face-to-face moment, the ego is involved in what J. B. Pontalis calls 'death work,' which involves the 'fundamental process of unbinding [of the ego], of fragmentation, of breaking up, of separation, of bursting' (cited in Ragland-Sullivan

1987, 70). Thus the specular moment between the armored, unified self and its repressed double – the fragmented body – is characterized by a kind of death-work, repetition compulsion in which the unified self continuously sees itself undone – castrated, mutilated, perforated, made partial. In this context, it is worth noting that the Venus tradition involves castration at its very origin. Aphrodite is said to have been born from the foam of Uranus's genitals which Cronus threw into the sea after castrating his father (Graves 1955, 49). The dynamic is clear. Male mutilation is mitigated by the creation of the desirable female body. The disabled body is corrected by the wholeness of the constructed body of the nude. But, as has been noted, the emphasis on wholeness never entirely erases the foundation of the Venus tradition in the idea of mutilation, fragmented bodies, decapitation, amputation.

If we follow these terms, the disabled Venus serves as an un-wanted reminder that the 'real' body, the 'normal body,' the observer's body, is in fact always already a 'fragmented body.' The linking together of all the disparate bodily sensations and locations is an act of will, a hallucination that always threatens to fall apart. The mutilated Venus and the disabled person, particularly the disabled person who is missing limbs or body parts, will become in fantasy visual echoes of the primal fragmented body – a signifier of castration and lack of wholeness. Missing senses, blindness, deafness, aphasia, in that sense, will point to missing bodily parts or functions. The art historian in essence dons or retains the armor of identity, needs the armor as does Perseus who must see Medusa through the polished shield. The art historian's defense is that mirror-like shield that conjures wholeness through a mis-recognition linking the parts into a whole.

What this analysis tells us is that the 'disabled body' belongs to no one, just as the normal body, or even the 'phallus' belongs to no one. Even a person who is missing a limb, or is physically 'different,' still has to put on, assume, the disabled body and identify with it.[74] The disabled body, far from being the body of some small group of 'victims,' is an entity from the earliest of childhood instincts, a body that is common to all humans, as Lacan would have it. The 'normal' body is actually the body we develop later. It is in effect a Gestalt – and therefore in the realm of what Lacan calls the Imaginary. The realm of the 'Real' in Lacanian terms is where the fragmented body is found because it is the body that precedes the ruse of identity and wholeness. Artists often paint this vision, and it often appears in dreams 'in the form of disjointed limbs, or of those organs represented in exosocy . . . the very same that the visionary Hieronymus Bosch has fixed for all time' (Lacan 1977, 4).

In understanding this point, we can perhaps see how the issue of disability transcends the rather narrow category to which it has been confined. Just as, I claim, we readers are all deaf, participating in a deafened moment, likewise, we all – first and foremost – have fragmented bodies. It is in tracing our tactical and self-constructing (deluding) journeys away from that originary self that we come to conceive and construct that phantom goddess of wholeness, normalcy, and unity – the nude.

One might even add that the element of repulsion and fear associated with fragmentation and disability may in fact come from the very act of repressing the primal fragmentariness of the body. As Freud wrote, 'the uncanny is in reality nothing new or foreign, but something familiar and old-established in the mind that has been estranged only [in] the process of repression' (Freud 1963b, 47). The feelings of repulsion associated with the uncanny, *das Unheimlich*, the unfamiliar, are not unlike the emotions of the 'normal' when they are visualizing the disabled. The key to the idea of the uncanny is in its relation to the normal. *Heimlich* is a word associated with the home, with familiarity – and with the comfortable predictability of the home. The disabled body is seen as *unheimlich* because it is the familiar gone wrong. Disability is seen as something that does not belong at home, not to be associated with the home. Freud notes that the terror or repulsion of the uncanny is ambivalent, is found precisely in its relation to and yet deviance from the familiar. That the uncanny can be related to disability is made clear when Freud cites specifically 'dismembered limbs, a severed head, a hand cut off at the wrist' as *unheimlich* (ibid., 49). What is uncanny about dismemberment seems to be the familiarity of the body part that is then made *unheimlich* by its severing. As Freud wrote, 'the *unheimlich* is what was once *heimisch*, homelike, familiar; the prefix "un" is the token of repression' (ibid., 51).

But in this equation I think Freud is actually missing the earlier repression of the inherently fragmentary nature of the original body *imago*. The homeyness of the body, its familiarity as whole, complete, contained, is based on a dynamic act of repression. Freud is assuming that the whole body is an *a priori* given, as he had done with the concept of the ego. But as Lacan has shown more than adequately, the ego is a multifaceted structure to be understood in its philosophical complexity. Likewise the ground of the body, its materiality given by Freud, needs a re-analysis. The route of disability studies allows for this revisioning. In this process, the *heimisch* body becomes the *unheimlich* body, and the fragment, the disabled parts, can be seen as the originary, familiar body made unfamiliar by repression. Dominant culture has an investment in seeing the disabled, therefore, as uncanny, as something found outside the home, unfamiliar, while in fact where is the disabled body found if not at home?

I have been concentrating on the physical body, but it is worth considering for a moment the issue of madness. While mental illness is by definition not related to the intactness of the body, nevertheless, it shows up as a disruption in the visual field. We 'see' that someone is insane by her physical behavior, communication, and so on. Yet the fear is that the mind is fragmenting, breaking up, falling apart, losing itself – all terms we associate with becoming mad. With the considerable information we have about the biological roots of mental illness, we begin to see the disease again as a breaking up of 'normal' body chemistry: amino acid production gone awry, depleted levels of certain polypeptide chains or hormones. Language production can become fragmentary, broken, in schizophrenic speech production. David Rothman points out that in eighteenth- and nineteenth-century America, insanity was seen as being caused by the fragmented nature of 'modern' life – particularly the pressures brought to bear on people by a society in which economic boundaries were disappearing. This fragmenting of society produced a fragmentation of the individual person. So the asylums that sprung up during this period recommended a cure that involved a removal from the urban, alienated, fragmented environment to rural hospitals in which order and precision could be restored. 'A precise schedule and regular work became the two characteristics of the best private and public institutions. . . . The structure of the mental hospital would counteract the debilitating influences of the community' (Rothman 1971, 144). As Rothman notes, 'Precision, certainty, regularity, order' were the words that were seen as embodying the essence of cure (ibid., 145). The mind would be restored to 'wholeness' by restoring the body through manual labor. However, needless to add, one had to have a whole body to have a whole mind. The general metaphor here continues to be a notion of wholeness, order, clean boundaries, as opposed to fragmentations, disordered bodies, messy boundaries.

If people with disabilities are considered anything, they are or have been considered creatures of disorder – monsters, monstrous. Leslie Fieldler has taken some pains to show this in his book *Freaks*. If we look at Mary Shelley's *Frankenstein*, we find some of the themes we have been discussing emerge in novelistic form. First, we might want to note that we have no name for the creation of Dr Frankenstein other than 'monster.' (This linguistic lapsus is usually made up for in popular culture by referring to the creature itself as 'Frankenstein,' a terminology that confuses the creator with the created.) In reading the novel, or speaking about it, we can only call the creature 'the monster.' This linguistic limitation is worth noting because it encourages the reader to consider the creature a monster rather than a person with disabilities.

We do not often think of the monster in Mary Shelley's work as disabled, but what else is he? The characteristic of his disability is a difference in appearance. He is more than anything a disruption in the visual field. There is nothing else different about him – he can see, hear, talk, think, ambulate, and so on. It is worth noting that in popular culture, largely through the early film versions of the novel, the monster is inarticulate, somewhat mentally slow, and walks with a kind of physical impairment.[75] In addition, the film versions add Ygor, the hunchbacked criminal who echoes the monster's disability in his own. Even in the recent film version by Kenneth Branagh, the creature walks with a limp and speaks with an impediment. One cannot dismiss this filtering of the creature through the lens of multiple disability. In order for the audience to fear and loathe the creature, he must be made to transcend the pathos of a single disability. Of course, it would be unseemly for a village to chase and torment a paraplegic or a person with acromegaly. Disabled people are to be pitied and ostracized; monsters are to be destroyed; audiences must not confuse the two.

In the novel, it is clear that Dr Frankenstein cannot abide his creation for only one reason – its hideous appearance. Indeed, the creature's only positive human contact is with the blind old man De Lacey, who cannot see the unsightly features. When De Lacey's family catches a glimpse of the creature, the women faint or run, and the men beat and pursue him. His body is a zone of repulsion; the reaction he evokes is fear and loathing. The question one wants to ask is why does a physical difference produce such a profound response?

The answer, I believe, is twofold. First, what is really hideous about the creature is not so much his physiognomy as what that appearance suggests. The *corps morcelé* makes its appearance immediately in the construction of the monster. Ironically, Dr Frankenstein adapts Zeuxis's notion of taking ideal parts from individuals to create the ideal whole body. As he says, 'I collected bones from charnel houses. . . . The dissecting room and the slaughter-house furnished many of my materials' (Shelley 1990, 54–5). From these fragments, seen as loathsome and disgusting, Frankenstein assembles what he wishes to create – a perfect human. It is instructive in this regard to distinguish the Boris Karloff incarnation of the creature – with the bolt through his neck – or Branagh's grotesquely sewn creature, from the image that Mary Shelley would have us imagine. Dr Frankenstein tells us:

His limbs were in proportion, and I had selected his features as beautiful. Beautiful! – Great God! His yellow skin scarcely covered the work of muscles and arteries beneath; his hair was of a lustrous black and flowing; his teeth of a pearly whiteness; but these luxuriances only formed a more horrid contrast with his watery eyes, that seemed almost of the same colour as the dun white sockets in which they were set, his shrivelled complexion and straight black lips. (ibid., 57)

What then constitutes the horror? If we add up the details, what we see is a well-proportioned man with long black hair, pearly white teeth, whose skin is somewhat deformed – resulting in jaundice and perhaps a tightness or thinness of the skin, a lack of circulation perhaps causing shriveling, watery eyes and darkened lips. This hardly seems to constitute horror rather than, say, pathos.[76]

What is found to be truly horrifying about Frankenstein's creature is its composite quality, which is too evocative of the fragmented body. Frankenstein's reaction to this living *corps morcelé* is repulsion: 'the beauty of the dream vanished, and breathless horror and disgust filled my heart' (ibid., 57). Frankenstein attempted to create a unified nude, an object of beauty and harmony – a Venus, in effect. He ended up with a Medusa whose existence reveals the inhering and enduring nature of the archaic fragmented body, endlessly repressed but endlessly reappearing.

Why does the appearance of the monster produce so powerful an affect? Routinely, one might view a deformed person, even a multiply deformed one, without desiring to kill that person. Here we see a man whose skin is strange or unnatural being transposed into the category 'monster.' The element of skin reminds us that the monster as a disturbance in the visual field is linked to the tactile field. The disruption in the skin's surface immediately translates into a threat of touching, of being touched. The idea of touch always initiates a dialectic of attraction and repulsion, of fear, hatred, or erotic attraction. Indeed, from a psychoanalytic viewpoint there is not much difference between these choices. So, inevitably, the disabled body becomes a site of the erotic, as instantly it is perceived in either the Venus or the Medusa scenarios.[77] In Shelley's novel, after the creation, Dr Frankenstein has rather a peculiar response – he goes to sleep and has a dream about his fiancée:

> I thought I saw Elizabeth, in the bloom of health, walking in the streets of Ingolstadt. Delighted and surprised, I embraced her, but as I imprinted the first kiss on her lips, they became livid with the hue of death; her features appeared to change, and I thought that I held the corpse of my dead mother in my arms; a shroud enveloped her form, and I saw the grave-worms crawling in the folds of the flannel. (ibid., 58)

The rather incredible set of associations made by Dr Frankenstein would take pages to explore thoroughly, but what we might want to note here is that the immediate flight from the Medusa image of the monster's fragmented body leads immediately to the Venus body of Elizabeth, seen as frankly erotic. However, upon the first sexual contact the Venus myth immediately deconstructs, and Elizabeth's body initially changes to a corpse, then to the decomposing corpse of Frankenstein's dead mother. The visual leads to the tactile, which then contaminates the normal body. And all these moments lead back to the decomposing, fragmenting body. Later in the novel, when the creature demands a spouse, Frankenstein again creates the fragmented, now female, body. But at the last minute 'trembling with passion, [I] tore to pieces the thing on which I was engaged' (ibid., 168).[78] Frankenstein's explicit reason for failing to give the monster a mate is fear that a race of deformed creatures would populate the earth and threaten the human race.[79] Thus the risk of the erotic touch, of the frankly erotic agenda for the creature, is seen as a contaminating danger to 'normal' people. So, the fragmented body is hacked up, exploded, into the fragments that make it up.

The work of Didier Anzieu, a psychoanalyst, might help to amplify how touch and skin contribute to the concept of the disabled body. Frankenstein's creation is driven out largely because of the nature of his skin, his covering, made hideous by its color, texture, and incompleteness. Anzieu postulates that skin is in effect an *imago* of the ego. As such, when the infant hallucinates the whole body, he or she actually uses the concept and the reality of skin as a metaphor for wholeness, completeness, total enveloping of a unitary self. The skin is in effect a 'narcissistic envelope' (Anzieu 1989, 39). As Anzieu notes:

> the boundaries of the body image (or the image of the body's boundaries) are acquired in the course of the child's detaching itself from its mother and they are to some degree analogous to the Ego boundaries which Federn has shown as being de-cathected in the process of depersonalization. (ibid., 32)

For Anzier, the skin is the metaphor and the reality of the intact ego. Any perforation or alteration of the skin's entirety signals the deconstruction of the concept of unity, of envelopment.

> In my view, the skin that has been torn from the body, if it is preserved whole, represents the protective envelope, the shield, which one must take from the other in phantasy either simply to have it for oneself or to duplicate and reinforce one's own skin. (ibid., 50)

The disabled body presents in both visual and tactile terms the rupture of the skin-ego, whether that disruption is lack of limbs or dysfunction of sensory organs. Indeed, seeing is related to touching, as Freud has noted,[80] as is hearing – each of which connects an observer to an object that may be out of range of touch. Anzier tries to account for a prohibition on touching in Western culture, citing biblical injunctions, Christ's *noli me tangere*, incest and masturbation prohibitions, and even Freud's renunciation of touching as a therapeutic technique. The point to be made is that touching involves the contact of one's ego, literally in this case, with the ego of the object. In the case of the perceptual realms involved in the disability transaction between subject and object, the specular moment leads to the tactile moment. Thus, touching represents an opening up of the ego, a kind of risk that the envelope may fail to contain the subject because of the moment of contact. 'The prohibition on touching separates the region of the familiar, a protected and protective region, from that of the strange, which is troubling and dangerous' (ibid., 146). Our touch is familiar, but the touch of the Other is *unheimlich*; so the disabled touch is seen as both contagious and erotic.

That this touch is eroticized and connected with the Oedipal moment is significant.

> The most primitive form of the tactile prohibition seems to run: do not stay clinging to the body of your parents . . . [but] the Oedipal prohibition reverses the elements of the prohibition on touching: what is familiar, in the first sense of familial, becomes dangerous . . . (ibid., 146–7)

Around the Oedipal moment swirl the images of castration, mutilation, and a general prohibition against 'generalized contact, i.e. on the embracing, conjoining and confusing of bodies' (ibid., 147). Touch represents a fragmenting of the body, a threat of mutilation, and a fear of losing one's boundaries, one's bodily integrity. In this sense, touching the creature, touching the disabled body, is both an erotic lure and a self-destroying gesture.

We can return, again, to the Venus, neatly enclosed in its marmoreal skin and thus representing an unperforated body, despite the mutilations that have disfigured it. Most of the visual arts eschew disability and disabled images, except perhaps for the romanticized images around madness. The work of Mary Duffy, a contemporary artist without arms, provides one notable exception to this reluctance to think of Venuses without arms as the equivalent of Medusa. In the first plate of a photographic series entitled *Cutting the Ties that Bind*, we see a standing figure draped entirely in white cloth against a dark background so that the figure beneath the drapery is not visible. In the second plate, the drapery is partially removed so that it covers mainly the thighs and legs revealing us a female body, the artist's, without arms. The figure is clearly meant to reproduce the Venus de Milo in the flesh. The third picture in the series shows the figure stepping away from the drapery with a triumphant smile. The work serves to show how the female disabled body can be reappropriated by the artist herself. Duffy writes:

> By confronting people with my naked body, with its softness, its roundness and its threat I wanted to take control, redress the balance in which media representations of disabled women [are] usually tragic, always pathetic. I wanted to hold up a mirror to all those people who had stripped me bare previously . . . the general public with naked stares, and more especially the medical profession. (cited in Nead 1992, 78)

The Medusa gaze is rerouted so that it comes not from the object of horror, the monstrous woman, but from the gaze of the normal observer. It is the 'normal' gaze that is seen as naked, as dangerous. And unlike Perseus slaying Medusa by holding up a mirror, it is now the 'object of horror' who holds the mirror up to the 'normal' observer.

This reappropriation of the normal gaze was further carried out by the photographer Jo Spence. Recognizing the inherent and unstated pose of normalcy imposed by the camera and by the photographic session, Spence revisioned her photography to be capable of representing the nude model as a person with disabilities. Her work, detailed in many shows and in her book *Putting Myself in the Picture: A Political, Personal, and Photographic Autobiography* (1986), partly focuses on her mastectomy. Spence links this operative and post-operative process to an understanding and participating gaze that seeks to touch, not recoil from, bodily changes. In addition to the simple fact of the partial mastectomy, Spence includes in her work photographs and texts that question assumptions about age and beauty. Her body is middle-aged, irregular, and defies the canons of ideal feminine beauty. Her work is involved with 'explaining my experience as a patient and the contradictions between ways in which the medical profession controls women's bodies and the "imaginary bodies" we inhabit as women' (Spence 1986, 156).

The visual arts have done a magnificent job of centralizing normalcy and of marginalizing different bodies. As we have seen, initially the impulse came from a move to idealize the body and make up the perfect body out of perfect sub-units. Then with the rise of hegemonic normalcy, the impulse veered from ideal to normalizing representations. Either of these paradigms pushes the ordinary body, the abnormal body, out of the picture. Photographer David Hevey has written about the paucity of images of the disabled in photographic anthologies. He concludes that 'disabled people are represented but almost exclusively as symbols of "otherness" placed within equations which take their non-integration as a natural by-product of their impairment' (Hevey 1992, 54). When he looked for any images of disabled people, he found either medical photographs in which the 'patients' appear 'passive and stiff and "done to", the images bear a bizarre resemblance to colonial pictures where "the blacks" stand frozen and curious, while "whitey" lounges confident and sure' (ibid., 53), or images like those of Diane Arbus that show the disabled as 'grotesque.' Ungrotesque, routine pictures of disabled people in advertising, 'art' photography, films and so on are hard to find. With the same regularity that bodies of color were kept out of the mainstream (and even the avant-garde) media in the years before the civil rights movement, so too are disabled bodies disqualified from representing universality.

One of the ways that visual images of the disabled have been appropriated into the modernist and postmodernist aesthetic is through the concept of the 'grotesque.' The word was used by Bakhtin to describe the aesthetic of the Middle Ages, which reveled in presenting the body in its nonidealized form. The grotesque, for Bakhtin, was associated with the common people, with a culture that periodically turned the established order upside down through the carnival and the carnivalesque. Gigantic features, scatological references, inverse political power were all hallmarks of the grotesque – an aesthetic that ultimately was displaced by humanistic notions of order, regularity, and of course power during the Renaissance.

While the term 'grotesque' has had a history of being associated with this counterhegemonic notion of people's aesthetics and the inherent power of the masses, what the term has failed to liberate is the notion of actual bodies as grotesque. There is a thin line between the grotesque and the disabled. Hevey examines, for example, how critics have received Diane Arbus's photographs of the disabled. Susan Sontag writes that Arbus's 'work shows people who are pathetic, pitiable, as well as repulsive, but it does not arouse any compassionate feelings.' Later she adds, 'Do they see themselves, the viewer wonders, like *that*? Do they know how grotesque they are?' (Hevey 1992, 57). The grotesque, in this sense, is seen as a concept without the redeeming sense of class rebellion in Bakhtin's formulation. Here it is simply the ugly, what makes us wince, look away, feel pity – more allied with its dictionary definition of 'hideous,' 'monstrous,' 'deformed,' 'gnarled.' Though artists and writers may use the grotesque, they rarely write about that state from the subject position of the disabled. The grotesque, as with disability in general, is used as a metaphor for otherness, solitude, tragedy, bitterness, alterity. The grotesque is defined in this sense as a disturbance in the normal visual field, not as a set of characteristics through which a fully constituted subject views the world. One problem with terms like 'disability' and 'the grotesque' is that they disempower the object of observation. The body is seen through a set of cultural default settings arrived at by the wholesale adoption of ableist cultural values.

In no area is this set of cultural values related to the visual more compelling than in film. Film is a medium whose main goal, one might say, is the construction and reconstruction of the body. The abnormal body plays a major role in the defining of the normal body, and so one might assume that film would be concerned with the issue of disability. Martin F. Norden has recently published the most complete account to date of disability in the film industry, *The Cinema of Isolation: A History of Physical Disability in the Movies* (1994). The remarkable thing about this book is the staggering number of films that have been made about the issue of disability.

When I first began to consider the issue of how the disabled body is depicted in film, I came up with my own list of twenty or so films, and I thought that I would mention the occasional way in which the disabled were included in a film industry that mainly focused on the normal body. In other words, I thought I was dealing with a parallel situation to, say, the depiction in cinema of African-Americans – a marginalized group who rarely appeared in Hollywood films until recently[81] and, if they did, played mainly minor characters or supernumerary roles.

But the facts about the depiction of disability are quite the opposite of what I had thought. The film industry has been obsessed with the depiction of the disabled body from the earliest silent films. The blind, the deaf, the physically disabled were singled out from the very beginning of cinema. Norden finds movies about disability from as early as 1898, and the earliest one-reeler silent films of the period 1902–1909 include such representative titles as *Deaf Mute Girl Reciting 'Star Spangled Banner'* (1902), *Deaf Mutes' Ball* (1907), *The Invalid's Adventure* (1907), *The Legless Runner* (1907), *The One-legged Man* (1908), *The Hunchback Brings Luck* (1908), *The Little Cripple* (1908), *A Blind Woman's Story* (1908), *The Blind Boy* (1908), *The Cripple's Marriage* (1909), *The Electrified Humpback* (1909), to name only a few. Later multi-reeler silent films routinely told the stories of the disabled. D. W. Griffith made a few disability-related films, culminating his efforts in the famous *Orphans of the Storm* (1921) in which two hapless sisters (Lilian and Dorothy Gish), one of whom is blind, try to survive on the streets of Paris. But the noteworthy fact about this film is not merely its disability-related content but that Griffith's version was the *fifth* filmic remake of the 1874 French play *Les Deux Orphelines*. With film only in its infancy, this particular disability story had been told afresh approximately once every four years from 1900 through 1921.

Norden's book lists about six hundred disability-related films in its index, a far cry from my twenty or so. And if one stops and thinks about the subject, one realizes that films concerning people with disabilities are almost always playing at any given time. For example, at the moment I write this sentence on 5 January 1995,

I can go see movies about the deaf Beethoven in *Immortal Beloved*, the linguistically deprived girl in Jodie Foster's *Nell*, the emotionally impaired monarch in *The Madness of King George*, and of course the lovable, mentally challenged *Forrest Gump*. In recent years films like *My Left Foot*, *Lorenzo's Oil*, *Rainman*, *Children of a Lesser God*, *Elephant Man*, *Mask*, *Awakenings*, *Stanley and Iris*, to name only a few better-known films, have become major hits. In addition to films centrally about disabled people, there are hundreds of films in which characters, mainly evil, are depicted as using wheelchairs, missing limbs or eyes, walking with a limp, stuttering, and so on.

The point that Norden's book made clear to me is that the cinematic experience, far from including disabilities in an ancillary way, is powerfully arranged around the management and deployment of disabled and 'normal' bodies. Disabled stories, stories of people's bodies or minds going wrong, make compelling tales. But more than that, as with any obsession, there has to be an underlying reason why films are drawn obsessively to the topic of disability. In order to understand why film makers routinely incorporate disabled bodies into films, it might be relevant to ask what else routinely appears in films. The answer is more than obvious: sex and violence. While it is fashionable for liberals to decry the violent content of films, and conservatives to decry the sexual, it might be more accurate for them to think of films as vehicles for the delivery of images of the body in extreme circumstances. The inherent voyeuristic nature of film makes it a commodity that works by visualizing for viewers the body in attitudes that it is otherwise difficult to see. Few people in quotidian life see couples making love on a regular basis, but that is a routine experience to filmgoers. Likewise, most middle-class citizens rarely see dead, mutilated, bleeding bodies, but the average viewer has no shortage of such images.

So films, one could say, are a streamlined delivery system that produces dramatically these bodily images in exchange for a sum of money (as the Coca-Cola industry can be said to be a system for delivering caffeine and sugar, or as cigarettes are really time-release delivery systems for nicotine administration). As novels were seen to be mechanisms for the cultural production of normativity, so films have to be seen in the same regard, with the addition that the phantasm of the body is particularly subject to these normativizing activities.

Films enforce the normal body, but through a rather strange process. The normal body, invented in the nineteenth century as a departure from the ideal body, has shifted over to a new concept: the normal ideal. This normal ideal body is the one we see on the screen. It is the commodified body of the eroticized male or female star. This body is not actually the norm, but it is the fantasized, hypostatized body of commodified desire. In order to generate this body and proliferate its images, films have constantly to police and to regulate the variety of bodily differences. These bodies are the modern equivalents of the nude Venuses, and to keep them viable, to think on and obsess about them, the Medusa body has constantly to be shown, reshown, placed, categorized, itemized, and anatomized. In short, we cannot have Sharon Stone without Linda Hunt; we cannot have Tom Cruise without Ron Kovic; we cannot have the fantasy of the erotic *femme fatale*'s body without having the sickened, disabled, deformed person's story testifying to the universal power of the human spirit to overcome adversity. As Norden points out, when films about disabled people are made, more often than not the disabled characters get cured by the end of the film (1994, 59). The tension between the whole and the fragmented body, between the erotic, complete body and the uncanny, incomplete body, must be constantly deployed and resolved through films.

The film *Boxing Helena* provides some interesting ways of seeing these tensions worked through. In the film, the surgeon Nick (Julian Sands) amputates the legs of Helena (Sherilyn Fenn), the bitchy, sexualized woman with whom he is obsessed but who rejects his advances. He performs the amputation initially to save her life after a car accident, but then goes on to amputate her arms as a way of keeping her and containing her – of rendering her helpless so he can take care of her.

A replica of the Venus de Milo decorates Nick's family mansion and is used as a double symbol. In one sense, it is an illustration of the beauty of the dismembered Helena. But it also represents idealized female beauty (in its wholeness) and is associated with Nick's mother whose blatant sexuality was used to humiliate her son when he was young. The film maker wants us to see the dismemberment of Helena partly as an act of revenge against the castrating mother, whose legacy shows up in Nick's premature ejaculation syndrome (which in that sense renders him disabled). The mother, who has died, later returns to Nick's gaze, seen from the back as the naked and armless Venus, and the statue itself at one time falls on Nick and in another moment explodes from within, thus illustrating the repressed reality of the fragmented body.

The salient point is that when Helena is amputated, that is, becomes the Venus, she becomes merely idealized. Whereas before her dismemberment she is a rapacious fantasy of female sexuality unencumbered by the traditional female values of caring, nurturing or sweetness, after her dismemberment, she loses her sexuality. In a typical ableist moment, she says after her amputation, 'How can I ever look at myself and think of myself as worthwhile?' Her worth in this case is her sexuality, which is lost. Her disability is actually created and owned by Nick.

In another instance of bourgeois, ableist celebration of the discursivity of sexuality, both she and Nick regain their sexual function (thus becoming undisabled) through eros. He buries his head in her lap, which of course despite all the mutilation leads us to realize that everything that is conventionally part of female sexuality is still intact – and in a moment of his fantasy she comes alive sexually, a trope which is equated with her suddenly having arms and legs. She caresses his head, walks, and whispers the answer to Freud's question 'What do women want?' telling him how women want to be made love to. Her whispered erotic litany begins to release the bad dream of disability. But it is only he, as the owner of her body, who can fully accomplish this release, and so she begs him: 'I want to feel like a woman. Give me back what you've taken away.' The supplement that has been missing is returned like the Lacanian phallus by Nick in a very Lacanian moment. As Helena watches through a semi-opened door, Nick makes love to another woman (who in the credits is called 'fantasy woman'), and we see he is no longer sexually dysfunctional. Helena's self is reconstituted through a triangularization of desire in which her mirror imago of the whole body is re-created by viewing the desire of the Other. The other woman represents her wholeness, and the entire issue of functionality is blurred into sexual ability.[82]

As trendy as the director Jennifer Lynch is trying to be, she cannot separate herself from traditional views of people with disabilities. Never does the surgeon have to catheterize Helena or change her tampon; more tellingly, Helena is never allowed to be both naked and disabled – as her body was so openly revealed before her amputations. Her double-amputated body is partly held up as an object of beauty, but not of sexuality – and therefore it can never be seen naked as she had been revealed to the camera's gaze before the operations. Unlike Mary Duffy or Jo Spence, Lynch cannot allow herself to show us the naked, disabled body. This would be too great a primal-scene moment, in which the true nakedness of disability, its connection with the nakedness of the unwhole fragmented body, would be unavoidable and unable to be repressed.

The film ends with the revelation that the entire narrative has all been Nick's dream. Helena was hit by a car, but in actuality she was taken to hospital, and at the end of the film she remains physically intact. Disability is just a bad dream, as she herself had cried out when she first discovered she had had her legs amputated. She is cured.

The film returns to the whole, untarnished body because that is always seen as the norm. In general, when the body is mentioned in literature or depicted in drama and film, it is always already thought of as whole, entire, complete, and ideal. In literature, central characters of novels are imaged as normal unless specific instruction is given to alter that norm; where a disability is present, the literary work will focus on the disability as a problem. Rare indeed is a novel, play, or film that introduces a disabled character whose disability is not the central focus of the work.[83] More often, the disability becomes part of a theme in which a 'normal' person becomes romantically involved with a person with a disability and proves that the disability is no obstacle to being attractive. At its most egregious, this theme is taken up in works such as W. Somerset Maugham's *Of Human Bondage*, in which the character's sexual life is cleared of problems only when the disability is removed. With an only slightly more educated view, films like *My Left Foot* confirm the character's inner worth when he attracts a wife at the end of the film. And Jennifer Lynch's *Boxing Helena* is simply part of this parade.

Throughout this chapter, I have tried to show that the concept of disability is a crucial part of the very way we conceive of and live in our bodies. In art, photography, film, and other media in which the body is represented, the 'normal' body always exists in a dialectical play with the disabled body. Indeed, our representations of the body are really investigations of and defenses against the notion that the body is anything but a seamless whole, a complete, unfragmented entity. In addition to the terms of race, class, gender, sexual preference and so on – all of which are factors in the social construction of the body – the concept of disability adds a background of somatic concerns. But disability is more than a background. It is in some sense the basis on which the 'normal' body is constucted: disability defines the negative space the body must not occupy, it is the Manichean binary in contention with normality. But this dialectic is one that is enforced by a set of social conditions and is not natural in any sense. Only when disability is made visible as a compulsory term in a hegemonic process, only when the binary is exposed and the continuum acknowledged, only when the body is seen apart from its existence as an object of production or consumption – only then will normalcy cease being a term of enforcement in a somatic judicial system.

7

Conclusion:

Uneasy Positions: Disability

and Multiculturalism

I have been trying to make the argument that the concept of
disability has been relegated to a sideshow, a freak show at that,
far away from the academic midway of progressive ideas and
concerns. While the main attractions of race, class, and gender
continue to grab the attention of professors and students, as well
as of the general public, the concept of disability is safely hidden
on the sidelines away from much scrutiny. I have been directing
the spotlight not so much on disability, which is the end result of
a series of complex cultural, social, and political processes and
obfuscations, as on the notion of normalcy that makes the idea of
disability (as well as the ideas of race, class, and gender) possible.

Further, I have been trying to show how deeply tied to the
normalized body are the assumptions we make about art, language,
literature, and culture in general. In recent years, hundreds of texts
have claimed to be rethinking the body; but the body they have
been rethinking – female, black, queer – has rarely been rethought
as disabled. Normalcy continues its hegemony even in progressive
areas such as cultural studies – perhaps even more so in cultural
studies since there the power and ability of 'transgressive' bodies
tend to be romanticized for complex reasons. Disabled bodies are
not permitted to participate in the erotics of power, in the power
of the erotic, in economies of transgression. There has been
virtually no liberatory rhetoric – outside of the disability rights
movement – tied to prostheses, wheelchairs, colostomy bags,
canes, or leg braces.

Of course, multiculturalism and the multicultural curriculum are by no means unproblematic spheres of activity. The general solution to problems raised around multiculturalism has been to include as many different groups as will fit into any curriculum, anthology, political party, or group. Although there are certainly differences of politics and aims among these multicultures, there is a general political, ideological, and social consensus that may be described, to the horror or glee of conservatives, as progressive.

So how, once the profoundly destructive marginalization of people with disabilities is recognized, may a new attention to the disabled body be included in the already crowded theater of multiculturalism? What can be done to accomplish this inclusion? Measures can be taken analagous to the familiar steps taken before with other groups: highlighting narratives, lyrics, and representations of disability in literature courses, teaching the politics of disability in courses that deal with social and political issues, making conscious efforts to include people with disabilities in media, and so on. Important as well would be the attempt to teach disability across the curriculum so that this subject does not remain ghettoized in special courses. This aspect of inclusion involves a reshaping of symbolic cultural productions and ideology.

In addition, legal measures can deal with issues of discrimination. In fact, in the United States, the centerpiece legislation concerning disability has already been passed. The Americans with Disabilities Act (ADA) of 1990 is a powerful piece of legislation that bans discrimination based on disability in the workplace and in public spaces. Its effect is that access has to be provided, accommodations have to be made, for people with disabilities. In a sense, the legal battle has been won (it is ironic that the law received strong support from conservatives as well as from liberals, partly because it was promoted by Senator Robert Dole, himself a person with disabilities). But remedies are not really so easily achieved. The ADA is only as effective as its enforcement. But there is no federal agency to enforce the provisions of this law. The situation remains today that the weight of the law can only be brought to bear through a lawsuit or the fear of a lawsuit. But lawsuits are costly and time-consuming, and to bring them is beyond the means of most people with disabilities.[84] The somewhat predictable result is, according to the *New York Times* (23 October 1994), that after four years in effect, the ADA has 'not significantly increased' the number of people with disabilities entering the work force' (A:22). The *New York Times* cites a survey finding that only 31 percent of people with disabilities aged from sixteen to sixty-four were working part time or full time, down slightly from 33 percent in 1986 when the law was not in effect. In other words, discrimination against people with disabilities remains in full force.

The same is largely true in relation to the curriculum. The conventional attempts to demarginalize disability, to include disability in multicultural endeavors, might seem like logical steps to take in the direction of progressive political aims. But the reality is a bit different. It has been the experience of a number of disability activists that when attempts are made to include disability in university diversity requirements, for example, there may be considerable opposition. What is interesting is that the opposition often comes not from conservatives but from people of color, feminists, Marxists, or those in queer studies. Simi Linton, Susan Mello, and John O'Neill point out (1995) that 'the critics [of including disability studies in diversity requirements] are those who are the strongest proponents of diversifying the curriculum. What is even more disturbing is that the criticisms previously heard from proponents of the traditional canon are now being used against the inclusion of disability in curriculum transformation efforts.' Linton et al. cite specific comments made in this regard:

> 'scholarship on disability will "water down" the diversity requirement; its purpose is to increase self-esteem, or capitulate to interest group pressure; it's not valid or rigorous scholarship; it's parochial, and will further anatomize the curriculum.' (*Radical Teacher* 47, 1995, 10)

Although we may envision an idealistic inclusion of people with disabilities into the multicultural family, in fact this family has some major dysfunctional aspects. What we discover when the subject of inclusion comes up is not simply the uneasy tension that arises. For example, in discussions about diversity requirements at my university, a faculty member of color recently said that disability did not have to be listed specifically along with race, class, gender, and so on because the category of disability was inherently included in a proposed document under the heading of 'other asymmetries of power.' In other words, disability is seen, even by those who are themselves the object of discrimination, as marginal, othered, and not really a valid category of oppression.

This point was made more clearly recently when the New York City Board of Education voted in February 1995 to exclude disability and sexual preference from its multicultural curriculum. The board, representing many of New York's minorities and ethnicities, did not think that people with disabilities or gays and lesbians represented the board's vision of a multicultural society.[85] And, as this book was being written, New York State's 1995 budget slashed subsidies to people with disabilities from its list of entitlements as well as reducing funding for special education. Republican proposals for fiscal reform include measures that would cut Supplemental Security Income to a quarter of a million children with disabilities (*Nation*, 27 March 1995, 406).

What is being missed in these multicultural discussions is the way that race and gender connect with disability. The point is not that disability is a subcategory of discrimination involving relatively few people. With between 35 and 43 million Americans defined as having disabilities (Shapiro 1993), one is talking about a substantial percentage of the population. Rather than being marginal, the issues around disability are central to the construction of normalcy: disability is tied to a process that defines us all. Furthermore, disability is not, as is commonly thought, equally distributed throughout the population. People in the lower classes tend to be born with more disabilities and to acquire more disabilities than middle- and upper-class people, and people of color tend to make up a disproportionate part of the poor. Women make up a disproportionate share of those who develop disabilities in mid-life (Fine and Asch 1988, 245). Moreover, Third World countries tend to have many more people with disabilities than do developed countries. Three-quarters of all disabled people now live in developing countries, and that proportion is expected to increase to four-fifths by the year 2000 (Nkinyangi and Mbindyo 1982). The social oppression experienced by many Third World women ensures that they have the most difficult lot of all. As N. Begum, a woman of color with disabilities, puts it (1990, 6): 'women with disabilities are perennial outsiders; their oppression and exclusion [render] them one of the most powerless groups in society.'

The point is that disability is not an area that can be simply included into the issues of race, class, and gender – it is already there in complex and invisible ways. There is no race, class, or gender without hierarchical and operative theories of what is normal and what is abnormal. So, simply trying to include disabilities into a multicultural curriculum may be an action, if it is indeed taken, that fails to see how an ableist view of society may be so ingrained that it permeates the already established categories of race, class, and gender.[86]

A disableist view of the cultural terrain may produce rather different readings of positions and events. While the race–class–gender grouping tends to coalesce around what might be termed 'progressive issues,' the disableist position may require realignments and rethinkings of some ideological 'truths.'

For example, and very tellingly, the position of people with disabilities on the issue of abortion and fetal screening is not seamlessly in accord with a liberal/progressive agenda. The idea of using amniocentesis to screen for birth defects and then aborting 'defective' fetuses is not a simple issue if one views it from a disabilities rights perspective. While most feminists would insist on a woman's right to abort a fetus that might be born deformed, mentally impaired, with Down syndrome, or some other defect, very few would agree with practices like those routinely performed in India in which parents screen for and then abort female fetuses. Indeed the general attitude of the American populace toward abortions when birth defects are detected is worth noting. In one study, while only 40 percent of people believed it was acceptable to have an abortion if no more children were wanted, a full 70 percent felt abortion should be allowed if a birth defect was detected (Fine and Asch 1988, 304). Even the language involved in this choice – 'birth defect' or physical 'deformity' – must alert us that we are very much in a world of opinion, of ideology, rather than a cool, scientific world of fact. One person's defect is another person's strength. The indiscriminate grouping together of traits – whether Down syndrome, deafness, or limblessness – creates a general category that belies the difference of various 'defects.' If one does not speak of high-functioning or low-functioning people with mental impairments, one again loses the notion of a disabilities continuum. All too often, differences are automatically labeled 'defects' or 'deformities.'

The fact is that many people with disabilities, say for example with Down syndrome, do not wish they were never born. And not all parents of Down syndrome children wish they had never had their child. The area of prenatal screening becomes greyer if the genetic traits for deafness or blindness are detected *in utero*. Is it ethical to abort a fetus if the child will be born unable to hear or see? If some people would find such an abortion abhorrent, why would they approve of one involving leglessness, spina bifida, or Down syndrome?

This argument can be taken further: What if children of color were born randomly to women? And what if there was a test to determine whether a child would be white or of color? Would it be ethical to abort a child of color? Few would answer 'yes,' but many more would argue for the termination of pregnancies in which the child to be born might be born deaf, blind, genetically impaired, or physically or mentally disabled.

There is another side to this coin. With the growth of political consciousness among the Deaf, the possibility has been raised by genetically Deaf parents that it might be better to abort hearing fetuses. The rationale, absolutely the same one used by 'normal' parents who do not want to have 'deformed' children, is that a Deaf child would thrive best in a Deaf family, that a hearing child would have trouble communicating with the parents, and that the family dynamic would be upset.

In addition, the gene for a kind of dwarfism has recently been isolated and the prenatal test for this gene has been made available to parents. The immediately obvious question is, should a 'normal' parent have an abortion if their child is to be born a dwarf? But other questions are posed. Parents who are themselves dwarfs have decided to use the test to make sure that their children will be dwarfs. The argument is that such parents often live in specially constructed dwellings built on a small scale which would be uncomfortable to 'normal'-sized people, and that remodeling could create a financial burden for the family. Furthermore, the oddity of a physically short family having to deal with, discipline, carry, and care for a rather large child might be disturbing to all concerned.

The position of progressive people with disabilities is that abortion is a woman's right and should not be tampered with. But at the same time complex ethical problems surround the use of prenatal screening to rule out the birth of a child with disabilities. As Fine and Asch put it (1988, 302):

> Every woman has a right to make this decision in whatever way she needs, but the more information she has, the better her decision can be. Genetic counselors, physicians, and all others involved with assisting women during amniocentesis should gain and provide far more and very different information about life with disabilities than is customarily available.

This position straddles a difficult divide. While progressive people with disabilities do not wish to side with right-to-lifers, they may nevertheless recognize that the use of abortions for eugenic purposes is problematic. Of course, though most progressives would not like to admit it, eugenics is still practiced, only now it is done at the prenatal stage rather than at a later date. It is also worth noting that the most stringent aspects of eugenics usually came down to encouraging 'superior' parents to mate or discouraging those who carried problematic traits from mating. What modern genetic testing has done is to move the discouragement or proscription of marriage (or of fertility) from the legislature to the genetic counselor's office. Nevertheless, the options remain the same: the limiting of fertility by birth control or sterilization. In effect, the offensive project of the Nazis to eliminate defectives is now practiced through the agency of modern medicine.

I want to make clear that I am not saying, nor are most progressive people with disabilities, that women should not have the right to abort fetuses identified as 'defective.' This choice is, as always, based on the individual woman's conscience, needs, and abilities. The problem is that since the general population is mostly 'ableist,' the choices made concerning abortion will necessarily be influenced in an ableist direction, by the prejudice that sees disabled people as living miserable lives, as objects of pity, as creatures whose birth it would have been a kindness to have prevented. This prejudice could, however, be overcome through the kind of changes in society at large that might foster an understanding of people with disabilities as whole, fully developed humans whose impairments place them within a continuum of ability of which everyone is part. The changes I am advocating involve not just goodwill or understanding, but definite government support so that the special problems of children and families with disabilities can be addressed. Moreover, as I argued earlier, disabilities appear or are highlighted in environments that produce disability. If our society were one in which difference could be more easily handled, impairments might not be seen as so 'devastating' as they are today.

Another area of uneasy positioning centers on euthanasia. The traditional liberal/progressive position is that we should have a law in place that permits euthanasia so that, for example, terminally ill people in comas should not have to suffer. Usually what is recommended is that people in comas should be detached from support systems and allowed to die naturally. In other cases, it is said, people who are severely impaired or dying should have the right to a physician-assisted suicide. This position is challenged by some people with disabilities. They feel that simply because a person is in a coma, his or her life should not be terminated. Many people with disabilities, who themselves have experienced the unkind hand of institutional medicine, doubt the ethical right or even judgment of doctors and families to decide who should die. They identify with the otherness of the coma patient, and see the attempt to detach support systems as part of a similar system that might in fact like to cut financial support from disabled children or to rid the world of anyone who has a serious disability. They link such actions to those in which mentally impaired people were sterilized or unwillingly made the subjects of medical experiments. Furthermore, the detaching of support systems may itself cause pain through suffocation and starvation. (One might want to recall that it was official medical policy until fairly recently to cause babies born with severe spina bifida or other birth defects to die by withholding infant formula from them in the first days of life.) Thus many people with disabilities believe that decisions about life and death should not be made by 'normal' people. Rather, a person with disabilities should act as guardian for the patient facing court-decided euthanasia.

In the case of people requesting their own death, as have the patients of, most notably, Dr Jack Kevorkian, some of them may be reacting to the natural depression that comes from the loss of mobility, limbs, sight, hearing, and other bodily functions. But this depression, and the feeling that the quality of life is low, is partially the product of an ableist society that places a great premium on being 'normal'. If such people had access to the kind of support systems that disabilities activists draw upon, they might not feel the need to kill themselves, to carry out society's death warrant against difference.

Obviously, the argument about the relation between disability and euthanasia is a great deal more complicated than the position I am quickly sketching here. And let me emphasize, I am not saying that euthanasia is a bad thing, but rather that until we understand the social and political implications of disability, we cannot always make rational decisions about the right to die. The point of laying out these arguments is not to condemn abortion or euthanasia, but to show the nature of the uneasy positions that arise when one takes into account a disabilities perspective. I also want to make the point that the simple inclusion of disabilities studies into a multicultural curriculum or the inclusion of a disabilities perspective into political agendas amounts to more than adding some demands to a list.

The difficulties abound. Take this example. At the 1995 Modern Language Association convention a group of Deaf scholars, who attended specifically to be part of a panel on 'deafness and textuality' as well as to attend an organizational meeting of disability studies scholars, found that the interpreters secured to translate were unable to understand academic discourse. These interpreters had been used routinely to assist deaf people appearing in court trials, and at social service hearings, weddings and funerals. Faced with discussions about discursivity, clitoral readings, and cyborgs, they literally threw up their hands in frustration. The Deaf scholars were thus unable to follow the presentations. If PhD-level interpreters, such as are found at Gallaudet University, had been available, this situation would not have occurred. But the larger point is that very few professional organizations are prepared to accommodate members with impairments. Few teachers in universities think about providing visual or aural supports for blind or deaf students. The environment is not open to the possibility of disability, or, put another way, far too often the environment creates the possibility for disability. Fairly sophisticated means exist to facilitate communication between hearing and deaf people, including real-time captioning, sign language interpretation, and pre-recorded speeches; there is also the very simple means of the distribution of papers in advance. The fact that most of these possibilities are not made available on a regular basis tells much about the priorities of academics and their organizations.

Another area of uneasy positioning is found in the judicial system. This system is set up with the expectation that the people processed through it will be in the possession of some linguistic ability – whether that be Spanish, American Sign Language, or

Korean. But when this 'normal' expectation is thwarted, the judicial system grinds to a halt. Throughout the USA hundreds of people, most of whom are poor and members of minorities, are languishing in jails and mental hospitals, their rights to a speedy trial, due process, and justice abandoned. These people have two things in common – they are deaf and they cannot sign or speak.

The assumption has been made throughout this book that the Deaf constitute a linguistic minority. But that argument can only be true if the deaf person has learned sign language. But some deaf people have never learned to sign. Take the following case:

José Flores, aged twenty-nine, has been in jail in Passaic County, New Jersey, since June 1992 awaiting trial on charges of kidnapping, burglary, and sexual assault of minors. Flores, profoundly deaf, has not received a speedy trial because he cannot read, write, or use sign language. Raised in a remote rural area of Puerto Rico, Flores had neither access to appropriate education or a Deaf community, both necessities to foster language in deaf children. Like the Wild Child of Aveyron, Kaspar Hauser, or Genie (in Russ Rymer's book of the same name), such people deprived of language until after puberty, find it very difficult to acquire language as adults. Because Flores could not communicate, his lawyer claimed that his client could not aid in his own defense and therefore should not stand trial. Although Flores has been evaluated by experts who are confident that he cannot understand concepts like 'guilt,' 'innocence,' 'trial,' and 'jury,' the prosecutors' attitude was that he would have to stand trial.

In New Jersey, as in most states, the only grounds for waiving a trial is 'mental incompetence,' that is, either insanity or mental impairment. This catch-22 results in the ridiculous consequence that if Flores were found to be incompetent, he would have to be confined in a mental hospital until he somehow miraculously learned American Sign Language on his own. On the other hand, if he were found competent to be tried, he would sit in the defendant's chair and watch a meaningless blur of activity, that to him would signify nothing.

The specter of the mental hospital is a very real threat to

inmates without sign language. Junius Wilson serves as a *memento mori* of what can happen when deaf people with limited language skills are treated as mentally incompetent. Wilson, at the age of ninety-three, was 'discovered' in 1993 in Cherry Valley mental hospital in North Carolina, where he had been 'lost' since 1925. In that year he had been arrested for attempted rape, but because he was deemed mentally incompetent to stand trial he was remanded to a state mental hospital, where he was eventually castrated as a sex offender, although he had never been tried. John Wasson, a social worker, discovered Wilson and made arrangements for his release. Four other similarly warehoused deaf people were 'found' in the North Carolina system as a result of a lawsuit brought by Wasson.

It is probably a safe estimate to say that there must be hundreds of such people scattered throughout the mental institutions of the United States; others are trapped within the penal system. No state, so far as I can discern, has a penal code that includes the concept of linguistic incompetence. So each case must be dealt with under the mental incompetence statute on an *ad hoc* basis, with each official cobbling together some solution. In addition, there currently exist no facilities in the United States established to teach deaf inmates sign language, even though the Americans with Disabilities Act specifies that disabled people must be provided with communication assistance to stand trial.

The fact that people without formal language end up in the prison system really should come as no surprise. After all, law is really a highly elaborated form of language. The broader question then is how are people without language making it to adulthood without education? Most of the cases of this kind concern poor rural or inner-city people who either never had access to or who were allowed to drop out of an educational system. These silent inmates are the products of an amazing failure of the educational and social service systems. It is appalling that people like José Flores could grow up in a world where no one taught them language. But it is even more appalling that these men should end up being punished for a situation they hardly brought about.

I pointed out these incongruities in an article, 'Prisoners of Silence,' in the *Nation* two years ago, and since that time no action has been taken to address this problem. The uneasy position is not so quickly made easy because the judicial system cannot allow for the idea that it may not be possible to try a whole category of people fairly, and because the Deaf community has largely shied away from its nonlinguistic brothers and sisters, since they represent an otherness to the notion of Deaf people as a linguistic minority.

Perhaps it is fitting to end with a meditation on this man, José Flores, in jail. He is incarcerated for being a person with a disability. He cannot hear, yet he is not Deaf. He is a Latino, a poor person, one of the most marginalized people in the world. His very existence, his lack of language, leads him to arrest. He is arrested for not being normal, for not having a language. Yet he was never taught to sign, a skill that would have turned his disability into merely an impairment. His lack of normality makes it impossible for him to be processed through the judicial system. Had he just been either poor and Latino, he would have fit the known categories and been tried and, given prevailing attitudes, convicted. But José Flores's impairment means that he is disabled, so profoundly disabled that he can never be released from jail, never be tried. Like part of a jigsaw puzzle that has been lost, he fits into no system. He is guilty of disability, and under a system that demands normality he will remain in limbo. In a recent discussion with his attorney, I found out that he will probably be committed to prison under a civil action as a danger to himself and others and placed in jail until such time as he is no longer a danger. Given the fact that he will never be taught sign language, that means he will be in jail for the rest of his life.

Flores is only one person in a world ruled by the norm. The hegemony of normalcy is, like other hegemonic practices, so effective because of its invisibility. Normalcy is the degree zero of modern existence. Only when the veil is torn from the bland face of the average, only when the hidden political and social injuries are revealed behind the mask of benevolence, only when the hazardous environment designed to be the comfort zone of the normal is shown with all its pitfalls and traps that create disability – only then will we begin to face and feel each other in all the rich variety and difference of our bodies, our minds, and our outlooks.

Notes

1. I will try to follow the practice of the Deaf community and capitalize Deaf when it applies to the group of people who are deaf (that is, without a significant degree of hearing) and also culturally Deaf. Cultural Deafness implies belonging to a community of deaf people who share a similar language (American Sign Language, British Sign Language, etc.), a common community, a similar education in a Deaf setting, and a common cultural and social history – in short, the linguistic, cultural subgroup known as the Deaf.

2. Ableist is a political term used by people with disabilities to call attention to assumptions made about normalcy.

3. *The Disability Rag* is a radical journal in the field, and its use of the term at least gives me something to go on.

4. I am using the term 'audist' as a parallel to terms like 'racist,' 'sexist,' 'classist.' My assumption here is that the hearing establishment, of which almost all readers are members, is biased toward the auditory mode of communication.

5. With the current evisceration of the welfare state, poor people do have to justify their personal culpability in their economic victimization.

6. I am working on a memoir which may or may not see the light of day.

7. I use the term 'disabled person' to describe the object of 'normal' people's scrutiny, as I indicated in the Preface.

8. I use the term 'temporarily abled' in referring to 'normal' people. Throughout this book I will put the word 'normal' between quotation marks where necessary. The point is, obviously, that there are no normal people and that such a term enforces the rigid categories of 'normal' and 'disabled.'

9. The United Methodist General Conference has recently revised its hymnal to delete 'dumb,' 'lame,' and other references offensive to people with disabilities (Shapiro 1993, 30).

10. I am going to use the term 'disabled body' throughout the text. The alternative 'body with disabilities' seems to be pushing a political corrective too far. My point is that a certain body has been constructed by society and that

body is most succinctly referred to as a 'disabled body.' The aim of disability studies is, of course, to think of bodies with disabilities rather than disabled bodies, but the aim of this work is to analyze the way this society forms certain kinds of bodies for its own taxonomical purposes.

11. This denial of the continuity of disability has rather bad consequences not only for the 'disabled' but also for the 'abled.' For example, I am always saddened when I see the older person who sits quietly during the din of the dinner table because her hearing aid cannot function well in large, noisy groups. Because these people do not consider themselves Deaf they have not learned sign language and will not associate with other Deaf people. Consequently their deafness really is a form of isolation caused mainly by audist assumptions about the divide between hearing and deaf.

12. I find it particularly telling that academic conferences usually provide no services for scholars with disabilities. Since there is a growing body of Deaf scholars, in all fields, the absence of sign-language interpreters is a clear message that 'normal' scholars do not even conceive of the possibility that Deaf colleagues might have anything to say. Since I have been writing this book and other articles on the Deaf, I have tried to get sign-language interpreters for all the papers I present. Most of the time conference organizers cannot come up with any. If they do, the interpreters are not sufficiently versed in academic discourse to provide much help. There is a dreadful double bind involved here: if conferences do not provide sign-language interpreters, then no deaf people will come, and if no deaf people come then there is no necessity for interpreters. Likewise, if blind people wish to attend lectures on dance, theater, film, or art there need to be visual interpreters present for their complete participation.

13. Of course, as I have already observed, some disabilities are invisible, or temporarily invisible. People with dyslexia, nonvisible diseases or ones that are in remission, deaf people who are not at the moment talking or listening, seated paraplegics, and so on are not immediately seen as disabled.

14. This thinking obviously is still alive and well. During the election of 1994, Newt Gingrich accused President Clinton of being 'the enemy of normal Americans.' When asked at a later date to clarify what he meant, he said his meaning was that 'normal' meant 'middle class' (*New York Times*, 14 November 1994, A:17).

15. The concept of the 'norm' should not be confused with Aristotle's idea of the 'mean.' The Aristotlean mean is a kind of fictional construct. Aristotle advocates that in choosing between personal traits, one should tend to choose between the extremes. He does not however think of the population as falling generally into that mean. The mean, for Aristotle, is more of an heuristic device to assist in moral and ethical choices. In the sense of being a middle term or a middle way, it carries more of a spatial sense than does the term 'average' or 'norm.'

16. This rather remarkable confluence between eugenics and statistics has been pointed out by Donald A. MacKenzie, but I do not believe his observations have had the impact they should.

17. See Chapter 6 for more on the novel *Frankenstein* and its relation to notions of disability.

18. Many of our own prejudices against the learning-disabled date from the second half of the nineteenth century. The founder of the intelligence test still in use, Alfred Binet (1857–1911), was a Galton acolyte. The American psychologist Henry H. Goddard (1866–1957) used Binet's tests in the USA and turned the numbers into categories – 'idiots' being those whose mental age was one or two, 'imbeciles' ranging in mental age from three to seven. Goddard invented the term 'moron' (which he took from the Greek for 'dull' or 'stupid') for those whose mental age was between eight and twelve. Pejorative terms like 'moron' or 'retarded' have by now found their way into common usage (Kevles 1985, 78). And the term 'mongoloid idiot' to describe a person with Down's syndrome was used as recently as the 1970s not as a pejorative term but in medical texts as a diagnosis. (See Michael Bérubé's fascinating article 'Life As We Know It' (1994) for more on this phenomenon of labeling.)

19. If this argument sounds strangely familiar, it is because it is being repeated and promulgated in the neoconservative book *The Bell Curve* (Richard J. Herrnstein and Charles Murray, 1994), which claims that poverty and intelligence are linked through inherited characteristics.

20. This assumption is based on my previous works – *Factual Fictions: Origins of the English Novel* and *Resisting Novels: Fiction and Ideology* – as well as the cumulative body of writing about the relationship between capitalism, material life, culture, and fiction. The works of Raymond Williams, Terry Eagleton, Nancy Armstrong, Mary Poovey, John Bender, Michael McKeon, and others point in similar directions.

21. The issue of people with disabilities in literature is well documented and I want generally to avoid it in this work. Excellent books abound on the subject, including Alan Gartner and Tom Joe, eds, *Images of the Disabled, Disabling Images* (New York: Praeger, 1987), and the work of Deborah Kent, including 'In Search of a Heroine: Images of Women with Disabilities in Fiction and Drama' in Michelle Fine and Adrienne Asch, eds, *Women with Disabilities: Essays in Psychology, Culture, and Politics* (Philadelphia: Temple University Press, 1988).

22. And if the main character has a major disability, then we are encouraged to identify with that character's ability to overcome his or her disability.

23. The genealogical family line is both hereditary and financial in the bourgeois novel. The role of the family is defined by Jürgen Habermas thus: 'as a genealogical link it [the family] guaranteed a continuity of personnel that consisted materially in the accumulation of capital and was anchored in the absence of legal restrictions concerning the inheritance of property' (1989, 47).

The fact that biological connectedness and financial connectedness are conflated in the novel only furthers the point that normality is an enforced condition that upholds the totality of the bourgeois system.

24. I will deal with the *corps morcelé* of Lacan later, in Chapter 6, where I show the relation between the fragmented body and the response to disability. At this point, let me just say that Stevie's turning into a fragmented body makes sense given the fear 'normal' observers have that if they allow a concept of disability to associate with their bodies, they will lose control of their normalcy and their bodies will fall apart.

25. See Chapter 4 for more on the relation of freak shows to nationalism, colonialism, and disability.

26. So, deafness did not 'exist' before the eighteenth century for two reasons. First, the isolated deaf person was simply seen as an aberration in his or her town or family. He or she was first and foremost a nonperson. However, the deaf person in an extended group of deaf might not be thought of as deaf since that person was part of a functioning system. For example, Nora Ellen Groce's book *Everyone Here Spoke Sign Language: Hereditary Deafness on Martha's Vineyard* describes how an inherited trait brought to the island in 1633 resulted in the deafness of a substantial minority of people living on Martha's Vineyard. Because the minority made up a substantial number, the deaf were actually not visible as deaf. One resident responded to the author's question about what the hearing thought of the deaf by saying, 'Oh, they didn't think anything of them, they were just like everyone else,' and went on to describe – to the author's amazement – how everyone on Martha's Vineyard used sign language.

27. The radical difference between the blind and the deaf goes back to antiquity. The Egyptians, for example, used the blind as musicians, artists, and masseuses. There is documentation to show that priests at Karmah trained the blind for these purposes, but of the deaf, it was written, 'There is no use wasting words upon the dumb' (Winzer 1993, 13). Aristotle set the tone for much of Western treatment of the deaf versus the blind. He said that the deaf were 'senseless and incapable of reason,' and 'no better than the animals of the forest and unteachable,' while the blind were thought of as having equal intellect to the sighted (ibid., 18). Saint Augustine added to the denigration of the deaf by denying them membership in the Church: he interpreted the statement of Saint Paul, 'Faith comes by hearing' to mean that those without hearing can never have faith. Until the twelfth century a deaf person's marriage within the Church was only possible through papal dispensation (ibid., 22).

28. It is telling, too, that the language of the deaf, sign, was an indigenous language that arose spontaneously where groups of deaf people formed a community. The language taught in deaf schools was more or less a standardization of that autochthonous language. Braille, by contrast, was a system invented by a seeing man, Charles Barbier, who developed this form of writing during

wartime to enable messages to be read at night without the use of light, which would betray soldiers' positions to the enemy. In 1830, Barbier brought the system to the Institution des Enfants Aveugles in Paris, where a blind student, Louis Braille, developed and promulgated Barbier's plan. In this sense, deaf language is a special issue, whereas Braille is actually a system not exclusively 'blind' in its applications.

29. Nicholas Mirzoeff points out in his article 'Body Talk: Deafness, Sign and Visual Language in the Ancien Régime' that there was a long-standing tradition in French theater of portraying deaf characters. Mirzoeff points out the appearance of Le Sourd as early as the sixteenth century. But, as he also notes, 'these "deaf" characters normally spoke and often were pretending to be deaf in order to deceive others in pursuit of a love affair' (1992, 570). So we can assume that these depictions were not of the Deaf *per se* but of comic imitators of deafness.

30. See Harlan Lane, *The Mask of Benevolence: Disabling the Deaf Community* and my review of it in the *Nation* (6 July 1992).

31. The fact that Duncan Campbell was a huckster who only pretended to be deaf and who made his money by duping people has little bearing on the attitudes toward the deaf that Defoe espouses. Defoe is a writer whose ambivalence to fact and fiction only makes his work more interesting to a modern reader. For more on this ambivalence, see my *Factual Fictions: Origins of the English Novel*, 1983, 154–73.

32. The family story goes a bit deeper. Defoe's daughter Sophia married Henry Baker (1698–1774), who learned about the methods of Wallis from reading *Duncan Campbell*. Baker then went on to educate the deaf daughter of a relative, one Jane Forester. After succeeding with her, Baker became a teacher of the deaf as his sole livelihood, and was in fact the first professional teacher of the deaf.

33. See Joseph Allen Boone, *Tradition Counter Tradition: Love and the Form of Fiction*, and Nancy Armstrong, *Desire and Domestic Fiction: A Political History of the Novel* along with my *Resisting Novels: Fiction and Ideology* for examples of this shift to textual forms of assimilating ideology.

34. Martin Jay, in his *Downcast Eyes: The Denigration of Vision in Twentieth-Century French Thought*, details a general historical trend that conceives of the Middle Ages as biased toward hearing or touch, and the Enlightenment as favoring sight. For example, Roland Barthes in *Sade, Fourier, Loyola* wrote concerning Ignatius Loyola that 'in the Middle Ages, historians tell us, the most refined sense, the perceptive sense, *par excellence*, the one that established the richest contact with the world was hearing: sight came in only third, after touch. Then we have a reversal: the eye becomes the prime organ of perception (Baroque, art of the thing seen, attests to it)' (1976, 46). But Jay questions this simplifying tendency on the part of writers like Barthes, although Jay does end

up affirming that something happens in European culture to the question of vision. One of the areas he pinpoints is the separation of the visual and the textual – what he calls 'the secular autonomization of the visual as a realm unto itself' (Jay 1993, 44). This point fits well into the idea that the eighteenth-century text, though requiring vision, is actually more about the issue of hearing. The vision of reading, then, is not necessarily the vision of seeing. Indeed, the vision of reading is in effect one that is more about incorporating hearing language through the eyes than it is about seeing objects.

35. Further technological advances like those provided by computer networks, fiber optics, and other advanced forms of communications have completely shifted the ground from spoken language to semiological representations. As electronic mail, computer bulletin boards, and other computer-based forums for communication develop, we will find ourselves less and less reliant on spoken language. Computer literacy has already become a valuable, if not indispensable, skill in many areas of culture.

36. See Leland Warren, 'Turning Reality Round Together: Guides to Conversation in Eighteenth-Century England,' *Eighteenth Century Life*, new ser., Vol. VIII (May 1983), 65–87.

37. I cite all further quotes of Desloges's text from Harlan Lane, *The Deaf Experience*.

38. In a sense, Jacques Derrida deals with a similar phenomenon in his book *Memoirs of the Blind*. Derrida says of the work of Antoine Coypel and others who draw the blind, 'the operation of drawing would have something to do with blindness, would in some way regard blindness. . . . Every time a draftsman lets himself be fascinated by the blind, every time he makes the blind a *theme* of his drawing, he projects, dreams, or hallucinates a figure of a draftsman, or sometimes, more precisely, some draftswoman' (Derrida 1993, 2). Drawing blindness involves blindness in the process of drawing and points to the blindness in drawing as well as the sightedness in the concept of blindness. In a similar vein, writing from the deaf point of view reveals the deafness in writing, while concealing the deafness of the writer.

39. See my *Factual Fictions: Origins of the English Novel*, 11–24, for a discussion of this notion of denial as a hallmark of fictional ambivalence.

40. See Benedict Anderson, *Imagined Communities: Reflections on the Origin and Spread of Nationalism* (London: Verso, 1983).

41. Ironically, it was Mussolini who said, 'National pride has no need of the delirium of race' (cited in Stille 1991, 22).

42. So ethnic and linguistic minorities may consider themselves nationalities, and while women cannot claim separate nationality, they may consider themselves separately from the total national identity. As Trinh T. Minh-ha says of women having to choose between ethnicity and gender: 'The idea of two illusorily separated identities, one ethnic, the other woman . . . partakes in the

Euro-American system of dualistic reasoning and its age-old divide-and-conquer tactics' (Trinh 1989, 104). Fractionalized groups such as women or the Deaf shared certain features of nationality during a period of national consolidation in Europe in the eighteenth and nineteenth centuries.

43. Harlan Lane makes a telling comparison between the colonization of Africans and the treatment of the Deaf (Lane 1922, 35–66). He particularly examines descriptions of both groups and shows how the deaf and the native African are constructed in similar ways.

44. It is ironic that, as a recent study shows, approximately 50 per cent of Americans are virtually illiterate in that they lack the skills necessary to write a simple letter or read a bus schedule (*New York Times*, 10 September 1993, A:1). Thus, the concept of a linguistic community exists really only in some kind of ideal form – at least at the level of writing and reading. One might better speculate on the degrees by which individuals are included or excluded from the ideal community of language users, rather than assume that all normal members of the community are users of language and all deaf are not.

45. It is worth remembering that nationalism is a two-edged sword. It cuts a broad cloth out of divergent peoples and creates the pattern for imperialism and colonialism. However, nationalism in the Third World has been an important means of resisting domination by imperialist countries. (See Simon During, 'Literature – Nationalism's other? The case for revision' in Bhabha 1990, 138–53.)

46. All three steps have in fact taken place. Deaf education in the nineteenth century was taken away from Deaf educators. Oralism was made official at the 1880 Congress of Milan. And more recently US educational policy has emphasized the mainstreaming of deaf children in hearing schools. This pattern coincides with an effort to nationalize other 'non-national' populations by removing their own ideological apparatuses.

47. See Chapter 5 of my *Resisting Novels: Fiction and Ideology*.

48. This argument is made today again as if it were new thinking in three books: *The Bell Curve: Intelligence and Class Structure in American Life* (New York: Free Press, 1994) by Richard J. Herrnstein and Charles Murray; *Race, Evolution, and Behavior* (New Brunswick, NJ: Transaction Publishers, 1994) by J. Philippe Rushton, and *The Decline of Intelligence in America: A Strategy for National Renewal* (Westport, Connecticut: Praeger, 1994) by Seymour W. Itzkoff. All these works maintain that intelligence levels are declining since the members of the under-class, poor and disproportionately of color, are dragging the 'norm' down by their rapid reproduction of low intelligence and social dysfunctionality. The wonder is that anyone thinks these arguments are any more than the old eugenicist saws brought out with very little resharpening.

49. The extent of the colonizing of these non-Western peoples included giving them names so that their 'disabilities' might be identified. Thus the

'Ubangi' women famous for their enlarged lips, achieved artificially by means of a tribal beautification practice involving the insertion of increasingly large disks into their lips, turn out to have not been 'Ubangi' at all. These women were from the Congo, but the press agent for Ringling Brothers Circus, Roland Butler, was looking at maps of Africa and found an obscure district named Ubangi, several hundred miles from the tribe's actual location. The name sounded properly exotic and so, in Butler's words, 'I resettled them.' This act of renomination also represented their own beauty practices as 'freakish' disabilities. They were presented as 'Monster-mouthed Ubangi savages' and as 'Crocodile Lipped Women From the Congo' (Bogdan 1988, 193–4).

50. Paul Tsongas's cancer became an issue that detracted from his candidacy in 1992. Although he tried to commandeer the media coverage to show him swimming every day, he was unable to beat the perception that he was disabled by his disease. More recently, Dan Quayle's complications from phlebitis had to be given some spin and could not be 'blamed' in his decision not to run for president.

51. As with categories of otherness, people with disabilities are often granted moral and spiritual powers that are supposed to offset the oppression of their group. For example, deaf people in literature or film are often the moral center for the world around them, as blind people are attributed capacities of second sight. The equivalent is of course the sagacity of the black slave or the moral rectitude of the Victorian mother. But the point is that the attribution of up-lifting virtues is precisely part of the oppression.

52. Obviously, reading can be accomplished by the blind through the use of Braille, and now with the use of computer scanners, audio tapes, and so on. But, in common parlance, reading requires sight.

53. Here I am using the body to signify a range of practices that define themselves as oppositional to rational, positivistic, phallocentric modes of cultural production. This is not to say that the body, in and of itself, represents some primal ground of resistance. Like any signifying term, it is always part of a chain of signification that it can influence and by which it in turn is defined.

Another way of putting the general point is to say that the blinded critic's insight is masculine, systematic while the deafened critic's 'context' is roving, clitoral, transgressive. The blinded critic would always find the road to insight through the palace of discursive wisdom, while the deafened critic is on another route leading to the colonized territory, the realm of the Other. As Trinh Minh-ha (1989) states, female critics and writers must be language stealers, must appropriate the language of the systematic for their own purposes. In that sense, they become allied with the deafened critic, who must reinscribe language on the body, in the materiality of the sign as it is embodied in the larynx or the hand.

54. The notion that the text is inherently visual is balanced by a Western prejudice against the notion of the reader who visualizes. Ellen J. Esrock notes in

The Reader's Eye: Visual Imaging as Reader Response (1994, 5) that 'such a dismissal of visual images by literary scholars is characteristic of our time.' Martin Jay makes a similar point about the tendency to denigrate the visual reception of art in our time. So, while reading is visual, the resulting knowledge should not be visual but linguistic.

55. It is almost paradoxical, then, that the first systematic education program for the blind, initiated by Valentin Hauy at the end of the eighteenth century in Paris, emphasized printing as a vocation for the blind. However, one activity was the printing of books with relief characters, that is, embossed typography, so that the blind could create a kind of print they could read (Paulson 1987, 102).

56. It would be wrong to say that all silence is transgressive or punitive. There is a pleasure in silence. The retreat one takes from community, the silent vows of monks, the silence of vastness and the sublime – all of these represent an erotics of silence. But one must add that this silence is voluntary and is not entirely silent. There is in all these scenarios the presence of a mediating term: art, nature, contemplation, writing, sketching, interior monologue, prayer, devotion. These are silences within language – only the manifestations of an alternative – perhaps not silence in its arbitrary and continuous form.

57. Of course, there are occasions in public when silence is required: silence in the men's room, silence in the elevator among strangers, and so on. But the discomfort of those who must keep that silence is equally obvious.

58. The notion of writing 'under erasure' (*sous rature*) is deliberately not silence – as in the case of certain writings by Derrida or Victor Shklovskii's *Zoo, or Letters Not About Love*, in which Letter Nineteen is printed with a large X effacing it – since the original trace is left to be read and then erased.

59. Attributed to Coleridge by Thomas Allsop in *Letters, Conversations and Recollections of S. T. Coleridge* (London: 1864). Notice that the wife is presumed to be garrulous, that trait being culturally assigned to women. The blindness is also seen as an inherent criticism of women – implying that they find fault with what they see. This saying has some currency in English history, being cited earlier in *Florio His First Fruites* (1578) and again in John Heywood's *Collection of English Proverbs* (Grant 1987, 86).

60. We can identify many minor figures too. In fact, it would seem that a stock character in the novel is the talkative (often old) woman. For example, there is Mrs Mercer in James Joyce's 'Araby' ('She was an old garrulous woman. . . . I had to endure the gossip of the tea table.') (Joyce 1964, 33). In 'The Dead' Joyce mentions Mrs Malin whose 'tongue rambled on' (ibid., 190).

61. Interestingly, there is no word in English to describe the silent sounds of thought. The best we can do is turn to poetry as in 'When to the sessions of sweet silent thought . . . '

62. I have to point out my own bad faith up to this point. I have perhaps

tricked the reader into assuming that deafness is silence, that not to hear is to be in silence. I have done this on purpose so that the reader might assume what the hearing world assumes. But this is an audist assumption because deafness is not at all silent – deaf people experience life filled with speech. But what they speak is sign language.

63. I am deliberately using the pejorative term. Deaf people would prefer the absence of any term – since most deaf do not think of themselves as 'dumb' or even 'mute.' The term 'deaf and dumb' or 'deaf–mute' came about because there was a general perception that deaf people were not simply deaf but that there was something almost physical that stopped them from speaking. In the gospels (Mark 7:31) Christ cures a man who 'was deaf, and had an impediment in his speech.' Christ puts his finger into the man's ears, spits and touches the man's tongue. 'And straightaway his ears were opened, and the string of his tongue was loosed, and he spake plain.' This passage expresses the idea that dumbness is a physical disability connected to deafness and seemingly unrelated to the deprivation of spoken language and the subsequent inability to learn by imitation. Of course, the Deaf do not regard themselves as mute since they can 'speak,' although perhaps not in the way that hearing people want.

64. How ironic that the words 'oral' and 'aural' are ones that in a hearing mode cannot be distinguished. Their difference is only revealed in writing, in a deafened mode. In this modality, there is no difference between speech and hearing, there is only reading and writing.

65. See Baynton 1992, 223ff., for examples of this usage among the teachers of the deaf in the nineteenth century.

66. Historically, the profession for which the deaf were prepared in residential schools was printing, particularly typesetting, a profession for which they were believed to be especially suited. Currently, computer programming is seen as a fit profession for the deaf. These are jobs in which signs can be produced without reference to the sense of hearing. The irony should not escape us that the printing trade employed the very icon of its own being.

67. In the same way, people who are color-blind, for example, remind us that color is an arbitrary arrangement assigned to a particular set of wavelengths that our human eyes just happen to be capable of seeing. Other cultures arrange those wavelengths that make up visible light quite differently, so that, for example, the frequencies that we call orange and red are grouped as the same color. Furthermore, there are animals that cannot see color, but can see light and dark far better than we can. Cameras that can photograph ultra-violet or infra-red radiation show us that we have privileged a certain range of wavelengths, assigning them qualities and meanings that clearly are not inherently determined by their physical nature alone.

68. Other Greek women 'write' in tapestry, most notably Helen, Penelope, and the Fates.

69. A parallel moment in later history occurs when Freud sees Dora's cough as a site of sexual encounter. Herr K. and Freud both colonize this location as their site of power: 'the conclusion was inevitable that with her spasmodic cough, which, as is usual, was referred for its exciting cause to a tickling in her throat, she pictured to herself a scene of sexual gratification *per os* between the two people whose love-affair occupied her mind so incessantly' (Freud 1963, 65).

Likewise, Dora's mutism is attributed to the same sexual origin, and like Philomel's, her mutism then leads to writing. 'Dora's aphonia, then, allowed of the following symbolic interpretation. When the person she loved was away she gave up speaking; speech had lost its value since she could not speak to *him*. On the other hand, writing gained in importance, as being the only means of communication with the absent person' (ibid., 56).

Thus the throat is the site of an eroticized, male-induced power; the recourse to a type of somatic writing, the hysterical symptom of aphonia, is then transferred to paper and script. The flow of power and the course it takes shows how mutism and femininity are again linked.

70. The pairing of beauty with ugliness is further carried out in Venus's marriage to Vulcan, who is himself both ugly and disabled by his lameness. Lameness tends also to be associated in an ableist way with impotence – as it is for example in W. Somerset Maugham's *Of Human Bondage*.

71. This phenomenon corresponds to the filmgoer's experience of watching stories of disability. As Norden points out (1994, 59ff.), when disability is depicted in film, there is a strong tendency to erase or fix the 'problem' by the end of the film. For example, no one recalls that Luke Skywalker in *Star Wars* lost his lower arm in a battle with his father Darth Veder. At the end of the film, a techno-intensive prosthesis is fitted on his stump, and for the sequels he acts as if his hand had grown back. No short-circuits or balky fingers are ever a problem in the sequels.

72. The Medici Venus had been reconstructed, so the eighteenth-century men did not have to face the incompleteness of their erotic object.

73. The term *corps morcelé* is a bit more vivid than 'fragmented body,' the now-standard translation of the term into English. *Morceler* is defined as 'to divide up into pieces.' It more actively carries the concept of chopping, cutting, or hacking. Thus the *corps morcelé* might more accurately be called 'the cut-up body.' However, I will retain the standard usage, for the sake of uniformity.

74. Irving Kenneth Zola pointed out that people with disabilities are mostly born into 'normal' families. Thus they are socialized into an ableist culture and have to adopt their disabled identity. 'We think of ourselves in the shadows of the external world. The very vocabulary we use to describe ourselves is borrowed from that society. We are *de*-formed, *dis*-eased, *dis*-abled, *dis*-ordered, *ab*-normal, and most telling of all an *in*-valid' (I. K. Zola 1984,144).

75. According to Martin Norden (1994), Robert Florey, a writer who contributed to the original *Frankenstein* script, came up with the idea of having Dr Frankenstein's assistant Fritz break into a medical school to steal a brain. He finds the 'normal' brain the doctor wanted but then drops it and takes one marked 'abnormal' instead.

76. Indeed, one could argue that the function of horror films is to remove the element of pity in the visual transaction between 'normal' viewer and disabled object. In the place of pity, pure repulsion is made allowable by turning the object with a disability into a criminal, a horror, a monstrosity. While everyone may enjoy a good horror movie now and then, there is a case to be made that horror films involving physically disabled characters are in fact the equivalent of racist films. The counterbalanced compassionate films showing people with disabilities triumphing over their disability is just the other moment in the same dialectic.

77. Women with disabilites are often the target for sexual or physical abuse; children with disabilities or Deaf children are often the victims of child abuse. This impulse to touch is unfortunately seen quite dramatically in these situations.

78. The fragmented body appears again in Conrad's *The Secret Agent*. Stevie, the mentally delayed brother-in-law to Verloc, ends up blown to bits when he stumbles during the transportation of a bomb. His body is so fragmented it has to be collected with a shovel. Stevie's impairment is, even before the explosion, linked to a fear of chaos. As Stevie sits drawing circles, the narrator comments that the drawings 'by their tangled multitude of repeated curves, uniformity of form, and confusion of intersecting lines suggested a rendering of cosmic chaos, the symbolism of a mad art attempting the inconceivable' (Conrad 1968, 76). The chaos implicit in Stevie's disability is then transmuted to virtual chaos in his action which throws Verloc's plans into disarray, as his dismemberment becomes a visual symbol of that chaos.

79. Later in the century Alexander Graham Bell would raise the same specter in regard to a deaf race taking over should deaf people be allowed to marry each other.

80. 'The same holds true of seeing – an activity that is ultimately derived from touching' (1900–, 156).

81. That is, with the exception of that burst of films made in the 1940s aimed specifically at African-American audiences.

82. This scene has a variation in Roman Polanski's *Bitter Moon*. Oscar (Peter Coyote) falls in lust with Mimi (Emmanuelle Seigneur), a young dancer. The couple go through a period of kinky sexual experimentation followed by Oscar's loss of interest in Mimi, and then his sadistic use of her. Ultimately she revenges herself by pulling him out of his hospital bed and turning him into a paraplegic. The story of their affair is narrated to a young British man (Hugh Grant) on a cruise to India. Grant's wife ends up in bed with Mimi. Oscar's disability is made

to seem sinister and perverse, and he manipulates the others around him into scenes where he can observe and even directly watch their sexual encounters. In a sense, rather than being made whole from this voyeuristic encounter, Oscar ends up even more alienated – and 'disabled' – and thus kills himself and Mimi as she lies in post-orgasmic sleep next to Grant's wife and under Grant's gaze.

83. For a further discussion of the image of the disabled in literature, film, and journalism see Alan Gartner and Tom Joe, *Images of the Disabled, Disabling Images*, and Michelle Fine and Adrienne Asch, *Women with Disabilities: Essays in Psychology, Culture, and Politics*.

84. And with current Republican attempts to limit liability and make the loser pay court costs, future lawsuits may be even harder to bring.

85. How ironic is this grouping, considering that the Nazis included both homosexuals and people with disabilities along with targeted ethnic groups and nationalities for extermination.

86. Of course, it is equally possible to say that any of these categories will permeate any other of the same categories. But the latter statement is more likely to be taken as true than the former in the current intellectual and political climate.

List of Works Cited

Adorno, Theodor. 1967. *Prisms*. Translated by Samuel and Shierry Weber. Cambridge, MA: MIT Press.

———— and Max Horkheimer. 1972. *The Dialectic of Enlightenment*. Translated by John Cumming. New York: Herder and Herder.

————. 1984. *Minima Moralia: Reflections from a Damaged Life*. Translated by E. F. N. Jephcott. London: Verso.

Althusser, Louis. 1977. *For Marx*. Translated by Ben Brewster. London: Verso.

Anderson, Benedict. 1983. *Imagined Communities: Reflections on the Origin and Spread of Nationalism*. London: Verso.

Anzieu, Didier. 1989. *The Skin Ego*. New Haven: Yale University Press.

Armstrong, Nancy. 1987. *Desire and Domestic Fiction: A Political History of the Novel*. Oxford: Oxford University Press.

Austen, Jane. 1985. *Emma*. London: Penguin.

Balibar, Etienne, and Immanuel Wallerstein. 1991. *Race, Nation, Class: Ambiguous Identities*. London and New York: Verso.

Barrell, John. 1989. '"The Dangerous Goddess": Masculinity, Prestige, and the Aesthetic in Early Eighteenth-century Britain.' *Cultural Critique* 12: 101–31.

Barthes, Roland. 1976. *Sade, Fourier, Loyola*. Translated by Richard Miller. New York: Hill and Wang.

Bartine, David. 1989. *Early English Reading Theory: Origins of Current Debates*. Columbia, SC: University of South Carolina Press.

Baudrillard, Jean. 1975. *The Mirror of Production*. Translated by Mark Foster. St Louis: Telos Press.

Baynton, Douglas C. 1992. '"A Silent Exile on This Earth": The Metaphorical Construction of Deafness in the Nineteenth Century." *American Quarterly* 44:2 (June), 216–43.

Begum, N. 1990. 'Burden of Gratitude: Women with Disabilities Needing Personal Care.' *Social Care: Perspectives and Practical Critical Studies*, Warwick: University of Warwick. Cited in Len Barton, Keith Ballard, and Gillian

Fulcher, eds, *Disability and the Necessity for a Socio-political Perspective.* Monograph of International Exchange of Experts and Information in Rehabilitation, No. 51.

Bell, Alexander Graham. 1969. *Memoir upon the Formation of a Deaf Variety of the Human Race.* Washington, DC: Alexander Graham Bell Association for the Deaf.

Benjamin, Walter. 1969. *Illuminations.* New York: Schocken.

Bérubé, Michael. 1994. 'Life As We Know It: A Father, a Son, and Genetic Destiny.' *Harper's* December: 41–51.

Bhabha, Homi. 1990. *Nation and Narration.* New York: Routledge.

Blacker, C. P. 1952. *Eugenics: Galton and After.* Cambridge, MA: Harvard University Press.

Bogdan, Robert. 1988. *Freak Show: Presenting Human Oddities for Amusement and Profit.* Chicago: University of Chicago Press.

Boone, Joseph Allen. 1987. *Tradition Counter Tradition: Love and the Form of Fiction.* Chicago: University of Chicago Press.

Boswell, James. 1936. *Boswell's Journal of A Tour to the Hebrides.* New York: Literary Guild.

Bowe, F. 1980. *Rehabilitating America.* New York: Harper and Row.

Brass, Paul. 1991. *Ethnicity and Nationalism: Theory and Comparison.* London: Sage.

Browne, S. E., D. Connors, and N. Stern, eds. 1985. *With the Power of Each Breath: A Disabled Women's Anthology.* Pittsburgh: Cleis Press.

Burke, Edmund. 1980. *Reflections on the Revolution in France.* New York: Penguin.

Clark, Kenneth. 1964. *The Nude: A Study in Ideal Form.* New York: Pantheon.

Connor, Walker. 1992. 'The Nation and its Myth.' *International Journal of Comparative Sociology* 33 (January/April): 48–57.

Conrad, Joseph. 1924a. 'An Outpost of Progress' in *Tales of Unrest*, Garden City: Doubleday, Page.

———. 1924b. *Youth.* Garden City: Doubleday, Page.

———. 1957. *Under Western Eyes.* London: Penguin.

———. 1968. *The Secret Agent.* London: Penguin.

———. 1986. *Lord Jim.* London: Penguin.

Davis, Lennard. J. 1983. *Factual Fictions: The Origins of the English Novel.* New York: Columbia University Press.

———. 1987. *Resisting Novels: Fiction and Ideology.* New York: Methuen.

———. 1993. 'Prisoners of Silence.' *Nation*, 4 October: 25–27.

Deegan, Mary Jo, and Nancy A. Brooks. 1985. *Women and Disability: The Double Handicap.* New Brunswick and Oxford: Transaction Books.

Defoe, Daniel. 1974. *The History and Life and Adventures of Mr Duncan Campbell.* New York: AMS Press.

————. 1975. *Robinson Crusoe*. New York: Norton.

Derrida, Jacques. 1967. *De la grammatologie*. Paris: Editions de Minuit.

————. 1972. *Marges de la philosophie*. Paris: Editions de Minuit.

————. 1993. *Memoirs of the Blind: The Self-Portrait and Other Ruins*. Translated by Pascale-Anne Brault and Michael Naas. Chicago: University of Chicago Press.

de Man, Paul. 1971. *Blindness and Insight: Essays in the Rhetoric of Contemporary Criticism*. Oxford: Oxford University Press.

de Vos, George. 1975. 'Ethnic Pluralism.' In George de Vos and Lola Romanucci-Ross, eds, *Ethnic Identity: Cultural Continuities and Change*. Palo Alto: Mayfield Publishing.

Dickens, Charles. 1884. *Little Dorrit*. New York: Pollard and Moss.

————. 1975. *Great Expectations*. London: Penguin.

Diderot, Denis. 1966. *Letter on the Deaf and Dumb*. In *Diderot's Selected Writings*. Edited by Lester G. Crocker and translated by Derrick Coltman. New York: Macmillan.

Doyal, L. 1983. 'The Crippling Effects of Underdevelopment.' In O. Shirley, ed., *A Cry for Health: Poverty and Disability in the Third World*. Rome: Third World Group and ARHTAG.

Dubois, Page. 1988. *Sowing the Seed: Psychoanalysis and Ancient Representations of Women*. Chicago: Chicago University Press.

Edwards, Martha L. 1995 (forthcoming). 'Ability and Disability in Ancient Greek Warfare.' In Lennard J. Davis, ed., *The Disability Studies Reader*. New York and London: Routledge.

Eisenstein, Elizabeth. 1968. 'Some Conjectures about the Impact of Printing on Western Society and Thought: A Preliminary Report.' *Journal of Modern History* 40:1 (March), 1–56.

Engels, Friedrich. 1968. *The Condition of the Working Class in England*. Translated by W. O. Henderson and W. H. Chaloner. Palo Alto: Stanford University Press.

Esrock, Ellen J. 1994. *The Reader's Eye: Visual Imaging as Reader Response*. Baltimore: Johns Hopkins.

Farb, P. 1975. *Word Play: What Happens When People Talk*. New York: Bantam.

Farrall, Lyndsay Andrew. 1985. *The Origin and Growth of the English Eugenics Movement 1865–1925*. New York: Garland.

Fine, Michelle and Adrienne Asch, eds. 1988. *Women with Disabilities: Essays in Psychology, Culture, and Politics*. Philadelphia: Temple University Press.

Finger, Anne. 1994. 'Comrade Luxemburg and Comrade Gramsci Pass Each Other at a Congress of the Second International in Switzerland on the 10th of March, 1912.' Unpublished manuscript.

Flaubert, Gustave. 1965. *Madame Bovary*. Translated by Paul de Man. New York: Norton.

Foucault, Michel. 1965. *Madness and Civilization*. Translated by Richard Howard. New York: Random House.

Freud, Sigmund. 1900–. *Standard Edition*. London: Hogarth Press.

———. 1963a. *Dora: An Analysis of a Case of Hysteria*. New York: Collier.

———. 1963b. 'The Uncanny.' *Studies in Parapsychology*. New York: Collier.

———. 1977. *Introductory Lectures on Psychoanalysis*. Translated by James Strachey. New York: Norton, 1966, reprinted 1977.

Gallagher, Hugh Gregory. 1985. *FDR's Splendid Deception*. New York: Dodd, Mead.

Gallop, Jane. 1988. *Thinking Through the Body*. New York: Columbia.

Gartner, Alan, and Tom Joe, eds. 1987. *Images of the Disabled, Disabling Images*. New York: Praeger.

Goffman, Erving. 1963. *Stigma: Notes on the Management of Spoiled Identity*. Englewood Cliffs, NJ: Prentice Hall.

Grant, Brian, ed. 1987. *The Quiet Ear: Deafness in Literature*. London: André Deutsch.

Graves, Robert. 1957. *The Greek Myths*. New York: Penguin.

Groce, Nora Ellen. 1985. *Everyone Here Spoke Sign Language: Hereditary Deafness on Martha's Vineyard*. Cambridge, MA: Harvard University Press.

Guillaumin, Collette. 1972. *L'idéologie raciste. Genèse et langage actuel*. Paris: Mouton.

Gwaltney, J. 1970. *The Thrice Shy: Cultural Accommodation to Blindness and Other Disasters in a Mexican Community*. New York and London: Columbia University Press.

Habermas, Jürgen. 1989. *The Structural Transformation of the Public Sphere: An Inquiry into a Category of Bourgeois Society*. Translated by Thomas Burger. Cambridge, MA: MIT Press.

Hawkins, Bisset. 1989. *Elements of Medical Statistics*. Canton, Massachusetts: Science History Publications.

Herder, Johan Gottfried. 1966. 'Essay on the Origin of Language.' In *On the Origin of Language: Two Essays by Jean-Jacques Rousseau and Johan Gottfried Herder*. Translated by John H. Moran and Alexander Gode. New York: Unger.

Herrnstein, Richard J. and Charles Murray. 1994. *The Bell Curve*. New York: The Free Press.

Hevey, David. 1992. *The Creatures Time Forgot: Photography and Disability Imagery*. London: Routledge.

Hugo, Victor. 1978. *Notre-Dame of Paris*. Harmondsworth: Penguin.

Hunter, J. Paul. 1990. *Before Novels: The Cultural Contexts of Eighteenth Century English Fiction*. New York: Norton.

Jaworski, Adam. 1993. *The Power of Silence: Social and Pragmatic Perspectives*. Newbury Park: Sage.

Jay, Martin. 1993. *Downcast Eyes: The Denigration of Vision in Twenthieth-Century Thought*. Berkeley: University of California Press.

Joyce, James. 1964. *Dubliners*. New York: Viking.

Kevles, Daniel J. 1985. *In the Name of Eugenics: Genetics and the Uses of Human Heredity*. New York: Alfred A. Knopf.

Kittay, Jeffrey, and Wlad Godzich. 1987. *The Emergence of Prose: An Essay in Prosaics*. Minneapolis: University of Minnesota Press.

Kitto, John. [1845] 1852. *The Lost Senses: Deafness and Blindness*. New York: Robert Carter.

Lacan, Jacques. 1977. *Écrits: A Selection*. Translated by Alan Sheridan. New York: Norton.

Laclau, Ernesto, and Chantal Mouffe. 1989. *Hegemony and Socialist Strategy*. New York and London: Verso.

Lane, Harlan, ed. 1984a. *The Deaf Experience: Classics in Language and Education*. Translated by Franklin Philip. Cambridge, MA: Harvard University Press.

———. 1984b. *When the Mind Hears: A History of the Deaf*. New York: Random House.

———. 1992. *The Mask of Benevolence: Disabling the Deaf Community*. New York: Knopf.

Lawrence, D. H. 1984. *The Virgin and the Gypsy*. New York: Vintage.

Liachowitz, Claire H. 1988. *Disability as a Social Construct: Legislative Roots*. Philadelphia: University of Pennsylvania Press.

Linton, Simi, Susan Mello, and John O'Neill. 1995 (forthcoming). 'Disability Studies: Expanding the Parameters of Diversity.' *Radical Teacher* (Fall 1995).

Lowe, Donald. M. 1982. *The History of Bourgeois Perception*. Chicago: University of Chicago Press.

MacKenzie, Donald A. 1981. *Statistics in Britain, 1865–1930*. Edinburgh: Edinburgh University Press.

Mallory, Bruce, et al. 1993. *Traditional and Changing Views of Disability in Developing Societies: Causes, Consequences, Cautions*. Monograph 54. Durham, NH: International Exchange of Experts and Information in Rehabilitation.

Marks, Elaine, and Isabelle de Courtivron, eds. 1980. *New French Feminisms*. New York: Schocken.

Marx, Karl. 1970. *Capital*. Vol. 1. Translated by Samuel Moore and Edward Aveling. New York: International Publishers.

———. 1964. *Economic and Philosophical Manuscripts of 1844*. Translated by Martin Milligan. New York: International Publishers.

Meyrowitz, Joshua. 1985. *No Sense of Place: The Impact of Electronic Media on Social Behavior*. New York: Oxford University Press.

Mirzoeff, Nicholas. 1992. 'Body Talk: Deafness, Sign and Visual Language in the Ancien Régime.' *Eighteenth Century Studies* 25:4 (Summer 1992), 561–86.

Murphy, Robert F. 1990. *The Body Silent*. New York: Norton.

Nead, Lynda. 1992. *The Female Nude: Art, Obscenity and Sexuality.* London and New York: Routledge.

Nkinyangi, J. A., and J. Mbindyo. 1982. *The Condition of Disabled Persons in Kenya: Results of a National Survey.* Nairobi, Kenya: Institute for Developmental Studies.

Norden, Martin F. 1994. *Cinema of Isolation: A History of Physical Disability in the Movies.* New Brunswick: Rutgers University Press.

Oliver, Michael. 1990. *The Politics of Disablement: A Sociological Approach.* New York: St Martin's Press.

Ong, Walter. 1967. *The Presence of the Word.* New Haven: Yale University Press.

Padden, Carol and Tom Humphries. 1988. *Deaf in America: Voices from a Culture.* Cambridge, MA: Harvard University Press.

Paulson, William R. 1987. *Enlightenment, Romanticism, and the Blind in France.* Princeton: Princeton University Press.

Pinker, Steven. 1994. *The Language Instinct: How the Mind Creates Language.* New York: Morrow.

Pittinger, R. E., C. F. Hockett, and J. J. Danehy. 1960. *The First Five Minutes: A Sample of Microscopic Interview Analysis.* Ithaca: Paul Martineau.

Porter, Theodore M. 1986. *The Rise of Statistical Thinking 1820–1900.* Princeton: Princeton University Press.

Ragland-Sullivan, Elie. 1987. *Jacques Lacan and the Philosophy of Psychoanalysis.* Urbana: University of Illinois Press.

Rothman, David. 1971. *The Discovery of the Asylum: Social Order and Disorder in the New Republic.* Boston: Little Brown.

Rousseau, Jean Jacques. 1966. 'Essay on the Origin of Languages.' In *On the Origin of Language: Two Essays by Jean-Jacques Rousseau and Johan Gottfried Herder.* Translated by John H. Moran and Alexander Gode. New York: Unger.

Ryan, J., and F. Thomas. 1980. *The Politics of Mental Handicap.* Harmondsworth: Penguin.

Sacks, Oliver. 1989. *Seeing Voices: A Journey into the World of the Deaf.* New York: HarperCollins.

Said, Edward W. 1993. *Culture and Imperialism.* New York: Knopf.

Sedgwick, Eve Kosofsky. 1985. *Between Men: English Literature and Male Homosocial Desire.* New York: Columbia University Press.

Shapiro, Joseph. 1993. *No Pity: People with Disabilities Forging a New Civil Rights Movement.* New York: Times Books.

Shelley, Mary. 1990. *Frankenstein, or The Modern Prometheus.* Oxford: Oxford University Press.

Shirley, O. ed. 1983. *A Cry for Health: Poverty and Disability in the Third World.* Rome: Third World Group and ARHTAG.

Shklovskii, Victor. *Zoo, or Letters Not About Love* 1971. Translated by Richard Sheldon. Ithaca: Cornell University Press.

Silverman, Kaja. 1990. 'Historical Trauma and Male Subjectivity.' In E. Ann Kaplan, ed., *Psychoanalysis and Cinema*. New York: Routledge.

Spence, Jo. 1986. *Putting Myself in the Picture*. London: Camden Press.

Stalin, Joseph. 1934. (A. Fineberg ed.) *Marxism and the National and Colonial Question*. New York: International Publishers.

Stallybrass, Peter. 1987. 'Patriarchal Territories: The Body Enclosed.' In Margaret W. Ferguson, Maureen Quilligan, and Nancy J. Vickers, eds, *Rewriting the Renaissance: The Discourse of Sexual Difference in Early Modern Europe*. Chicago: Chicago University Press,.

——— and Allon White. 1987. *The Politics of Transgression*. Ithaca, NY: Cornell University Press.

Steiner, George. 1967. *Language and Silence: Essays on Language, Literature, and the Inhuman*. New York: Atheneum.

Stigler, Stephen M. 1986. *The History of Statistics: The Measurement of Uncertainty before 1900*. Cambridge, MA: Harvard University Press.

Stille, Alexander. 1991. *Benevolence and Betrayal*. New York and London: Penguin.

Topliss, E. 1979. *Provision for the Disabled*. Oxford: Blackwell.

Trinh, T. Minh-ha. 1989. *Women, Native, Other*. Bloomington: Indiana University Press.

US Bureau of Census, *Current Population Reports* Series P-23, 127. Labor Force Status and Other Characteristics of Persons with a Work Disability. Washington, DC: US Government Printing Office, 1982.

Van Cleve, John Vickrey, and Barry A. Crouch. 1989. *A Place of Their Own: Creating the Deaf Community in America*. Washington, DC: Gallaudet University Press.

Varley, John. 1978. *The Persistence of Vision*. New York: Dial Press.

Walby, Sylvia. 1992. 'Woman and Nation.' *International Journal of Comparative Sociology* 33 (January/April): 81–100.

White, Hayden. 1973. *Metahistory: The Historical Imagination in Nineteenth-Century Europe*. Baltimore: Johns Hopkins University Press.

Winzer, Margaret A. 1993. *The History of Special Education: From Isolation to Integration*. Washington, DC: Gallaudet University Press.

Youngs Jr, Frederick A., Henry L. Snyder, and E. A. Reitan 1988. *The English Heritage*. Arlington Heights, Illinois: Forum Press.

Zola, Emile. 1964. *The Experimental Novel and Other Essays*. Translated by Belle M. Sherman. New York: Haskell House.

———. 1993. *The Masterpiece*. Translated by Thomas Walton. London: Oxford University Press.

Zola, Irving Kenneth. 1984. 'Communication Barriers Between "the Able-Bodied" and "the Handicapped."' In Robert P. Marinelli and Arthur E. Dell Orto, eds, *Psychological and Social Impact of Physical Disability*. New York: Springer.

Index

abortion 162–3, 164–5, 166
access for disabled 10–11
Achenwall, Gottfried 25
Adams, John Quincy 55
Adorno, Theodor 14–15, 23, 101, 111
age of Reason 51
Alberti, Solomon 54
Allsop, Thomas 180
Althusser, Louis 81
American Sign Language 17
Americans with Disabilities Act 1990 3, 131, 159, 160, 169
Ammon, Johan 54
Anderson, Benedict 75, 76, 177
Anzieu, Didier 146–7
Aphrodite, *see* Venus
appearance modality 11, 12
Arbus, Diane 150, 151
Aristotle 52, 55, 126, 173, 175
Armstrong, Nancy 174, 176
Arnoldi, J.L.F. 54
art 177
   see also photographic art
Asch, Adrienne 8, 9, 10, 161, 163–4, 174
asylums 86
attractiveness and disability 131
Augustine, Saint 52, 175
aural communication 16, 17, 20
   fetishizing 19
   see also sign language

Austen, Jane 114
average *see* norm

Babbage, Charles 29
Baker, Henry 176
Bakhtin, Mikhail 3, 30, 137, 150, 151
Balfour, A.J. 37
Balibar, Etienne 75, 77, 78, 80, 81, 82, 94
Balzac, H. de 42
Barbier, Charles 175–6
Barnum, P.T. 90
Barrell, John 137
Barthes, Roland 61, 176
Bartine, David 61
Baudrillard, Jean 118
Baynton, Douglas C. 82, 113, 118–19, 181
Beaumarchais, P.A.C. de 53
beauty
   and ugliness pairing 131, 154, 182
   see also Venus
Beckett, Samuel 115
Beethoven, Ludwig van 7, 9, 153
Begum, N. 162
Bell, Alexander Graham 32, 38, 81, 183
bell curve 29, 30, 32, 33, 174
Bender, John 174
Benjamin, Walter 93, 138
Bernhardt, Sarah 9

and theory *see* deafness and insight
work-related 7
disabled
  body term 172–3
  category xv
  depicted in novels 39–41, 174
  depicted in negative light 41, 124
  as minority group 98
  person term xiii
  term 10
discrimination in workplace and
  public spaces 159–60
diversity requirements 6, 160–1
Dole, Robert 159
Down syndrome 163, 174
Doyal, L. 85
Dubois, Page 138
Duffy, Mary 148–9, 156
dumbness 45, 118, 119, 121
  not tolerated in writing 123
  see also mute; Philomel;
  Shakespeare, William: *Titus
  Andronicus*
Durant, Will 96
During, Simon 178
dwarfism 164
dysfunctionality of the deaf 78

Eagleton, Terry 174
Edwards, Martha L. 89, 102
ego 147
eighteenth century 3, 20, 82
  and industrialization 87
  and madness 142
  notions 24
  prejudice of hearing over sight 113
  published works of the deaf 108
  see also universalizing marginality
Eisenstein, Elizabeth 62
emptiness 112
Engels, Friedrich 87–8
Enlightenment 51, 70, 71, 83
eroticism 145–6, 148, 154
'error curve' 32
'error law' 26, 29
'error theory' 32

Esrock, Ellen J. 179–80
ethnicity 36, 45, 77, 78, 79, 80
eugenics 29–31, 33, 35–7, 44, 80, 91,
  174
  and abortion 164–5
  eugenic gaze 46
  of the minds 39
  notion of normativity 42
  and race and ethnicity 45
  testing 47
  as way of repairing declining stock
  88–9
euthanasia 165–6

Fabian Society 35
facilities, lack of for disabled
  173
Factory Act 1833 29
Farb, P. 89
Farrall, Lyndsay Andrew 31
Federn 147
feeblemindedness 36, 38
female critic 179
feminism xi
fetal screening 162–3, 164
Fieldler, Leslie 143
films depicting disability 151–4
  see also Boxing Helena
Fine, Michelle 8, 9, 10, 161, 163–4,
  174, 184
Finger, Anne 128
finger spelling 59
fingerprinting 31, 32
Fisher, R.A. 29
Flaubert, Gustave 39, 40–1, 101
Flores, José 168–70
Florey, Robert 183
Fontenay, Saboreux de 59
Ford, John 6
Foucault, Michel 2, 51, 63, 128
fragmented body 138–42, 148, 154,
  175, 182, 183
  Frankenstein's monster 145, 146
fragmented torso *see* visualizing
  disabled body
freak shows 90–1, 92

non-ideal status 29
Norden, Martin F. 6, 98, 151–2, 153,
   154, 182, 183
norm or average concept 24–5, 27,
   28, 29, 30, 35, 43, 173
norm, deviations from 29, 30, 32, 33,
   34, 36, 52
'normal' body 141, 154
normal distribution 29
   curve 32, 33, 35
normal gaze 149
normal ideal body 154
nude 132–3, 134, 141
   fragmentary nature 137
   see also Venus

Odysseus 111
Oedipal moment 148
Oedipus 101
'ogive' 34
Oliver, Michael 85, 130
O'Neill, John 160
Ong, Walter 107
oppression xix, 68, 179
oralism and sign debate 84
ostracism 101

Padden, Carol 118
Paulson, William R. 53, 180
Pearson, Karl 29, 35–6
penal system 169
Pereire, Jacob 65
perfectibility of human body 31, 35
Perlman, Itzak 9
'person with disabilities' term xiii
perversion 38–9
'phantom limbs' 135, 137
Philippe, Louis 26
Philomel 119–20, 121, 122,
   123
philosophical reflection and deafness
   55, 61
photographic art depicting disability
   148–9, 150–1
phrenology 45
physical identity 92

physical impairment 1, 3, 7, 82, 129,
   152
'physical minorities' term 3
Pinker, Steven 19
Pittinger, R.E. 110
pity 1–2, 63
Pliny 25, 137
poetry 119, 120, 121
Polanski, Roman 183
political bonds and activity xx
political consciousness among the
   Deaf 163–4
politics of disability xiii
politics of power and fear 4
Pontalis, J.B. 139
Poor Law 1834 29
Poovey, Mary 174
Pope, Alexander 6
Porter, Theodore M. 25, 27
positive extremes 33
Pound, Ezra 117
poverty and disability 85, 86
power 2, 4, 11, 158
prose 16–17, 18, 20, 21
psychoanalysis 39
psychology 44
public displays of deaf students
   54–5, 56
published works of the deaf 108
putative blindness 107

Quayle, Dan 179
queer studies xi
Quetelet, Adolphe 26, 27, 28, 29, 30,
   32, 35

race 23, 24, 45, 73, 86, 90, 92, 158,
   161, 162
   concept 79, 80
   norm 15
   see also race, class and gender below
race, class and gender triad with
   disability as missing term 1–22
   appearance modality 12
   categorizing disability 5–10
   concept of disability 1–3